Gun Digest Book of
GREEN SHOOTING

A PRACTICAL GUIDE TO NON-TOXIC HUNTING AND RECREATION

Rick Sapp

©2010 Krause Publications, a division of F+W Media, Inc.

Published by

Gun Digest®Books

An imprint of F+W Media, Inc.
700 East State Street • Iola, WI 54990-0001
715-445-2214 • 888-457-2873
www.gundigeststore.com

Our toll-free number to place an order is (800) 258-0929.

Library of Congress Control Number: 2009937517
ISBN-13: 978-1-4402-1362-5
ISBN-10: 1-4402-1362-3

Designed by Paul Birling
Edited by Corrina Peterson

Printed in the United States of America

DEDICATION

For my two kids – Jason and Morgan – and for yours as well. May they live in a healthy world where all inhabitants fall asleep with full bellies and rise the next day to sunshine, a slight breeze and a hint of rain.

ABOUT THE AUTHOR

According to author Rick Sapp, the subject of "green shooting" is a wolf in sheep's clothing. It has a niche sound – as if it might only interest shooters, hunters, competitors, manufacturers – but in actuality it has a broad and fascinating basis in chemistry, biology and esoteric topics such as group dynamics. "That's the beauty of being a freelance writer," Rick says. "I've had the privilege of studying children's hospitals and taking African safaris, shooting frangible bullets and interviewing bicycle designers, paraplegics and mink farmers … and when I write about these topics, someone pays me! Not much and it's often late and the market is shrinking, but it is the only thing I have ever really wanted to do with my life." Rick's background includes newspaper reporting and publishing, editing magazines, 20 books and an advertising and public relations agency.

Gun Digest ® Book of GREEN SHOOTING

TABLE OF CONTENTS

FOREWORD

It's too bad about lead ammunition, really. I mean, lead is plentiful. It's cheap. It works superbly as intended in this application.

And then, if it gets into your physiological system, it can poison you. Although quite slowly. Nothing dramatic, obvious, like a pie in the face.

I suppose that, in the long run, the furor over lead as a component of recreational shooting could result in a healthier environment. I'm not sure of that, however. We live in a very complex world in which situations are not always as they appear. And changes inevitably have consequences, some of which, especially in complex systems, can turn out to be real surprises (consider, for example, the ill-fated foray into tungsten bullets by the military).

If the effort to develop effective shotshells and cartridges without relying on lead is successful, we (presumably) would all have one less thing to think about. If it results in thousands of people giving up shooting in frustration, no one will be happy; not even, paradoxically, the anti-gun and animal rights groups – they are not one and the same – which need those of us who enjoy guns and shooting and hunting to help power their fund-raising.

And while we accept that some ducks may have died from lead poisoning, we do not know how many; we do not know how many were saved by switching to "non-toxic" shot, or how many that may have been lost to lead poisoning would have died prematurely from other causes. Indeed, it is not impossible to find creditable waterfowl biologists who quietly maintain that the waterfowl issue was blown dramatically out of proportion.

Neither do we fully understand the relationship between the endangered California condor and lead bullet fragments in the remains of harvested deer and elk, the vaunted "gut piles." A condor may occasionally feed on a pile of entrails and, in a universe of infinite possibilities it might die because of that. The evidence is far from conclusive, but it is possible and it has become justification for sweeping efforts to restrict lead ammunition far out of proportion to the conclusiveness of the evidence.

It is not that I am insensitive to the death of an endangered species. I am not. I do not want to live in a world without whales and hummingbirds; without grizzly bears and sable antelope. I do realize that a small alteration here, a minor change there – a concrete dam destroys a bamboo forest and pandas starve, tourism declines taking the local economy with it – and suddenly officials are wondering why the region is experiencing social unrest. It can happen so slowly that we blink and look again, but still can't see it, and when we do, it appears to have happened overnight.

I do not want to gift a world to my children wherein their only animal companions are cockroaches and flies. Still, as I get older, I become more sensitive to hidden complexities and less convinced by "we have to act now – we can't wait until we understand the situation" arguments.

So now comes *Gun Digest® Book of Green Shooting,* which looks at the state of non-toxic ammunition. "Green" being a code word for non-toxic, as in non-lead. The book may not say enough about dove hunting, and may perhaps discuss waterfowl in an overly-long section. Nevertheless, it maintains a steady focus on the issue, bringing lawsuits and patents, lead dust and deer hunting, into rough alignment.

This book is only a snapshot of a running conservation and health argument, a moving issue about which we learn more each year. Therefore, by definition, the book will become outdated at the speed with which the issue evolves. However, it is a good snapshot that will, in some ways, hasten its own obsolescence by its sincere effort to find and speak the truth at our present level of understanding. Not perfect, but not bad and I recommend that.

Richard K. "Dick" Peddicord, PhD
President, Environmental Range Protection
Heathsville, Virginia
January 2010

ACKNOWLEDGEMENTS

Many people assisted with information, photos, suggestions and corrections for this book. I would like to make note of the following individuals however, who were especially helpful:

Randy Brooks,

Jessica Brooks,

Chandler Bates, III and Preston Bunker, Barnes Bullets;

John Powers, RUAG (Precision Ammo); Peter Pi, Dakota Ammo;

Dan Tercho, Nice Shot;

Jay Menefee, PolyWad;

Alex Papp, Classic Shotshell/RST;

Jeffery Mullins, Extreme Shock;

Mike Hetrick, ICC;

Joe Benini and Joe Kugler, Sinterfire;

Ron Petty, Hevi-Shot;

Tim Brant, ATK;

Grant Fackler, Ballistic Products;

Mike Brady, North Fork Bullets;

Ron Shema, Gainesville Target Range;

Dr. William Cornatzer, SD;

Jim Pearce, ORNL;

Dr. Peter Proctor;

Sandra Washek, ND DOH;

Gary Caughman, artist;

Bill Brassard, Jr. and Ted Novin of the NSSF;

Steve Wagner, Blue Heron Communications;

Jon Walusiak and Chad Mangers, W Design;

Jody Lyle, National Park Service;

Tom Roster, ballistician and writer;

Don Friberg, U.S. FWS biologist and friend of many years;

Cheryl Irwin, OASD-PA;

Amanda Baribeau, MN PCA;

Mary Jane Williamson, ASA;

John Steinhorst, Sporting Clays magazine;

Larry Pratt, Gun Owners of America;

Dr. Richard Peddicord;

Lianna Sandy, MT2;

Stuart Cohen, Environmental & Turf Services;

Capt. Steve Johnson, Texas Gulf Duck Hunting;

Tracy Blake, SwanHunting.com;

Matt Kostka, Top Gun Guide Service;

Brad and Diane Finneman, Honker Down Guide Service;

Rick Stockstill, NSSA/NSCA;

Don Oliver, Box O' Truth;

Frank Tripoli, Tripoli Triggers;

Robin Ball, Sharp Shooting Indoor Range & Gun Shop;

and finally, the professionals at Krause/F&W Publications –
Corrina Peterson,
Dan Shideler,
Bonnie Tetzlaff.

INTRODUCTION

I want to do the right thing. I imagine you do, too.

The problem, of course, is that we may not agree on what is right.

And if we do agree on that, we will almost certainly disagree about how to get there from here.

I don't really give a damn about the California condor. Or the snail darter. Or Salim Ali's fruit bat. Or Salim Ali either. Do I care about whales or Florida panthers or even "the human race?" I'm not sure....

I do care about my children. If they were hungry and those endangered animals were all there was to eat, they'd be goners, even if they were the very last of their species. It isn't personal.

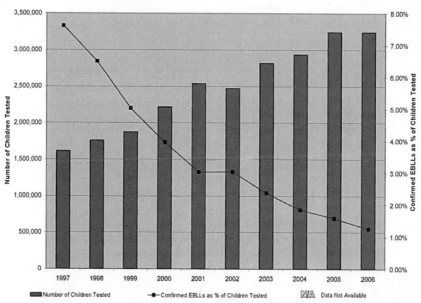

U.S. Total Blood Lead Surveillance Report 1997 - 2006

Children have very low tolerances to lead and its effects on them can be terrible. Thus, it has been banned from toys and glass, from gasoline and paint. Nevertheless, it has not been demonstrated that incidental contact via reloading or shooting, or eating venison taken with traditional ammunition, has any affect on children ... or adults. A graph from the Centers for Disease Control and Prevention indicates that in the 10-year period between 1996 and 2006 levels of lead in the blood of children fell dramatically. (CDC graph from www.cdc.gov)

You may or may not feel the same way. But regardless of how you feel, you would kill every sea otter, every bison, every loggerhead turtle to feed your hungry family.

Of course, like Ender Wiggin in Orson Scott Card's novel *Ender's Game*, the criticism would never end. That would be personal. Long after you were dead, people would remember and condemn you, even perhaps some of those you saved.

The controversy about toxins in the environment is similar to the endangered species argument and the climate change argument. Indeed, at some level they are linked. Species are disappearing and the climate is changing, though not rapidly or with immediately catastrophic consequences. Shooting does deposit lead on the ground and in the atmosphere. Lead isn't a healthy element for living things, but the sky is not falling.

We are going to be forced to compromise. We have, in fact, already done so with glass and gasoline, with paint and toys. In 10th grade science class the teacher poured a few drops of mercury into your palm; you marveled at its

The author after a hard day at the range: eye and ear protection plus a wide-brim hat and sun-screen for protection against UVA/B ... and now concerns about toxic primers and lead shot. Where does it end? Many outdoor ranges have not yet embraced lead removal, but with states becoming more sensitive to environmental concerns about lead leaching into aquifers or in runoff after a heavy rain, that indifference could become legally costly. In addition, recovered lead is sold for recycling, which helps keep the cost of clean-up manageable.

ability to maintain its shape and then passed the silvery metal to a classmate. Today men in hazmat suits would descend on the school; the teacher would lose his license.

This book discusses the issue of shooting lead, and the options. It draws upon material from many sources here in the U.S. and from around the world. Lead in the bloodstream or in our drinking water will poison us, slowly, cruelly, but it isn't clear what the role of recreational shooting is, nor are the solutions readily apparent. Indeed, it isn't 100 percent clear that there is a problem, although there is a 100 percent argument.

What seems obvious is that we spend a great deal of time name-calling when a less emotional discussion would be in our long-term best interest. Pro-shooting groups and anti-gun groups employ hysteria effectively to rally support, but digging trenches prevents everyone from doing the right thing or even talking about it. Is there a vocal group that would like to use the debate about lead in the environment to ban guns and shooting when the more direct approach has failed? Almost certainly, there is. Is there a broad sentiment in the shooting sports that any possible change or hint of change is an attack against the bedrock of their liberties? No question about it.

This book, *Gun Digest® Book of Green Shooting,* looks at the issue of non-toxic shooting from the point of view of our tools: ammunition for shotgun, rifle and handgun. It begins with the controversies – waterfowl poisoning, lead leaching into the aquifer, elevated lead levels among shooting range personnel – and reviews the current alternatives to lead ammo.

As an authentic gun carrying liberal, I hope that this book has a measure of objectivity and that it can bring a fresh perspective to the issue of non-toxic or green shooting to millions of readers.

Rick Sapp
Gainesville, Florida
January 2010

SECTION I:
THE IMPORTANCE
OF GOING GREEN

CHAPTER 1

THE HUNTER – OUR ENVIRONMENT'S BEST FRIEND

Deep in the hardwood forests of the Apalachicola watershed, a man and a woman move cautiously through the snake-filled palmetto. They are thirsty and soaked with sweat. Their backs strain in the ungainly, bipedal posture that evolution has bestowed on humans. Eyes search ahead and above; ears strain for a call, but not just any call – The Call. In the first flush of morning, their binoculars fog with dew and warm breath. They are hunting for the ivory-billed woodpecker, the stunning bird thought to be extinct for a hundred years. Maybe it is; maybe it isn't.

Inside an enclosed leopard blind in the Selous Game Reserve a woman fidgets. A .375 is cradled across her lap. Beside her sits an African, a man who has guided many Americans, Europeans and Asians, all visiting his country to hunt, possibly to kill something of great value. Tanzania is, after all, still rich in wildlife. Zebra and wildebeest migrating by the thousands, the tens of thousands, are hunted by lions and leopards and cheetah, by hyenas and wild dogs.

Blood flows freely at an international conference of wildlife managers and NGOs, individuals with programs and agendas, plus the occasional movie star – which lends the gathering celebrity and therefore "news-worthiness" – where every attendee jockeys for the conservation spotlight. Experts scratch for weakness in their opponents; they gouge eyes, hit below the belt for media attention, because celebrity results in contracts, grants, university positions and the National Geographic spotlight. This, too, is a hunt, a chase, and occasionally a kill. Here, professionals understand that hunting is simply another term for politics: competition, self-preservation and allocation of resources.

So who is a "real hunter," a true hunter?

Every human, every consuming animal and plant, from the most ravenous shark to the least microbe, from the mass murderer to the most committed vegan, is a hunter. To live is to hunt.

The giant live oak shades the seedlings of the pine, and its root system, growing for a century and a survivor of flood and fire, plow and axe and drought, starves the seedlings of moisture and nourishment. They wither or they wait. The oak is hunting and so, too, of course, are the seeds.

MOTHER IS CALLING....

The web of life is so interconnected and so precariously balanced that the wolf's self-interest is both in killing a caribou and preserving the herd. Taking and feeding from the individual while ensuring that the group thrives. The pirate spider consumes all of the other spiders until there are none left alive; then, it too perishes. And its young.

The wolves must not become too numerous or too efficient, too gluttonous or too lazy, and yet they must cull the herd, must keep it moving toward the distant calving grounds or the caribou will overgraze and destroy their habitat. This would be disaster for the hare and the mouse, the fox and the owl, the lichens and the grasses, because the tundra and the cold north woods require many years to heal their scars.

The oak may not consciously lose limbs so that a few lucky and opportunistic pine seedlings find room to grow and mature, find their *lebensraum,* but it happens in every naturally occurring field and forest. The dolphin pod does not devour every fish in a school, although that is not for want of effort. The bird hunter takes quail with a blast from his shotgun, but calls the spaniel away and leaves birds to rebuild the covey. Birds burst from the brush again the next year.

And so each American sport hunter, each man and woman who goes into the field with gun or bow, hopes to take the finest possible specimen of deer or turkey … and yet expects that their efforts will preserve the species so that their children and their children's children will have the same opportunity. Even as they proudly pose beside the great rack, the monster skull, the rich pelt, they understand there are plenty more where that came from. The experience of killing is more meaningful because they have become part of a tradition, shared a heritage that is unimaginably ancient and, they hope, has an unlimited future.

The paradox at the heart of hunting – at the heart of life itself – is that some must inevitably die so that the race, the population, the species, may live. And thrive. Of course, all individuals eventually die, and a "natural death" on the steppe, in the jungle or the sea is no pretty picture, involving starvation or disease, or blood and pain and terror, or all of the above. It is only a cow and yet it is suspicious, frightened. I shoot the impala and it is surprised and feels pain. We understand. We can live with that.

The web of life is interconnected and precariously balanced.

And so, it is this dilemma — weighing the life of an individual animal in the same scale as the health of populations — that many humans are unable to appreciate. They project their personal expectations of joy and pain, of hope and suffering into the body of the Miura bull lumbering into the ring. It is the dainty English tourist, after all, not the resident Spaniard, though both flock in untold thousands to the spectacle of bull fighting, that pressures the Spanish king to drape the picador's horse with heavy quilts to prevent its goring. It is the vegetarian in the cloth coat who protests the management of the chicken farm and the harvesting of seal pups for fur. It is the non-participant who would outlaw fishing in England, bowhunting in America, shooting live pigeons in Italy.

Science tells us that species, too, die. It can be argued, for instance, that Paleolithic hunters were responsible for the collapse of the great New World mammals, the giant sloth and the mastodon, but it is more persuasively argued that over the course of millions of years of species life they perished because the climate changed; they had become specialized to cope with an environment that did not survive.

Every speck of white is a migrating animal in the Porcupine Caribou herd (Area 1002) on the coastal plain of the Arctic National Wildlife Refuge, with the Brooks Mountain range in the distance to the south. With so many targets, every hunter must stay calm to take his or her time and kill the very finest specimen possible, expecting that the thousands of dollars in licenses, tags, permits and fees paid will ensure the survival of *Rangifer tarandus.* (Photo Chuck Young, U.S. FWS)

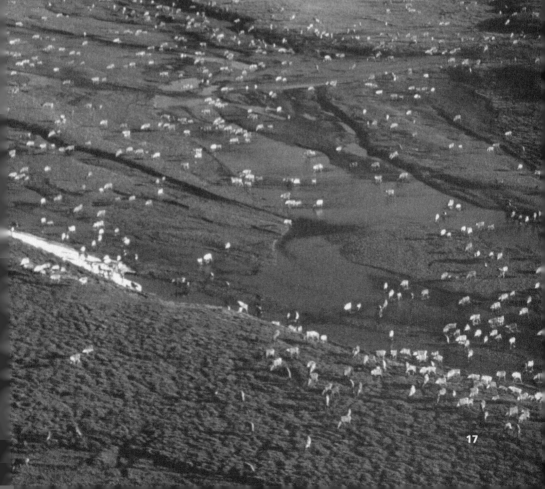

RMBS [Rocky Mountain Bighorn Society] President, Dan Larkin, presented a ceremonial check to Colorado Wildlife Commission Chairman, Brad Coors, and Colorado Division of Wildlife Director, Tom Remington, at the November [2009] Wildlife Commission meeting in Alamosa.

The check, totaling $134,575, represented the monies raised by the RMBS through auction and raffle sales of sheep and goat licenses chances during 2009. In addition, $5,500 was raised through sales of a statewide pronghorn license raffle.

The RMBS is authorized by the Secretary of State and the Division of Wildlife to promote and sell one bighorn sheep auction and raffle license, one mountain goat auction and raffle license and one pronghorn raffle license. Monies raised through your generous donations are used by the Colorado Division of Wildlife and the Rocky Mountain Bighorn Society for various projects, including habitat improvement, disease research, transplants and education. [1]

The white-tailed deer may number as many as 20 million in North America, brought back from the brink of extinction primarily by sport hunter/conservationists in the 20th century. (Photo Scott Bauer, U.S. Dept. of Agriculture)

It cannot be disputed that man has killed – directly – a variety of species. The great auk and the passenger pigeon were both destroyed for food and feathers. Wolves and lions were hunted to the brink of extinction to make the land safe for farms and ranches. The extinction list is unfortunately long and yet, because of the sport hunter, guided by a difficult century of debate and discovery, the populations waiting to join that list has paradoxically diminished.

THE "SPORT" HUNTER

The modern hunter – call him a sport hunter if you will, as there is no prejudice in that term even though it makes some participants squirm – understands the dilemma thoroughly. He makes every effort to kill the very finest example of his chosen game – deer with the largest antlers, for example – and yet is always first in line with contributions of time and sweat and money to support the preservation and enhancement of species. He pays handsomely to participate in the opportunity to hunt and joins conservation clubs by the tens of thousands to restore wetlands, preserve habitat and transplant healthy game animals.

Hunters and non-participants alike are concerned about the preservation of species, yet they demonstrate this in different manners. In this case, the sport hunter turns the model on its head, for it is the hunter who has rolled up his sleeves, donated her time and money, lobbied congress, and saved wildlife around the world.

Sadly, while non-hunters join and contribute money to conservation groups by the millions, a significant percentage of their effort is devoted to filing lawsuits, paying their executives and hiring celebrities.

It would be wrong however to understand the thousands of men and women who flock to National Wild Turkey Federation or Rocky Mountain Elk Foundation banquets as myopic self-serving enthusiasts: people whose only interest is saving turkeys or elk so that they can kill one. No amount of wild meat could ever pay for the cost of the local or national gatherings, the travel, the gear used, the licenses purchased. No flock of wild turkeys could ever fully compensate the artists who paint and sculpt and decorate wing bones; the writers who communicate the experience knowing in advance that their words, the images they build, the emotions they evoke will always be worth more than the pay.

A turkey gobbler in full strut, perhaps focused on your call, displays the thick and overlapping layers of feathers that make the head and neck shot advisable. The wild turkey has made a remarkable comeback from the verge of extinction, and it could not have done so without the active help of sportsmen.

The turkey or the deer are symbols of the hunter's commitment, her enthusiasm for hunting. To confuse killing with hunting is fundamentally erroneous, though killing is an occasional and necessary part of the politics of the hunt. It is the anticipation, the preparation, the development of and then the participation in a community of interest that defines hunting; that and the opportunity to participate in something both primitive and eternal.

In antiquity, and in many civilizations into the 20th century, hunting was generic, required and understood. It was an unquestioned part of the fabric of existence. One simply hunted in order to survive. Those who did not hunt – if not for fresh meat, at least as scavengers – lived bitterly on scraps and handouts, gnawed the bones left by the others. Maybe nothing has changed.

BY THE NUMBERS

Today, it is more difficult to express the need to hunt, but one can quantify it – at least as well as dying or new home sales and better than falling in love or home gardens planted. According to the U.S. Fish & Wildlife Service, 12.5 million Americans 16 years old and older went hunting in 2006. They hunted 220 million days, took 185 million trips and spent more than $22.9 billion on their sport. [2]

It is true that participation in hunting and shooting generally (and also in fishing, camping and other outdoors activities) have declined in the U.S. Reasons

Biggest bird in the world: Since 1996, six to 10 condors per year have been released in the vicinity of the Grand Canyon. Each carries two radio transmitters and is monitored by as many as 10 biologists. Lead poisoning, says the state of Arizona, is the leading cause of condor death and the main obstacle to a self-sustaining population. (Photos AZ Game & Fish and Ymaup at Wikipedia.org)

given are loss of accessible habitat due to urbanization and suburbanization; rise of the two-income family; pressure from electronic media; a dramatic (and often unjustifiable) increase in the cost of licenses and assorted permits, fees and tags; political antagonism from organized "animal rights" advocates and a gradual evolution away from a hands-on lifestyle.

The numbers, the reasons and arguments only scratch the surface of hunting and shooting in North America, though. The deeper impact is that outdoor people have marshaled their resources to preserve, indeed to enhance, wildlife populations around the world. This is a salient fact and it has never happened before in the history of man.

The testimony of sport hunting in North America is a living environment, filled with large and small game, and hundreds of animals, plants and insects that prosper in a symbiotic relationship with those animals. North American wildlife thrives due to the successful conservation efforts funded by sport hunters. No species has ever become extinct (in the U.S. or elsewhere) or even truly threatened because of regulated sport hunting.

Critically endangered California Condors – here feeding on a dead calf – can be poisoned when they eat carcasses of animals shot with lead pellets but not retrieved. Currently, all free-flying condors are captured at least once a year to be tested and, if necessary, treated for lead poisoning. (Photos AZ Game & Fish and Ymaup at Wikipedia.org)

At the turn of the century, it was believed in many areas that pronghorn antelope had become extinct.

Here are a few population facts about what are commonly known as North America's "un-endangered species," most of which have been hunted since man first populated the continent some 20,000 years ago[3]:

• By the turn of the 20th century, the white-tailed deer was rare in America. Estimates from surveys of its range suggested there were fewer than half-a-million. Today, by all reasonable estimates, this hardy species numbers 30 million. Indeed, they are so numerous that they are regarded as a pest in many suburban locations and the very people who speak out against hunters rail against deer in their vegetable gardens.

• The journals of Lewis and Clark mention elk in huge abundance as they made their way across the continent and back between 1804 and 1806. Shooting these animals for market consumption – and because, as far as they knew, there being no wildlife management in those days, there was simply no reason not to – in the 1800s decimated the population and numbers fell to an estimated 41,000 when they were at last surveyed in 1907. Today, because of the active support of sport hunters, engaging in transplantation efforts and the hard, inglorious and expensive work of habitat preservation, numbers in the U.S. and Canada are about 800,000 animals.

- It is a similar story for the pronghorn, which were so rare at the turn of the former century that in many areas it was believed they had become extinct. As few as 5,000 were believed to inhabit the Western plains whereas today, principally because of management efforts funded and backed by sport hunters, there are a million of the speedy antelope west of the Mississippi River.

- A truly astonishing recovery has been made by the wild turkey. At one time these animals were so numerous that even the redoubtable Philadelphian, Ben Franklin, believed them to be a "more respectable bird" than the scavenging bald eagle as a symbol of the new nation. In the late 1800s, the turkey was, for all intents and purposes, extinct. Today, because of the energetic support and funding of sport hunters for transplanting and husbanding the growth of wild flocks, there may be as many as seven million birds in America. While it is almost impossible to count individual birds, there are sufficient numbers to support hunting in every state except Alaska, which is outside the bird's natural range, Canada and Mexico. (Indeed, the greatest threat to the wild turkey and other ground nesting birds today is the coyote, which greedily gobbles eggs and chicks alike.)

- The Canada goose has more than doubled in population in the latter half of the 20th century, from as few as one million to 2.5 million, a number verified by flyway estimates required by international treaties. The goose is so numerous that quite a few municipalities have decided that it is a pest and have instituted special urban hunts.

Duck hunters rise to shoot from a hunting blind. Hunters have contributed millions of dollars to conservation in America through a self-imposed excise tax of 10 – 11 percent on sporting goods. This tax, loosely called the Pittman-Robertson Act, funds wildlife habitat restoration, hunter education and the development of shooting ranges. (Photo Dr. F Eugene Hester, U.S. FWS)

On the issue of reintroducing predators, the discussion is far from settled.

The reintroduction of predator species – wolves, bears, coyotes and even mountain lions – is significantly more controversial than bringing back the goose or the moose. Gray wolves roam the northern forests of Minnesota, Wisconsin and Michigan's Upper Peninsula – all relatively remote and under-populated areas – but the process continues to be extraordinarily controversial.

Truly, sport hunters by and large prefer to not see these species reintroduced. Even though wolves were part of the natural ecosystem, there is a reasonable fear that predators will take deer and moose by the uncounted thousands. This fear has a self-serving edge, but it also coincides with the fear of suburbanites that coyotes will kill and eat their dogs and cats, and with the concern – quite rational as it turns out, based on the Yellowstone experience – that wolves will sometimes prey upon cows and sheep. So on the issue of predators, including reintroduction of panthers (mountain lions) in Florida or Pennsylvania, the way is unclear and the discussion is far from settled.

WHERE RUBBER MEETS THE ROAD

"America means business." It is an old cliché and perhaps a bit tired, and while it can be understood in many different fashions, it suggests that this is a land of opportunity and that prosperity lies not at the end of a rainbow for every stumbling schmuck but at the limits of a person's sweat, ingenuity and perhaps luck. It also means that in this country – and it may well be true around the world – cash confers social value.

Thus, when the Federal Aid in Wildlife Restoration Act, commonly called the "Pittman-Robertson Act," was signed into law in September 1937, it definitely meant business for sport hunters … and for bird watchers, hikers, campers and photographers who, unlike their consumptive-oriented brethren, it must be said, contribute little financially. This single act of the U.S. Congress provides financial aid to states for hunter education, the management and restoration of wildlife (not just game species) and the development of shooting ranges.[4]

Pittman-Robertson levied an 11 percent excise tax on sporting arms and ammunition, and hunters and shooters have overwhelmingly supported it. The act has been amended to include handguns (1970), archery gear (1972) and crossbow arrows (1984). In fact, the dean of modern bowhunting, Fred Bear, *lobbied for the inclusion of archery in the act,* arguing that, for his sport to be taken seriously in the hunting world, it must step forward and pay its way.

Ultimately, the act has paid for the acquisition and improvement of wildlife habitat, introduction of wildlife into suitable habitat, research and surveys of wildlife problems, acquisition and development of access facilities and hunter education programs, including construction and operation of target ranges. All of this has taken place solely because hunters have paid an estimated $3 billion (with a matching $500 million from hunting license sales) into the program, and even if that money is not adjusted for inflation over the nearly 75 years since its passage (which could boost the a figure as high as $50 billion!) it is an astonishing self-tax.[5]

It is not just government however that sport hunters support with their time and money. Dozens of organizations benefit from hunter efforts in conservation or are themselves hunter initiatives (and dozens more support fishing through an act similar to Pittman-Robertson called Dingell-Johnson). Among the top in terms of membership, funding and national programs, are:

- Ducks Unlimited: With 780,000 members in North America, DU is the premier hunter-friendly conservation organization in the world. DU conserves, restores and manages wetlands and associated habitats for waterfowl and other wildlife. It estimates it has saved more than 12.6 million acres in the U.S., Canada and Mexico.

- National Wild Turkey Federation: Established in 1973, the NWTF now has more than 350,000 members. Together with its partners, sponsors and individual members, it has raised more than $286 million, upholding hunting traditions and conserving nearly 14 million acres of wildlife habitat. Since inception, the estimated number of wild turkeys in North America has risen from approximately 1,000,000 to more than 7,000,000.

- Rocky Mountain Elk Foundation: With more than 155,000 members nationwide, the RMEF has protected more than 5.6 million acres of wildlife habitat since its founding in 1984. It has helped restore elk to such places as Kentucky, Wisconsin and Ontario from which elk had been long absent.

- Safari Club International: Since its inception in 1979, SCI has raised $300 million for hunter advocacy and wildlife conservation, working with 45,000 members around the world to preserve habitat, study wildlife ecosystems, research outdoor issues and promote hunter access.

- Dallas Safari Club: In 2007 alone, DSC made grants in aid totaling nearly $300,000. Since its organization in 1970, its thousands of world-wide members have organized to conserve wildlife and wilderness lands, educate the public and promote and protect the interests of hunters.

NEXT STEPS

In the '70s, a great deal of heat was expended – at least in the U.S. – on the issue of "zero population growth." The world's population has grown by several billion people since then and now stands upwards of 6,793,485,080 individuals.[6]

Although the United Nations has predicted that world population will peak at around 11 billion, population researcher John McCarthy, professor emeritus of Computer Science at Stanford University, suggests that the world could support 15 billion people.[7]

While the world may be able to support 11 billion or even 15 billion humans, the image of billions of people (and their uncounted millions of pet dogs, cats and birds) living at the level of the population of Calcutta, India or Dhaka, Bangladesh is sobering … and frightening. Those would be our children and grandchildren. In the larger picture, a doubling of the world's human population would almost certainly doom the planet's wildlife to extinction – and because of the complex interconnectivity of life on this planet, humans would not be far behind.

"The indirect consequences of habitat loss and fragmentation may be less obvious but often carry grave consequences for animal welfare and for conservation. Maintaining functional ecosystems often requires the protection of vast

Experts disagree about the rate and impact of climate change for all earth-bound species – formerly referred to as "global warming" – but melting ice caps and glaciers certainly suggest the disruption of the flow of air and water around the earth that we have come to expect as "normal." The next decade should give us a map of consequences to come. (Photo of Hurricane Ida, November 9, 2009: NASA/NOAA)

expanses of land to meet the minimum habitat requirements of the largest, most widely roaming members of the ecosystem, including top carnivores such as eagles and cougars or large migrating herd animals such as elk."[8]

It may surprise hunters, fishermen and shooting enthusiasts that the above sentiment – surely shared in the outdoor community – is a statement by the Humane Society of the United States (HSUS). HSUS and its faithful otherwise bare their corporate fangs against all things related to sustainable harvest and our outdoor heritage.

So while we debate the larger issues – population growth, resource allocation, climate change – there are smaller subjects that we can tackle at home, and perhaps with some possibility of reaching a consensus. One of those issues is lead in the environment, and the so called green movement which has pushed this question into the hunting and shooting arena continues to shake establishments, from gasoline production to farming, to their core. It is no small wonder that we 12.5 million hunters and perhaps a few million clay and cowboy shooters beyond that find ourselves entangled in the debate.

We are few and the issues are vast, but not insurmountable.

CHAPTER NOTES

1. www.bighornsheep.org

2. Every five years, the U.S. Fish and Wildlife Service sponsors a "National Survey of Fishing, Hunting, and Wildlife-Associated Recreation." Questions are developed by a committee whose members represent every state and many nongovernmental organizations. The most recent survey was conducted in 2006.

3. Sources: U.S. Fish & Wildlife Service www.fws.gov, Wildlife Management Institute www.wildlifemanagementinstitute.org, Whitetails Unlimited www.whitetailsunlimited.com, Ducks Unlimited www.ducks.org, Dallas Safari Club www.biggame.org, Rocky Mountain Elk Foundation www.rmef.org and National Wild Turkey Federation www.nwtf.org.

4. Center for Wildlife Law, University of New Mexico http://wildlifelaw.unm.edu/

5. U.S. Fish & Wildlife Service, Southeast Region www.fws.gov/southeast/federalaid/pittmanrobertson.html

6. U.S. Census Bureau: www.census.gov/main/www/popclock.html.

7. McCarthy's paper and the U.N. survey are availabel at www-formal.stanford.edu/jmc/progress/population.html and www.un.org/popin.

8. www.hsus.org/wildlife/issues_facing_wildlife/habitat_loss_and_fragmentation/ According to the Florida Department of Agriculture & Consumer Services Gift Giver's Guide at http://app1.800helpfla.com/giftgiversguide/, HSUS has total revenues of $85 million a year. Last year, it held $45.5 million in its savings account and spent $21.8 million on program services, $1.2 million on administration and $17.4 million to raise more money. PETA raised a paltry $33.2 million, spent $27.5 million on program services, $1.4 million on administration and $4.0 million for fundraising.

CHAPTER 2

GREEN SHOOTING – IT'S THE LAW
(and if it's not, it soon will be)

ABOUT Pb

I t's all about lead – the element, not the aiming strategy; the element designated Pb[1]. At least that is the rationale.

Lead is soft, relatively speaking, malleable for a metal, very dense and corrosion resistant. It is also relatively cheap, costing – at the time of this writing in late 2009 – less than a buck a pound. The cost, in fact, is about the same as zinc and a tad more than aluminum. It is one-third the price of copper, one-sixth of tin and one-eighth of nickel. If all this sounds too good to be true, of course, it is.

Lead bricks are used to shield a radioactive sample of Cs-137. (Photo L. Chang, Wikipedia.org)

The metal has wonderful uses as bullets and shotgun pellets where, mixed with a tiny percentage of antimony, it gives shooters tight, thick patterns. Lead can also shield us from radiation. In small quantities, it has been used throughout human history in pewter, solder, glass, batteries, building materials, burial vault liners and even in compounds which, applied to the skin or hair, turned them a spectral white. Therein hides the genesis of a problem.

Lead is a naturally occurring metal. That does not mean that you want lead in your bloodstream. Meteors are naturally occurring, but you do not want one hitting you in the head. Lead, as it turns out, may be as natural as a rainbow or the soft skin of an infant's bottom, but it is also a deadly and insidious poison, one that accumulates in the body over time. Although it is a poison, it does not kill or maim quickly.

Lead falls into a class of poisons called neurotoxins, and has been documented in human remains and artifacts from ancient civilizations: Rome (in pipes and hair dyes), Egypt and Greece (in facial makeup), and China (in bronze weapons). A neurotoxin disrupts nerve cells, causing paralysis; interferes with the beating of the heart, the rigidity of bones and the elimination of waste; kills sperm and causes miscarriages.

Even with knowledge of these dangerous properties, the world has not ceased to mine and trade lead: the U.S. is a major international supplier. Indeed, the element has probably been mined for 8,500 years. About 123,000 metric tons of lead is extracted annually in the U.S., much of it in southeast Missouri, and another 1.2 metric tons is re-acquired from secondary production (recycling). As a whole, the world produces about 3.8 million metric tons a year – much of it now in lead-acid batteries, despite lead's known toxic properties – and that amount increases annually.[2]

Lead water pipes with taps from the Roman era are now in the Regional Archeological Museum of Palermo, Italy. (Photo Giovanni Dall'Orto at Wikipedia.org)

FOR THE BIRDS

A movement to find substitute materials has reduced the amount of lead used in construction, cables and containers, and all sorts of other products. The shooting sports and the industry that supports them have also made an initial move away from relying solely on lead for ammunition ... though that move is contentious and has not happened automatically or overnight. The problem of lead poisoning in waterfowl due to ingestion of lead shot was documented as early as 1894.

Not long after World War II, Winchester-Western began to study waterfowl losses which it had reason to believe were due to lead poisoning. It also researched options to conventional lead shot because, with so many war veterans returning home with an interest in hunting and firearms, the waterfowl situation had the potential to significantly worsen, even as their commercial business grew.

As it turns out, waterfowl react to lead in about the same way as humans react. This is especially true for duck species which are bottom-feeders or divers (scaup, redhead, canvasback), more than for the more numerous surface-feeders or dabblers (teal, pintail, mallard).

A duck ingests a lead pellet and the tiny BB finds its way into an organ known as the gizzard. Inside the gizzard, which is sort-of a secondary stomach where raw food particles are ground into tiny bits, the pellet helps – for a while – with digestion. Soon, however, the BB begins to erode and ultimately it dissolves. The lead is absorbed and enters the duck's bloodstream where it is carried to vital organs. Soon the animal begins to show symptoms of poisoning: it flies with difficulty and then not at all, quickly lapsing into paralysis and a prolonged and ugly death.

For a generation, Winchester-Western and researchers from various government agencies studied the problem of lead in waterfowl. In the '60s, the company began a serious focus on non-toxic alternatives to lead. It soon became apparent, from manufacturing and environmental points of view, considering the costs and effects as well as the performance characteristics understood at the time, that the best alternative to lead was steel.

The outdoor community actively resisted the move, however. To many people who did not shoot or hunt, and to some who did, it seemed a terrible contradiction: the community which prided itself on being the original American conservationists was fighting the development of an effective ammunition with obvious benefits to the animal species it professed to love, the very animals it killed and ate.

For waterfowl hunters, the problem lay not in the cost of steel loads – for although they were more expensive than conventional lead loads, that wasn't necessarily a huge issue – the problem was the molecular composition of steel.

Steel is iron plus, usually, a tiny amount of carbon; and iron, like lead, is a basic element. Steel is harder than lead, not as malleable, and is not poisonous.

The problem is that steel has a density of 7.874 gm/cm3 (weighing 490 pounds per cubic foot), whereas lead has a density of 11.34 gm/cm3 (weighing 708 pounds per cubic foot). Steel pellets of equal size thus shed energy and velocity faster than lead, and the larger the pellet the quicker its trajectory (energy and speed over distance) deteriorated. That's a difference of about one-third and, when shooting at a rapidly moving target at an uncertain distance on a breezy day while wearing bulky clothing, it can be critical. It's the difference between dropping a duck into the decoy spread where the Labrador can easily retrieve it andhaving it swim away into the reeds dragging a broken wing or leg. No hunter wants that, hence the resistance to early non-toxic loads.

The change from lead to non-toxic loads for waterfowl was promoted by the powerful National Wildlife Federation and became the law of the land in 1991. Waterfowl hunters had to adapt and it caused a significant amount of grousing that old hunters had to learn the ballistics of a new material. Long shots, shots beyond 50 yards, with the steel loads of those days were more difficult. Indeed, they were actively discouraged by shot manufacturers, in the sporting media and in conservation circles.

The NRA, in National Rifle Association of America vs. Kleppe (1972), challenged the Secretary of Interior's legal right to mandate non-toxic shot. The court upheld the regulations on the grounds that they had adequate factual basis and

By international treaty, the U.S. and Canada are required to conduct fly-over estimates of migratory waterfowl breeding zones to estimate numbers. Results allow wildlife management specialists to regulate hunting seasons and make other recommendations to sustain healthy populations. (Photo Donna Dewhurst, USFWS)

that even disagreement among experts was "not enough to invalidate an Environmental Impact Statement." [3]

Fortunately for waterfowl hunters, that was not the end of the story. Today, the loads and materials options are many, and the ballistics of shotshell loads has improved to the point that even old timers might approve.

The result of the half-century debate and study about waterfowl and lead is encouraging from the point of view of numbers of waterfowl, preservation of habitat and (we will touch more thoroughly on this in Section II) the diversity and effectiveness of loads.

According to the U.S. Fish & Wildlife Service (FWS) the most recent breeding population and habitat assessment survey of the U.S. and Canada is "very encouraging." To conduct the survey, 12 air crews flew 55,000 miles of transects over two million square miles of habitat across the U.S. (including Alaska) and Canada. The preliminary estimate of total ducks from the 2009 survey was 42 million, 13 percent greater than the 2008 estimate and 25 percent greater than the 1955-2008 average[4].

And it isn't just that production of ducks, geese and swans is on the rise in North America, but the number of waterfowl harvested has risen. FWS estimates more than 13.7 million waterfowl were harvested in the U.S. during the 2008-2009 season. While the duck harvest dipped slightly from 14.6 million the previous season, more than 3.8 million geese were harvested, an increase of 120,000.

WHAT'S YOUR COLOR?

We shooters are "going green," which means we are moving toward non-lead, non-toxic shot and bullets, whether we like it or not … and not just for ducks.

In 1991, FWS, which is the lead federal agency for enforcement of international treaties governing migratory wildlife, with jurisdiction over waterfowl in the U.S., banned lead shot for waterfowl hunting.

Looking back, some argue that the "obvious answer" may not in fact have been so obvious. Perhaps lead poisoning had as much to do with lead additives in gasoline – banned by 1986 – than in shotshells. The U.S. Environmental Protection Agency (EPA) reported that the elimination of lead from fuel removed thousands of tons of lead from the air, and that the level of lead in the bloodstream of America's children was down 70 percent.

But harmful as lead in the air was, it was not the primary reason that hundreds or thousands of ducks and geese sickened and died each year (mass waterfowl die-offs had been identified, though the cause was always hypothesized, never specifically identified or scientifically proven). Those deaths were a result of actual, physical pellets and it is these pellets – from shotguns, handguns and rifles – that EPA and FWS are studying and discussing now.

Concerning the physical deposition of lead projectiles on the ground, EPA says lead:
- oxidizes when exposed to air,
- dissolves when exposed to acidic water or soil,
- can move from firing ranges via storm-water runoff, and
- can migrate through soils to ground-water when dissolved.

"Recently, there has been a growing public concern about the potential negative environmental and health effects of range operations. In particular, the public is concerned about potential risks associated with the historical and continued use of lead shot and bullets at outdoor ranges.

Three traditional rifle cartridges for size comparison: 5.56x45 NATO, 30-30 Winchester and .308 Winchester. (Photo Boris Barowski, Wikipedia.org)

"This concern is not unfounded. An estimated 9,000 non-military outdoor ranges exist in the United States, collectively shooting millions of pounds of lead annually. Some ranges have operated for several generations. Historical operations at ranges involved leaving expended lead bullets and shot uncollected. Many of these ranges continue to operate in the same manner as in the past.

"It is estimated that approximately four percent (4%) (80,000 tons/year) of all the lead produced in the United States in the late 1990s (about two million tons/year), is made into bullets and shot. Taking into account rounds used off-range and rounds used at indoor ranges, it is clear that much of this 160,000,000 pounds of lead shot/bullets finds its way into the environment at ranges." [6]

Perhaps the fat lady has sung for lead and for primers which also contain toxic chemicals and it is only a matter of time until all recreational shooting "goes green."

THE FEDS – A SAMPLER

As a CEO, the U.S. president regulates the federal bureaucracy; everything from buying paper clips to invading a foreign country. In this capacity, he or she develops rules called Executive Orders for employees and agencies. Two of those orders – No. 13101 ("Greening the Government Through Waste Prevention, Recycling, and Federal Acquisition" September 14, 1998) and No. 13148 ("Greening the "Government Through Leadership in Environmental Management" April 21, 2000), both signed by Bill Clinton – said the U.S. government was

Camp Hansen Okinawa, Japan (Oct. 13, 2003) Utilitiesman 3rd Class Osborne fires off a 40mm round out of a M203 grenade launcher attached to an M-16 Assault Rifle during range qualifications. Osborne was assigned to Naval Mobile Construction Battalion Forty (NMCB-40), which is deployed to Okinawa and is working on construction projects throughout Japan. (Photo John P. Curtis, U.S. Navy)

going green, was going to use more environmentally friendly products[7]. The order included ammunition. Surprisingly, the marines and, to a lesser extent, the army were already studying the issue.

Every year the U.S. military reportedly fires between six and ten million training rounds, and that does not account for munitions expended in combat, which is exempt. The Department of Defense (DOD) is now required to develop and purchase non-toxic ammo and it has begun to fulfill that order at its training ranges.

MCB Camp Butler (June 7, 2006) Cpl. Christopher Fletcher loads an MK-19 40 mm grenade launcher June 7 at Camp Schwab's Range 10. Seventy-two Marines and sailors from various Okinawa-based units took part in pre-deployment training June 5-12 in preparation for upcoming deployments to support Operations Iraqi and Enduring Freedom. Fletcher is a motor vehicle operator with Headquarters Battery, 12th Marine Regiment, 3rd Marine Division. (Photo Scott M. Biscuiti, U.S. Marine Corps)

At training bases like Ft. Irwin, new cartridges, the Mk281 in two versions for high velocity (machine-fired) and the XM1110 for low velocity (shoulder-fired), are replacing the M918 for 40mm MK19 machine grenade launchers. The Mk281 is considered "non-dud-producing" and was requested by Fort Irwin commanders. The round is produced by American Rheinmetall Munitions – U.S. subsidiary of German-based Rheinmetall Defence – located in Stafford, Virginia south of Washington, DC and just down the street from the Quantico marine base. The production facility is located in Camden, Arkansas.

Reports from the training field indicate that the "green" 40mm cartridges have a realistic simulation and deliver good "hit signatures" without the problems of duds and the many "cease fire" alerts associated with conventional pyrotechnic cartridges. Not only does use of the new Mk281 reduce range clean-up, but commanders say it helps prevent training accidents and greatly reduces travel time to "hot" ranges because it can be used in many friendly environments.

It is not just the defense department that uses ammo, though. In 2009 Winchester won the contract to supply the Federal Bureau of Investigation (FBI) with .40 caliber rounds for their standard issue Glock 22s. This $54 million contract plus an earlier contract amounted to $108 million and included a significant volume of "reduced lead training ammunition."

It was "the single largest ammunition contract in the history of federal law enforcement, worth a maximum of $54 million. Winchester Ammunition will produce .40 S&W service ammunition, training ammunition, reduced-lead training ammunition and frangible ammunition for the FBI for one base year, with four, one-year renewal options...."

Agencies of the federal government such as the Federal Bureau of Investigation are now purchasing frangible non-toxic rounds for training purposes. (Photo FBI)

"Winchester's enhanced .40 S&W service ammunition is a 180-grain bonded jacketed hollow point round and was selected over all other rounds that were tested. The FBI tests [see Chapter 8: Non-Toxic – What's Available and What's Coming] the terminal ballistics of each round by shooting a specific test protocol through various barriers such as heavy cloth, wallboard, plywood, steel and auto glass into ballistic gelatin.

"In addition to the FBI, the contract impacts many agencies both inside and outside the Department of Justice, including the Drug Enforcement Administration, Bureau of Alcohol, Tobacco, Firearms and Explosives and U.S. Marshal Service."[8]

THE STATES – A SAMPLER

In December 2007, New York's Environmental Conservation Commissioner Pete Grannis announced that the state's 464 environmental conservation officers and forest rangers must use "green [non-lead] ammo" with non-toxic primers "to reduce the impact of lead at firing ranges." It is just "common sense," he said, to "protect public health and the environment from the effects of lead." The Department of Environmental Conservation estimates its officers fire more than 150,000 rounds annually, including during regional in-service training exercises, as well as at the 26-week residential basic training academy[9].

Chances are your state is not far behind. A Minnesota legislator has proposed banning lead shot for small game and upland bird hunting.

But isn't everyone against toxic substances in the environment? Certainly, but too much tungsten, bismuth or even iron in a diet eventually becomes toxic. Does this end only when shooting itself is banned?

Independent shooting sports retailers – perhaps the folks selling sporting goods in your home town – are far from unanimous in their position on non-toxic shooting or about their response.

The ventilation system of an indoor range must positively draw air, with the fumes and the practically invisible ash it carries as a result of shooting, from the shooter toward the target, where it can be vented outside or filtered using a method that removes impurities. (Photo Vladimir)

"We're the only range in Pennsylvania that shoots only green ammo that is open to the public," says Frank Tripoli, owner of Tripoli Triggers in Williamsport. "My whole focus is the safety and health of shooters. People are suing toy companies because of lead in paint and the last thing I want is to have a closed environment, even with a superb air handling system, where someone has the potential for lead poisoning. Plus, law enforcement will only use the range if it is lead-free. Pennsylvania's police only train with green ammo."

The cry of the loon may be the most beautiful and mysterious bird call in the world. "Lead poisoning in aquatic birds may occur when spent lead shot is mistaken for gravel (which is normally consumed to aid in digestion) and ingested. Birds may also be exposed to lead when feeding on fish attached to lead fishing gear such as sinkers or jig heads. The [Wildlife Clinic at the Cummings School of Veterinary Medicine, Tufts University] is conducting an ongoing study of the prevalence of lead poisoning in aquatic birds, particularly the Common Loon. In addition to loons, frequent victims of lead poisoning include swans, pelicans, geese, ducks, cormorants, cranes and herons." (Photo Steve Maslowski, U.S. Fish & Wildlife Service)

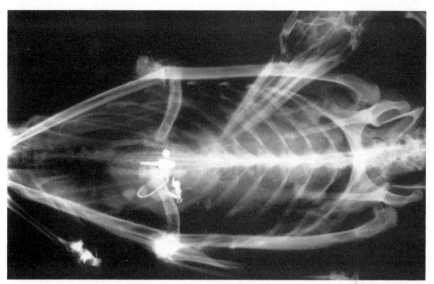

In this x-ray of a dead loon found on a northern Minnesota lake, lead fishing tackle is clearly visible. (Photo Minnesota Pollution Control Agency)

"I see us [hunting, shooting, law enforcement and military] going totally non-lead within our lifetime," says Robin Ball, owner of Sharp Shooting Indoor Range & Gun Shop in Spokane, Washington. "Science says lead from spent rounds has little environmental effect, but our side doesn't seem to have much of a voice against the environmental lobby. At our range, we only shoot lead. We make sure employees wash their hands and face before they eat. We monitor for airborne pollution and haven't run into any problems."

Lest you think someone is picking on hunters, New York and other states have banned small lead sinkers also. The Empire State's decision affected lead sinkers weighing less than half an ounce; Maine and Vermont soon followed. New Hampshire raised the bar to a full ounce and included lead jigs smaller than an inch. Massachusetts prohibits the use of all lead sinkers for the taking of fish in Quabbin and Wachusett Reservoirs, the two bodies of water that support the core of that state's loon population. FWS has banned lead sinkers in several national wildlife refuges and the National Park Service (NPS) in Yellowstone National Park. Concerned about their state bird, the common loon, Minnesota seems poised to enact restrictions.

The U.S. is not alone in attending to lead from fishermen. Great Britain has restricted the use of lead fishing weights weighing less than one ounce. In Canadian national parks and national wildlife areas, it is illegal to use lead sinkers and jigs weighing less than 50 grams (1.76 ounces). In Denmark, companies are now prohibited from importing and marketing any product containing lead.[10]

A WOLF IN SHEEP'S CLOTHING?

Not everyone is enamored of the move to green shooting, however, no matter how well intentioned the reasoning. "The sacred alter of 'green' ammo has sucked up tens of millions of dollars over many years in the nebulous pursuit of 'non-toxic' ammunition," writes Dr. Gary Roberts, a naval reserve officer and member of the staff at Stanford University Medical Center, who has extensive test experience for DOD related projects, "yet with a few … exceptions, has not resulted in any improvements in ammunition reliability, accuracy, or terminal performance – the factors that actually help win fights." [11]

Larry Pratt, Executive Director of the Gun Owners of America, says there is simply no science to support the efforts to force rifle and handgun shooting into non-toxic ammunition, and certainly not in the military, a move which he says would be funny if it weren't so serious. Pratt believes the green ammo movement is simply a back door method of gun control. "They can't outlaw guns so they're going to make the ammo as expensive and as hard to buy as possible."

Indeed, industry insiders wonder about a "lead scare" perhaps promoted by individuals with ulterior motives. "Certainly jacketed lead-core bullets are cheaper to shoot, and perhaps that's what keeps people shooting," says Jessica Brooks from Barnes Bullets, a company that has specialized in developing non-lead bullets for more than a generation. "If people have to pay a premium price for ammunition, then they're going to either put down their guns and not shoot or shoot sparingly. That doesn't do a whole lot to preserve this industry for future generations."

Which many believe is exactly the point.

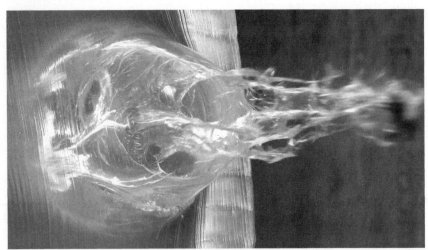

A 185-gr. Barnes XPB non-toxic copper bullet blasts through a block of ballistic gel. Is the push to restrict lead ammunition simply "back door gun control?" Larry Pratt, Executive Director of the Gun Owners of America, says this is precisely the hidden issue.

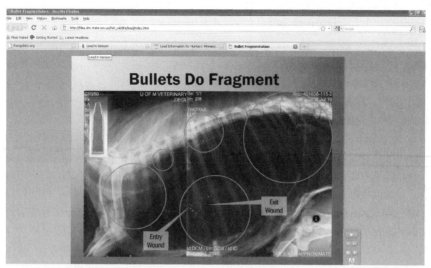

Screen capture of radiograph by Lou Cornicelli, Minnesota Department of Natural Resources big game program coordinator, showing fragmentation of rapid-expansion bullet: "Regardless of the type of ammunition used, this study showed that bullets do fragment. [Here] Lead fragments spread throughout the cavity, from shoulder to flank." (http://files.dnr.state.mn.us/fish_wildlife/ lead/index.htm)

Regarding lead deposition on shooting ranges, Peter Proctor, PhD, MD, from Houston, Texas, has worked with cases of heavy metal poisoning. As early as January 1994 he wrote a letter that is now posted on the Gun Owners of America web site[12] and which says, in part:

"First, metallic lead (e.g., in the form of lead bullets, shot, etc) is not a significant source of environmental lead contamination. This is for several reasons. Among these are the relative inertness of lead in metallic form. Thus, for example, lead containers are used in sulfuric acid manufacture because of the relative insolubility and inertness of lead even to strong acids. This is combined with the relative insolubility and immobility of lead salts in the soil environment. Thus, lead levels in water leaving the site were only 20 ppb.

"Lead contamination and/or lead poisoning can come from a variety of sources. These include such well known sources as the use of lead salts in ceramic glazes and paint chips ingestion by children. Such exposure involves actual oral consumption of non-metallic lead.

"As for metallic lead, there have been a few cases of probable mild chronic lead poisoning secondary to retained bullets following gun-shot wounds. These are rare enough to be "reportable." They illustrate the relative non-toxicity of metallic lead even under extreme conditions.

"In my literature search of over 5,000 papers, I could find no reference to outdoor shooting ranges as significant sources of environmental lead. How-

Big guns like this Barrett 50 caliber make a serious noise and, in the hands of a skilled marksman, can kill at more than a mile. Few shooting ranges in the eastern half of the U.S. can handle such a rifle, and traditional bullet fragmentation or dispersion following impact would be a true problem if the guns and their ammo weren't so expensive.

ever, there are debatable questions about chronic inhalation of particulate lead in poorly ventilated indoor shooting ranges. Perhaps someone got things confused.

"Thus, I must conclude that the proceedings brought against Mr. [Robert G.] Arwady and his shooting range [Southwest Tactical Training Range in Fort Bend County, Texas] lack any scientific basis. I am willing to testify to such if necessary."

It is apparent, although the letter and opinions are 15 years old, that the science did not then – and does not now – support a necessity to ban lead ammo from shooting ranges and that Dr. Proctor, who was one of only two board certified toxicologists in Houston, was willing to testify to that fact.

In mid-2009, the U.S. National Park Service (NPS) floated a suggestion to ban its employees from using lead ammo in big game culling operations on park properties – and to ban lead shot and lead sinkers also. They further considered requesting hunters at Grand Teton National Park and, in cooperation with FWS, at the National Elk Refuge, to voluntarily use non-lead ammo. NPS left open the option of requiring all shooting within U.S. Park Service properties to be green.

The National Shooting Sports Foundation (NSSF), the trade association for the firearms and ammunition industry, responded that they rejected NPS's categorization of "traditional ammunition" as a health threat[13]. NSSF noted that no scientific evidence supports restricting ammunition containing lead components and that banning such traditional bullets was arbitrary and "a drastic policy decision unsupported by science."

NPS also raised concerns that lead bullet fragments found in game might cause lead poisoning in humans. This suggestion is not borne out in scientific studies either, however, including recent Centers for Disease Control and Prevention (CDC) research on North Dakota hunters who consumed wild game. According to the NSSF, the CDC study showed there was no reason for concern about eating game taken with traditional ammunition, but other interpretations of the data present an entirely different view[14]. Still, there is no documented case of human lead poisoning among hunters who have eaten game harvested with traditional ammunition ... even though levels of lead in their blood is definitely elevated. (Additional study of this in context is presented in Chapter 7: Lead Ammo – The Truth is out There ... Somewhere.")

"While we're not opposed to voluntary measures, we maintain there is no need for them," said Steve Sanetti, president of NSSF. "The firearms industry supports science-based decisions about wildlife management. Under current regulations, there is no scientific evidence showing that the health of wildlife populations and humans is at risk from the use of traditional ammunition."

In a subsequent press release, Grand Teton National Park and National Elk Refuge officials encouraged hunters to voluntarily switch to "alternative ammunition" during the 2009 elk and bison seasons. The voluntary measures are being advocated even though the elk refuge manager said there have probably been no population impacts on ravens or eagles (which scavenge carcasses) connected with traditional rifle ammunition.

NSSF senior vice president and general counsel Lawrence G. Keane summed up the situation by saying: "In some areas today, wildlife management is being driven by fear of litigation, not by science."

A PAIR OF DUCKS?

The concept of "cleaning-up" outdoor shooting ranges which have for years been open to public and organized shooting is not as simple as it sounds. Lead is not attracted by a magnet, for instance, so recovering solid particles requires digging, filtering and separating by hand or machine.

Most states now have documents called Best Management Practices that guide shooting ranges in regard to lead ammo. Colorado's guideline, for example, states in part:

"During the active life of a shooting range, steps can be taken to reduce the amount of lead in the environment. A lead management program, which employs a variety of best management practices, should include bullet and shot containment, prevention of lead migration, and periodic lead removal and recycling. There are many techniques available to achieve these objectives, which can be designed to meet the specific needs of individual ranges. In addition to lead management practices, the use of lead-free shot should also be evaluated."[15]

Environmental & Turf Services is one of numerous companies that have expertise appropriate to the growing concern about lead in the environment. Company president Stuart Cohen is a certified ground water professional with a PhD in chemistry who has spoken at NRA Range Development Conferences. Cohen says concerns about lead's hazard to human health are real and that the risk is simply too great to keep lead as the principal "status quo" ammunition.

According to Cohen, there are numerous problems with long term use of lead ammunition on shooting ranges, as well as complications involved in an abrupt change from lead to rounds or shot pellets comprised of other materials: "If you have a range where you formerly shot lead and began shooting tungsten or steel, for instance, I would be concerned that soil pH could change once steel or tungsten shot begins to corrode. That would increase the acidity of the soil and cause the spent lead shot or bullets to leach into the aquifer. In other words, the change to green ammo could, potentially, mobilize the soil and move a situation from potentially to actually hazardous."

Curiously, using only lead-free ammo on a range, although it may reduce the cost of eventual range clean up and ease recycling efforts, may also create potential environmental problems. The long-term effects of spent tungsten, for example, are not well understood. In his company's compliance guide, Cohen notes that, while "the use of copper-jacketed bullets will inhibit the spreading of lead in the target/ backstop area ... it will complicate recycling efforts. (Facilities that melt the shot or bullets may view the copper as a contaminant in their process.)."

And even the vaunted steel shot comes with difficulties. Indoors or out: It poses a ricochet hazard because it is so much harder than lead. If steel shot is used in an area, the shotfall zone should not also include spent lead shot[16].

CHAPTER NOTES

1. The original Latin name for lead was plumbum, hence the designation Pb. Because lead was so frequently used in pipes and ornamental structures, the name was eventually imported into English as the word plumber.

2. U.S. Geological Survey (USGS – http://minerals.usgs.gov), Mineral Commodity Summaries, January 2009. A metric ton is 2,204.6 pounds or 204.6 pounds heavier than a standard U.S. ton: see http://minerals.usgs.gov/ds/2005/140/lead.pdf.

3. Defendants were Thomas Kleppe, Secretary of the Interior, who was responsible for approving Migratory Bird Treaty Act regulations, and Lynn Greenwalt, Director of the U.S. Fish & Wildlife Service (FWS), who was responsible for promulgating regulations. http://dc.findacase.com/research/wfrmDocViewer.aspx/xq/fac.%5CFDCT%5CDDC%5C1976%5C19761217_0000177.DDC.htm/qx

4. "Waterfowl Population Status 2009" FWS www.fws.gov/migratorybirds/NewReportsPublications/PopulationStatus/Waterfowl/StatusReport2009_Final.pdf

5. "Migratory Bird Hunting Activity and Harvest During the 2007 and 2008 Hunting

Seasons" FWS July 2009 (includes dove, woodcock and others) www.fws.gov/migratorybirds/NewReportsPublications/HIP/HuntingStatistics/Migratory%20bird%20hunting%20activity%20and%20harvest%20during%20the%202007%20and%202008%20hunting%20seasons.%20Preliminary%20Estimates,%20July%202009.pdf

6. www.epa.gov/region2/waste/leadshot/bmp3_7.pdf

7. Read the complete text of Executive Order Executive Order No. 13101 at www.epa.gov/epp/pubs/13101.pdf and Executive Order No. 13148 at http://frwebgate.access.gpo.gov/cgi-bin/getdoc.cgi?dbname=2000_register&docid=fr26ap00-129.pdf.

8. www.winchester.com/news/newsview.aspx?storyid=242

9. "DEC Announces Plan to Train with 'Green Ammo' Leading the Way for Other Law Enforcement Agencies in Switching to Environmentally Friendly Ammunition for Training" www.dec.ny.gov/press/40935.html.

10. Twenty-two percent of 202 common loons found dead in New England had ingested lead objects, principally sinkers and jigs: collected only from fresh water only, 57 percent of 74 adult birds. A single dose of 0.3 grams of lead per bird result in death. Lead sinkers and jigs generally weigh between 0.5 and 15 grams, hence the ingestion of even one sinker is fatal. University of Vermont, Vermont Legislative Research Group "The Effect of Lead Sinkers on Waterfowl" www.uvm.edu/~vlrs/doc/lead_sinkers.htm

11. You can read Dr. Roberts' report and other commentaries at Imminent Threat Solutions web site: www.itstactical.com.

12. http://gunowners.org

13. The NSSF maintains a file of press releases at www.nssf.org/news/.

14. As reported by Scott Streater in Environmental Health News, September 2009, at www.environmentalhealthnews.org/ehs/news/lead-in-game-meat.

15. "Corrective Action at Outdoor Shooting Ranges" Guidance Document – Version 1, Colorado Department of Public Health and Environment, January 2005 (The full text is available on line at www.cdphe.state.co.us/hm/shootingrange.pdf.)

16. www.environmentalandturf.com

SECTION II:
THE GREEN SHOTGUNNER

CHAPTER 3

ALTERNATIVES TO LEAD SHOT

No one can predict the future. No one knows whether a miracle composite will eventually be identified to perfectly replace lead, an element that is plentiful, effective and cheap. Lead has proven to be – over centuries of shooting for every kind of game in every kind of environment and weather – both highly effective and relatively inexpensive. Still, based on the demonstrated science of need and the conservation heart of hunters, including the manufacturers who supply them, "relatively effective" alternatives to lead are available on today's market.

Hevi-Shot calls Hevi-Metal a "pattern density breakthrough" specifically for scatter-gunners who like to shoot the ultra-dense tungsten compound.

Here's a look at what's available and how it performs.

STEEL AND STEEL SHOT

Steel was the original idea for a substitute metal for lead and may still be the best, but the longer it has been studied the more complications and options have come to light. Although lead is a denser and therefore heavier metal than steel, steel – iron plus carbon – is harder than lead. This is why a small amount, usually three to five percent, of antimony is added to lead when shot is poured: to increase its hardness.

Incredibly, a very small amount of arsenic, perhaps 0.5 percent (.005), is also added when manufacturing lead shot[1]. A simple explanation of shot manufacture is to pour molten lead, which has already been mixed with antimony and arsenic, through a shaking colander or screen. As they drip through the holes, the droplets become round and fall into a vat of water where they cool. Arsenic helps the falling drops of metal develop surface tension and become spherical – rather than oblong – by delaying the solidification of the molten lead, and thereby al-

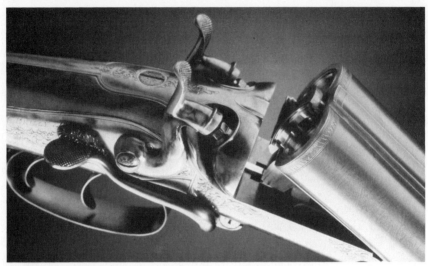

Older shotguns have barrels made from steel that is not as hard as that used in most modern guns. They have been fired thousands of times, perhaps have had parts replaced and have been dropped and polished and ... before using shot that is harder than lead, consider having them studied by a skilled gunsmith. (Photo AYA)

lowing it to flow more readily. The amount of arsenic used is so minute that it is not considered a health hazard.

For laymen, the production of steel shot seems more complicated. Steel (often scrap) is first annealed[2A] to the desired hardness and then melted, the molten steel being subjected to atomization – blasting it into tiny fragments – by a jet of high-pressure water. This is followed by a series of thermal and mechanical treatments to give the product final characteristics. It is dried, screened for size, spiraled to remove irregular shapes, quenched and tempered.

The alternative method of producing steel shot is to cut wire and stamp it to shape. Because steel is still a small minority of shot sold and manufacturers usually charge more for it, this is still economical.

Steel Performance

To understand how steel performs – and its performance is far superior today than original loads, which were sometimes reported as bouncing off waterfowl in flight! – and how it compares to lead, it is useful to sort through the parts of a typical shotgun and see what happens when you pull the trigger.

A shotgun barrel is made in one section, but it is described as four, each with a different function. The shotshell is seated in the chamber which is physically connected to the forcing cone and the bore. When you pull the trigger and the shell's powder ignites, the shot cup (also called a wad) and the shot are shoved out of the hull and into the forcing cone.

Patterning your shotgun with the load you plan to shoot during hunting season will help you find your point of aim and learn how loads perform at distance. (Photo Craig Endicott)

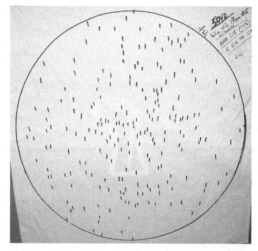

The forcing cone is a short, conical section that necks the barrel bore down in size from the chamber – which must accommodate the entire shell – to the bore – which must only accept what is inside the shell.

Next comes the barrel bore itself, by far the longest section. Here, the powder completes its burn, building pressure to the maximum for the load, and the shot reaches maximum acceleration.

Finally, at the muzzle is the short choke section, which is responsible for shaping the shot pattern and helping separate the wad from the shot. Unless a shotgun is very old or is built for a specialized purpose, it will have replaceable, screw-in chokes. This allows you to give your shot pattern a different shape or a different length (called a shot string).

When the gun's firing pin hits the primer in the base of the shotshell, the primer explodes and ignites the powder. The powder burns almost instantaneously, and the resulting scorching hot gas compresses the round shot inside the shell. Such an explosive compression deforms some of the lead pellets, especially those manufactured with lower percentages of antimony. Further compression as they mash together in the forcing cone and in the choke continues to deform pellets.

Steel shot is deformed not at all because it is practically as hard as the gun barrel. This means that steel patterns at almost any distance – guns and loads are often patterned at 40 yards – are typically more compact and consistent than lead; steel shot strings are also much shorter. A steel pattern typically has fewer "flyers" or pellets wandering far off course because they have been deformed in the barrel and thus are aerodynamically inconsistent.

While there is some question about whether the length of a string of shot is important because the majority of pellets are bunched in an initial spread, and it is a difficult thing to measure, a string of lead shot can be 10 to 12 feet long, including flyers. The length of a comparable string of steel (or other lead substitutes) will be much shorter, perhaps by half. This means a shooter may need to recalculate target lead when switching from one substance to another.

Any modern shotgun, especially a fine gun like the Weatherby Athena over/under 12-gauge, will handle any modern load for which it is chambered.

A steel load is typically built to be a little faster than lead – to make up for lack of density and therefore lack of energy at range, cartridge designers compensate by increasing velocity[3] – which seems obvious since lead is heavier, but velocity is also dependent upon shell components, especially the type of powder. Thus, unless you are hand loading and can research exact load recipes including powder burn rates for a particular barrel length and choke, relative velocities are difficult to compare. Remember that shot size is a standard whereas components – lead or steel pellets, for instance – vary in weight. Thus an ounce of #7 lead will have fewer pellets than an ounce of the same diameter steel: 299 to 422.

Typically, to make allowances for steel's lower density, an experienced shotgunner new to shooting steel will want to limit the range of his shots. If you can bring down a flying bird at 50 yards with a 12-gauge, practice self-discipline and limit shooting at first to 35 or 40 yards (realizing that in the field distances are difficult to estimate, especially looking upward with no points of reference). If you typically shoot #6, try shooting #5 or even #4. These steps will help you compensate for the knock-down power you have grown accustomed to with lead.

Ballistics Products says that choosing a steel pellet size for loads incurs additional considerations. While larger pellets contain more energy per pellet at a given range, larger pellets are more difficult to control for tight, consistent patterns. Select a pellet size with sufficient energy at the ranges you expect to be shooting without simply selecting the maximum size or even the fastest load.

Thus, when shooting steel shot for clays, a practice that is becoming more common, choose the largest size available, typically #7, which at this time is the only size commonly available. The only considerations are range, wind and whether you are shooting a tournament or registered targets (which often carry specific size stipulations). Large pellets stay on course longer.

Steel and Your Shotgun

Modern shotguns are built to handle almost any properly loaded shell that fits into their chamber. The barrel's steel is very hard; many barrels are chrome-lined; forcing cones have been lengthened and are often chromed as well; and a significant degree of research has gone into chokes – and a significant degree of choke education into shooters. Now, by and large, people understand that a gun with multiple screw-in choke options must not be shot without a choke in place, and the choke must be tight so that it aligns in a flush manner with the bore and that it must be occasionally removed and cleaned, including the threads of the choke and the barrel.

This hasn't always been the case. Many older shotguns – and there are millions of hand-me-down guns in closets across North America – were made with a steel that was not as hard as the steel shot going through it, and they would pit and scratch and bulge or even, in rare cases, explode when a heavy, high pressure load was fired. In addition, they had fixed chokes incompatible with steel. So for older guns, those with a date of manufacture prior to the steel era (say 25 years ago) the rule of thumb is not to shoot steel (or Hevi-Shot) through them at all.

Should you choose to shoot steel in an older gun, carefully consider the load's chamber pressure and opt for a lower pressure load. If you hand load, consider adding a buffer or a Mylar wrap inside the shot cup or perhaps dropping down in shot size, if possible. The objective is to keep steel pellets from coming into abrasive contact with the barrel as the burning gas propels it forward at a thousand miles per hour.

Some manufacturers offer newer barrels that will fit older guns. A well-maintained Remington 1100 that dates from the '80s might drop geese comfortably, but a new steel-proofed 26- or 30-inch barrel is only $253 retail and that is far less than buying a new 1100. (Remington says its Model 1100 Steel Shot Barrels are designed for use with 2 ¾- or 3-inch magnum steel – or lead – shot shells when used on magnum receivers, and 2 ¾- or 3-inch magnum steel or 2 ¾-inch lead shotshells when used on non-magnum receivers.)

A duck hunter has set out decoys and is framed by the rising sun over the Central (Mississippi) Flyway. It is widely suspected that some percentage (guesses as high as 10 to 15 percent can be found in the literature) of waterfowl hunters "cheat," refusing to shoot steel or other non-toxic loads. Instead, they hide lead shells in the woods near their blinds or simply hope that they will never be caught. In an era when state and federal conservation resources stretched almost beyond the breaking point, this would be a practice – if it is true – that no hunter or conservationist would condone. (Photo Dave Menke, U.S. FWS)

Of course, steel oxidizes; it rusts. Lead does not, at least not anywhere close to the rate of steel, which can develop a patina of rust overnight. Thus attention to old shells, the ones in the pocket of your game bag at the end of the day, is very important. If you end a waterfowl season with a partial box, store it in a low-humidity environment because firing a mass that is effectively welded together with rust can destroy your barrel. If you are lucky, it will only be the barrel.

And speaking of eating steel ... biting down on a #4 pellet inside a well-turned mallard breast means a trip to the dentist. With lead, you may be able to get away with the bite although you won't want to swallow the pellet – though if you do, it will almost certainly pass through your system within 24 hours leaving behind no detectable traces whatsoever.

It won't do to think of plated lead shot as non-toxic, either. Plated shot is simply lead with a fine coating or wash of copper or nickel. The advertised intent is to give soft lead pellets better flight and penetration characteristics by making them harder, thus preventing their acquiring flat spots during setback and the brief, scorching passage to the open air. In fact the practical effects of this hardening are difficult to demonstrate without resorting to a pattern board.

TUNGSTEN SHOT

In the search for non-toxic substitutes for lead pellets, tungsten compounds have risen to the top as a leading best-all-around candidate. Tungsten is much denser than lead and almost three times as dense as steel. This hardness is attractive, but also comes with a brittleness and, before developing it as a non-toxic

The bufflehead is the smallest wild duck flying over North America. Even with this small bird there is no evidence that tungsten has any negative health effects. (Photo Nauticashades, Wikipedia.org)

shot substitute, manufacturers had to learn to first grind the metal into a powder and find the right elements to mix with it.

In January 2003 the U.S. Fish & Wildlife Service took a significant step by approving tungsten-matrix shot for waterfowl: "We approve shot formulated of 65% tungsten, 10.4% iron, 2.8% nickel, and 21.8% tin as nontoxic for hunting waterfowl and coots.

"We assessed possible effects of the tungsten-iron-nickel-tin (TINT) shot, and we believe that it does not present a significant toxicity threat to wildlife or their habitats and that further testing of the shot is not necessary. Approval of this shot provides another nontoxic option for hunters.

"Currently, steel, bismuth-tin, tungsten-iron, tungsten-polymer, tungsten-matrix, and tungsten-nickel-iron shot are approved as non-toxic."

While there is little extant medical literature about the toxicity of tungsten, some has been published since original FWS approval. Acute poisoning from elevated tungsten levels in the blood is extremely rare, but a few cases have been documented. Tungsten causes the rapid onset of nausea, seizures, a clouded consciousness leading to coma and renal failure; complete recovery takes months.

Patterns from tungsten are still very tight at distances between 40 and 60 yards, where other non-toxic shot patterns tend to fall apart, indicating that the denser tungsten matrix pellets hold their energy longer and provide greater penetration on longer shots.

The long-term or chronic effects of tungsten pellet ingestion by waterfowl are virtually unknown, but do not appear to harm a bird ... which after all has a relatively short lifespan. There is some medical suspicion that a cancer risk exists if metal workers inhale powdered tungsten, but this, too, has been studied insufficiently to give a final scientific judgment. No safe or acceptable levels of tungsten in the human body have yet been established.

The case of the U.S. Army's nylon-wrapped tungsten 5.56 bullets made by ATK and tested at Camp Edwards on Cape Cod demonstrate that tungsten does indeed break down and dissolve into the underlying aquifer. Writing in the December 17, 2006, "Cape Cod Times," Amada Lehmert reported that a water sample taken from 30 meters beneath a small arms range on that National Guard training base held tungsten concentrations as high as 560 parts per billion. Shooting was halted at the base and the army halted acquisition of this green bullet.

Apparently the jury has convened to reconsider tungsten's toxicity or lack thereof. At this time, the shooting community has few truly sparkling options – cheap, effective, available – to lead other than steel.

Mixing Steel and Tungsten Pellets

Ballisticians for Federal hold hundreds, perhaps thousands of patents. Their U.S. Patent No. 6,202,561 titled "Shotshell having pellets of different densities in stratified layers" was published in March 2001 (www.freepatentsonline.com).

"A shotshell comprised of shot pellets of different densities and materials which provide increased effectiveness at both close and long range. Preferably the pellets are disposed in longitudinally stratified layers, with the more dense pellets located rearwardly (sic) of the pellets of lesser density. The pellets having the greater density maintain a closer pattern at long range, because they are preferably made of tungsten which has a high density and are located rearwardly (sic), while the pellets having lesser density are preferably made of steel, describe a much wider pattern because of their lower density and forward location, and are therefore most effective at close range."

Eventually, companies offered "duplex" loads with two sizes of shot in a single shell. Today, Remington Wingmaster uses a tungsten-bronze (copper and tin)-iron mix that improves on the concept of multiple size shot in a single load. At 12.0 gm/cm3 it is 10 percent denser than lead, a "scientifically proven optimum density for pellet count and pattern density." Scientifically proven ... or simply traditional.

HEVI-SHOT

In 1998 a metallurgist named Darryl Amick developed Hevi-Shot. It was a new, and in theory non-toxic technology using tungsten, nickel, iron and tin to

Even a cursory glance shows that pellets in Hevi-Shot loads defy conventional wisdom that shot must be uniformly round for best ballistics and energy delivery.

develop a slightly different, but super-dense pellet, a bit denser than lead. Obviously, such a load could deliver terrific energy at long distances – those 60-yard shots that old-time goose hunters were lamenting when forced to shoot steel – and thus Hevi-Shot developed exclusively at first as a bird hunting load.

The exceptionally dense nature of Hevi-Shot's tungsten formulation requires special handling and loading elements. Special shotcups, for instance, were required to eliminate pellet contact with the barrel or otherwise scrubbing and pitting were almost certain in older guns and even possible in the newer guns. Modern barrels rate around 116-117 BHN hardness on the Brinell scale compared to steel shot at about 75 BHN and to Hevi-Shot in the range of 150-162.

Like steel, but unlike some advertised soft tungsten loads, Hevi-Shot does not deform in its passage out the barrel, and consequently results in excellent patterns with few flyers. Thus, many experienced reloaders like to drop down a single size from the lead load – still the standard for performance and price – and perhaps a couple sizes smaller than steel. This is appropriate because the extra density being shot compensates for wind drift and friction.

Amrick is the principal inventor (with Haygarth, Fenwick and Seal) listed in U.S. Patent No. 5,527,376 "Composite shot" which was published in June 1996 for Teledyne Industries of Oregon. According to Amrick's paperwork, filed in October 1994: "Shot pellet or small arms projectile comprises 40-60% by weight of tungsten and 60-40% by weight of iron formed by sintering tungsten containing powders … to form a material consisting primar[il]y of an intermetallic compound of tungsten and iron or of a metal matrix of iron surrounding tungsten containing particles." In other words, the new Hevi-Shot.

The process for manufacturing Hevi-Shot is almost identical to that for producing lead shot. The binary alloy of steel-tungsten matrix is melted, heating to 1637° C (2979° F). The liquid is poured through a sieve. Droplets fall between 12 and 30 inches "through air, argon, nitrogen or other suitable gas into a liquid such as water at ambient temperature, causing the cooled shot to form into spheres of desired sizes. Though generally of the desired shape, they can be further smoothed and made more uniform by mechanical methods such as grinding, rolling, or coining." Hevi-Shot though is notoriously out-of-round, but with superior marketing sleight-of-hand and perhaps a willingness to question conventional wisdom the company has turned this negative to a positive.

BISMUTH

In combination with tin, this heavy, brittle metal is used as a substitute for lead shot, although it is not quite as dense. Nevertheless, it is easily twice as hard as lead. As a shot product, bismuth is superior to steel, with performance characteristics comparable to lead: it did not scar barrels, even with repeated shooting through older barrels, and any choke – even older fixed choke barrels – would work safely, but the price was often four times that of high quality lead rounds. That was a problem.

History notes that bismuth as an alternative to lead was brought to international attention by a Canadian waterfowl hunter, part-time carpenter and metallurgical tinkering genius named John Brown. Brown apparently did much of the initial work on the material in the '80s, including patenting his ideas, but bismuth was rejected by the major ammo companies – perhaps because Brown was an unknown without recognized ballistic credentials, or because his ideas came too early in the development of non-toxic shooting, or because bismuth is much more expensive than steel.

Nevertheless, Brown eventually got the attention of the legendary Bob Petersen, founder of Petersen Publishing Company, and Petersen formed the Bismuth Cartridge Company in the '80s. Unfortunately, when Petersen died in 2007, Bismuth Cartridge went out of business. The torch has recently been taken up by Pinnacle Ammunition, spearheaded by several of the former Petersen and BCC executives.

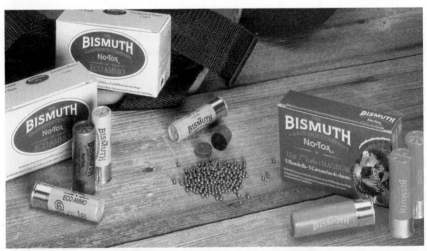

What's not to like about a non-toxic metal that shoots like lead? Bismuth shells have traditionally cost much more but the original company, which used lacquered paper shells and biodegradable fiber wads, went out of business with the death of founder Bob Petersen. Bismuth has since been resurrected as Bis-Maxx by the Pinnacle Ammunition Company.

Advertised as Bis-Maxx, the new bismuth shells are labeled "All guns, all gauges, all chokes," except for classic Damascus or twist-steel barrels. Bismuth, like tungsten, carries more energy downrange than steel – 24 percent, according to Pinnacle – and puts more pellets in a pattern than tungsten.

Bismuth has advantages over steel and over lead as well. Bismuth can be fired at waterfowl with lower velocities because it is denser than steel and thus retains its killing energy at greater distance. It also has the reputation of working well in sub-gauges like the 20 and 28 ... even the .410. And compared to lead or tungsten, though it is more expensive, it is definitely non-toxic and therefore universally legal.

Eley in Sutton Coldfield, England, is the manufacturer of all bismuth shot brought into the U.S. Eley uses the modified short drop Bleimeister process to make the smaller shot, #3 through #7. Shot larger than #3 must be die-cast because in larger diameter, the bismuth alloy tends to tear-drop or fall out-of-round. Even in its short history, bismuth loads earned a reputation for including a fair number of irregular pellets. This can make for some ugly patterns, but the delivery of energy in the pellets that remained in a pattern was impressive and effective.

Background: John Brown's Bismuth Patent

John Brown's U.S. Patent No. 4,949,644 was published in August 1990. Titled "Non-toxic shot and shot shell containing same," it explored bismuth as an effective pellet material: "Non-toxic wildlife shot pellets for shotgun shells are formed from bismuth or a bismuth alloy." Brown argued instructively that:

"Lead shot conventionally is employed in shotguns. The density of lead provides shot made therefrom (sic) with a ballistic efficiency which heretofore has not been matched by any other commercially available shot material, such as steel.

"Unfortunately, lead presents a serious toxicity problem to waterfowl. Spent shot lying on the bottom of shallow lakes and marshes within reach of feeding ducks and geese is sometimes ingested along with similar sized gravel and taken into the gizzard of the bird. After being broken down in the gizzard, the lead is absorbed into the bird's system, often in lethal doses. Studies have shown that the number of waterfowl which die from lead poisoning have been significant. As a result, steps have been taken in some areas of the United States to ban the use of lead shot in favor of non-toxic shot such as steel shot for hunting wildfowl.

"There have been a number of proposals for alleviating this problem," Brown's attorney wrote, noting that coating lead shot has not been successful because the coatings of tin, copper and magnesium are "quickly groun~ ~~ the abrasive action of the bird's gizzard." Efforts to coat shot wit~ impractical and "in the instance of one epoxy resin, hastened the de~ Even a light coating of nickel has proven to be of "insufficient har~

Today, the environmentally-friendlier options for waterfowl loads are many, and the ballistics of shotshell loads has greatly improved.

quickly ground off in the gizzard. Brown even notes that his own prior U.S. Patent No. 4,714,023 for a nickel-phosphorous coating – while proven effective – still covers a lead core.

"Iron and steel shot are non-toxic but are ballistically inferior to lead and damage shotgun barrels. Steel shot occupies a much greater volume than the same weight of lead shot and fitting a sufficient number of steel shot to provide adequate shot pattern into existing shell cases is a major difficulty. Solid copper shot is ballistically more efficient than iron and does little damage to gun barrels, but is almost as toxic as lead.

"There remains a need in the art for a completely lead-free shot that is ballistically similar to lead shot."

Brown had "discovered" bismuth: "An alloy was formed containing 99.9% by weight bismuth and 0.1% by weight tin. The alloy was melted and cast into pellets using an aluminum mold. The pellets were slightly harder than pure lead and heavier than lead. Loads were put together using heavier than normal powder charge and without buffering or the use of shot sleeves, in order to test the pellets under harsher than normal conditions. In testing, the shot produced good patterns, and recovered pellets showed substantially the same deformation characteristics as lead.

"The present invention provides non-toxic wildlife shot which performs ballistically superior to soft iron or steel shot. In fact, pellets according to the present invention can perform ballistically substantially the same as corresponding lead shot. Furthermore, the non-toxic wildlife shot containing bismuth … has deformation characteristics similar to lead. This provides shot … with similar animal stopping characteristics as lead, which is considerably better than the stopping characteristics of soft iron or steel shot, which does not deform."

Finally, Brown argues a point that has rarely mentioned during the height of the non-toxic debate: "This is of particular significance since there are some indications that the kill ratios may be about the same for birds which die of lead poisoning due to ingestion of lead pellets, and birds which are wounded by steel shot, yet escape and later die from their wounds."

Plated shot is not non-toxic. Plated shot is simply a lead ball with a fine coating or wash of copper or nickel. The intent is to give soft pellets better flight and penetration characteristics by giving them a harder coating and thus preventing their acquiring flat spots during the shot. The practical effects are difficult to demonstrate without resorting to a pattern board.

In the next chapter, we will look at the new non-toxic shot (and until the weight of scientific evidence proves otherwise, we still consider tungsten matrix materials as non-toxic) commercially available. Some is quite pricey, although that is not a surprise. What may be a surprise is that some steel loads are not at all expensive … are, in fact, cheap! Then, in the Chapter 5, we'll look at opportunities for hand loading non-toxic shells: why you should give it a try, what you'll need to begin and some tips for getting started.

CHAPTER NOTES

1. http://hyperphysics.phy-astr.gsu.edu/HBASE/pertab/as.html

2. Terms you will hear in the non-toxic discussion:

a. Annealing: heating solid metal to high temperatures and cooling it slowly so that its particles arrange into a defined lattice.

b. Metal Injection Molding (MIM): Spherical or semi-rounded metal powder is combined with a melted thermoplastic binder, extruded and cooled to form pellets which are then used in a plastic injection molding machine to form complex shapes. MIM parts have excellent mechanical and corrosion-resistance properties. The process is very efficient, using 97 percent of raw materials and reducing scrap or waste to a minimum.

c. Molding: raw material is compressed in a die to the shape of the desired part.

d. Sintering: forming objects from a metal powder by heating the powder for up to three hours at a temperature below its melting point. Powder particles join together to form a single solid object.

e. Sizing (coining or re-striking): reshape a part to a more precise form.

3. The formula for velocity is simply distance divided by time, $v = d/t$ as in feet per second (fps). This works perfectly well for an object covering equal distances in equal intervals of time in a specified direction. A string of shot however is more complicated because it accelerates to maximum velocity at the muzzle. From that point, it rises on a trajectory, and then falls, slowing down progressively. Shot (or a bullet) have variable velocity because they cover unequal distances in equal intervals of time.

Non-toxic shooting is not developing solely for waterfowl. Hevi-Shot says its Dead Coyote loads put "50-plus .20 cal pellets 'T' shots" in every load. Dead Coyote is also U.S. FWS approved non-toxic for waterfowl hunting or hunting in environmentally sensitive areas.

CHAPTER 4

NON-TOXIC SHOT IN TODAY'S MARKET

With all shotgunning on federal wildlife refuges designated as non-toxic, and with more states – Illinois, South Dakota, New York and others – inclined in that direction, hunters and shooters will begin to hear more about non-toxic brands and loads. While the wrangling about non-toxic shooting for waterfowl has by-and-large subsided, manufacturers will ramp up their research and development departments and we can eventually expect new shot options to squeeze out of their corporate offices. Here is the commercial state of the art as of January 2010.

Table 1: Quick Reference – Grains, Ounces & Grams		
Grains	Ounces	Grams*
218.75	½	13
293.21	2/3	19
328.14	¾	21
382.83	7/8	24
410.16	15/16	26
437.50	1	28
492.21	1 1/8	32
546.90	1 ¼	36
601.59	1 3/8	39
658.80	1 ½	42
710.97	1 5/8	46
765.62	1 ¾	50

* Numbers listed in this table are those used by manufacturers to designate loads on boxes of shells. They are general rather than precise, as, for instance, one ounce actually equals 28.349523125 grams.

Baschieri & Pellagri (B&P)

B&P has officially produced lead shotshells in Bologna, Italy, since 1891 and recently introduced five 12-gauge steel loads. B&P cartridges are imported into the U.S. by Kaltron Outdoors and the company has an extensive retail network.

B&P's Gordon System case has a shock absorbing base to reduce felt recoil. A wedge-shaped groove around the base's circumference compresses upon ignition. The company says this reduces recoil by a minimum of 10 percent and also reduces chamber pressures by improving powder combustion and overall ammunition performance. (Most other manufacturers rely on the wad for shock absorbing.)

The Steel Shot line up is listed by European designations. The 24 High Velocity is, for example, 24 grams or 7/8 ounce. Similarly for 28- (1 ounce), 32- (1 1/8 ounce), 35- (1 ¼ ounce) and 35-Magnum (1 ¼ ounce 3-inch). B&P recognizes the non-toxic movement by describing all of these shells as "to meet your needs for waterfowl hunting and for ranges and public and private upland land coming under non-toxic shot requirements." All five offerings are rated between 1330 fps and 1360 fps.

According to B&P, because steel shot weighs about 29 percent less than lead it has a smaller residual energy. This disadvantage can be offset by using a steel shot with a diameter that is 12 percent larger. By increasing the velocity roughly five percent, an equivalent residual speed and corresponding energy can be achieved. B&P says that with energy equivalent to that of lead, its steel penetrates 5-10 percent deeper in game. Thus, faster loads with reduced pellet counts provide a higher percentage of clean kills.

In addition, although its offerings are still somewhat limited in shot size options, B&P recognizes the potentially harmful scrubbing effect of hot shot streaming down a barrel: "Our wads are built … to insure the utmost protection by avoiding any contact between the shot and the shotgun barrel."

A carton of 250 2 ¾-inch, 32-gram #7 steel shells is listed at $103.95 or $.42 per shot. A case of 250 2 ¾, 32-gram #4 lead shells in the MB Classic line is listed at $90.95, or $.36 per pull of the trigger.

Clever Mirage (CM)

Founded in 1960, this company from Montorio, Italy, is not widely known or sold in the U.S. Still, it reports producing 130 million shotshells a year and is distributed in the U.S. by Gene Sears Supply.

Recognizing that the change from lead is not only taking place in duck blinds, CM has two 12-gauge 2 ¾-inch steel competition loads. Its Sport Soft Steel for trap and skeet is available in 19-, 24- and 28-grams while its Top Class comes in 24- and 28-grams.

CM's four T3 steel game loads are available chambered for in 2 ¾- (32-gram soft steel and 35-gram), 3- (36-gram) and 3 ½-inch (39-gram).

Tungsten is available in the CM Tung-Shot line. This Tungsten matrix material is slightly harder than a lead-antimony mix: 11.2 gm/cm^3 versus 10.8 gm/cm^3 (or bismuth at 9.6 gm/cm^3). The standard loads are 12-gauge 2 ¾ -inch, with 34 and 42 grams of shot. CM notes that it uses an extra-hard machine cut wad for the protection of the barrels, and that muzzle velocity is 1378 fps.

According to CM, patterns from tungsten are still very tight at distances between 40 and 60 yards, where other non-toxic shot patterns tend to fall apart, indicating that the denser tungsten matrix pellets hold their energy longer and provide greater penetration on longer shots.

If there is a disadvantage, CM suggests that tungsten patterns are too tight for close shooting unless you are more interested in vaporizing than deep frying your duck. The negatives with tungsten and other hard shot substitutes are that ricochets from hard surfaces – rocks in the berm behind the pattern board or the metal sides of the stand, for example – can be a problem; that it is not suitable shot for full-choked shotguns; and that the price is higher than lead or steel.

The 12-gauge 2 ¾- and 3-inch TinZinc shells which CM sells are softer than steel, but faster than lead. Because TinZinc is soft, there is little problem with ricochet or barrel scouring.

Estate

Estate Cartridge is now a division of Federal, with a half-dozen steel shells for the 12-gauge in chamberings 2 ¾- ($10-$11 per box), 3- ($12-$13 per box) and 3 ½-inch ($16-$17 per box). Because these shells are primarily used for waterfowl, and a large male Canada goose may weigh 15 pounds, shot is typically in the larger end of the size range: BB, #2, #4....

This trademark also builds steel shells for the uncommon 10-gauge (a 3 ½- loading of 1 5/8 ounce is $25.55) and two loads for the 20-gauge (a 2 ¾- with ¾ ounce is $10.43, whereas a 3-inch with one ounce is $12.43).

Estate Cartridge is a division of Federal in the ATK Group headquartered in Anoka, MN. Its responsibility in the company line-up is to produce the white-bread shotshell line.

Federal

Founded in 1922, Federal Premium is a subsidiary of ATK, Alliant Techsystems, a spin-off from Honeywell and a major player in the international aerospace and defense arenas. ATK also owns Alliant Powder, CCI/Speer, Champion,

Federal's Black Cloud FS Steel was designed to serve a market which was unhappy with the range and performance of cheap steel loads, but did not want to pay the high prices of new non-toxic shot compounds like bismuth.

Eagle Industries, Gunslick, Intensity, Nitrex, Outers, Ram-Line, RCBS, Shooter's Ridge and Weaver. (Recall that ATK built the innovative, but ultimately troublesome, 5.56 tungsten-nylon round for the U.S. Army.)

Federal certainly takes steel shot to the next level. It doesn't just build a few steel loads, though; through the years it has actively participated in both the hunting and the conservation solutions.

Its new Black Cloud FS Steel, for instance, was designed to serve a market which was unhappy with the range and performance of cheaper steel loads, but did not want to pay the high prices (up to $4 a shot!) of new non-toxic shot compounds like bismuth, some of which can, however, actually out-perform lead.

The Black Cloud line-up covers most waterfowl chambers and pellet sizes (BBB, BB, #2, #4) in 10-gauge (3 ½ – about $29 per box), 12- (2 ¾, 3, 3 ½ – about $16 to $28 per box) and 20-gauge (3 – about $19 per box) guns. About this steel shot, Federal warns: "Best performance is achieved with steel shot chokes that do not strip the wad or reduce muzzle pressure." It is a significant point when considering the purchase of a shotgun or a special-purpose barrel.

Black Cloud uses a new physical design for 40 percent of the shot in a shell. FliteStopper steel shot is stamped in an oblong shape with a tiny lip or cutting edge around its center, and its base and top are slightly flattened. Federal also says it is "staged with 60 percent premium steel" and is designed to cut and tumble in a game bird rather than just penetrate.

FliteStopper steel fills the lower portion of Federal's unique FliteControl shotcup. This solid wad has three petals near the base that open rearward and three flaps that flip open outward at the rear for rear-braking. The innovative wad design, Federal says, stays with the shot longer for tighter patterns and higher retained velocity.

Close-up of Federal 209A primers. Non-toxic shooting begins at the point of ignition when manufacturers substitute for highly toxic heavy metal compounds such as lead styphnate.

Federal also produces steel shot loads for varmints, predators and small game. Look for boxes of shells labeled Ultra-Shok, Wing-Shok (copper plated loads of both steel and lead) and Speed-Shok. It even loads a couple steel loads (FRS12) for "field or target" that, at one ounce of #6 or #7 may be light for turkeys but, properly choked, ought to bring down pheasants without a problem.

In the tungsten zone, the "coyote load" (PHC120) introduced in 2009 has a 15 gm/cm^3 density, 8 gm/cm^3 more than steel. It allows downsizing of shot, more pellets on target and greater payload energy. The shell itself is 12-gauge, 3-inch with 1 ½ ounces of BB which Federal rates sufficient for geese or coyotes.

The Heavyweight line features a density of 15 gm/cm^3, a third denser than lead. It is combined with the FliteControl wad for tight patterns and longer range. Federal says, for instance, that #7 puts more pellets on target while matching the density of #5 lead out to 40-yards. Available in 10-, 12- and 20-gauge.

Fiocchi

Lecco, Italy's Fiocchi manufacturing is part of the Prym Fashion Group, but in the U.S. it is represented by Fiocchi USA.

For about 130 years Fiocchi has manufactured a variety of lead shot. Today it has three principal target lines: Shooting Dynamics Clay (12-gauge, 2 ¾-inch with 3.0 percent antimony chilled shot); Nickel Plated (12-gauge, 2 ¾- with 3.2 percent nickel-plate); and its higher end Paper Target (12-gauge, 2 ¾, 5 percent magnum). By contrast, its steel target line has 12- and 20-gauge loads offering #6 and #7 shot.

In its steel waterfowl loads, Fiocchi shows some enthusiasm for produce offerings with both 12-gauge (2 ¾-, 3-, 3 ½-inch) and 20-gauge (2 ¾- and 3-inch) shells in the larger diameter shot that is customary for ducks and geese.

There are two zinc-plated, waterproofed shells for 3- and 3 ½-inch chambers for waterfowl (shot sizes in the BBB-#2 range) and two in the Golden Pheasant line-up for 2 ¾- and 3-inch with shot in the #3 - #4 size. Boxes of 25 12-gauge 3-inch #4 zinc-plated Golden Pheasant steel cost about $19.50.

Of its Tundra tungsten line, which Fiocchi calls "Green and Mean," the company speaks of three specific benefits:

1. It is not brittle and so "will not pulverize or break upon traveling along the barrel."

2. It can be utilized with any standard choke and barrel combination that shoots lead.

3. The shot pellet behaves like lead as far as deformation is concerned.

The Fiocchi line-up of 2 ¾- and 3-inch shells is divided into those with a specific weight superior to bismuth for waterfowl or pheasant – 9.5 gm/cc – and those with specific weight superior to lead, 12.5 g/cc. Both the Waterfowl and Golden Pheasant shells are 12-gauge 2 ¾- or 3-inch.

Gamebore

Founded in Hull, England, in 1973 and sold to Kent Cartridge America in 1998, Gamebore is serious about non-toxic shotgun loads and consequently is far ahead of the curve. Gamebore says it builds more than 150 million shotgun cartridges each year and has sold more than 100 million "rounds of steel shot cartridges world wide." Its U.S. headquarters is in West Virginia.

Gamebore's steel lines begin with seven competition loads that are available only in 12-gauge, 2 ¾-inch shells with plastic wads/shot cups except one #7 ½ in the Super Steel line. The new 3-inch Silver Steel load of plated #4 or #5 for pheasants or upland birds uses fully degradable components: a powder card, driving wad and fiber shot cup.

Stepping away from its all-12-gauge line-up, Gamebore offers one 20-gauge 2 ¾ shell of #5 in the Game & Wetland Steel line.

Gamebore believes that tungsten matrix is the best-all-around shooting alternative to lead because its formulation can be very close in density: 11.0 gm/cm^3 to 10.8 gm/cm^3. The matrix is "pure tungsten powder" mixed into a polymer (essentially, a plastic glue). Gamebore's formulation is designed, the company says, for uniform size, consistent density and maximum muzzle velocities; because it is malleable, it is safe for most older barrels. These shells also use a fiber shot cup which decomposes easily.

The English company has developed three 12-gauge #5 shot lines in their non-toxic tungsten. TMX mixes iron into the tungsten matrix so it is 20 percent cheaper to produce and gives 90 percent patterns at 40 yards. Impact Multi-Shot is a 60/40 iron/tungsten matrix mix. The third line is Tin Shot – Super Speed.

Hevi-Shot (Environ-Metal)

Oregon's Environ-Metal is responsible for the Hevi-Shot brand and, while they admit that steel is cheaper, maintain that tungsten-based Hevi-Shot is denser

and therefore gives better penetration at distance using smaller shot. "Hevi-Metal waterfowl loads," the company says, "put 20 percent more lethal pellets on-target at 40 yards than any steel ammunition."

While most loads are offered in 12-gauge – that is after all by far the most popular shotgun size in North America – additional 10- and 20-gauge loads, as well

Hevi-Shot has introduced three sets of screw-in ventilated choke tubes. Scattergunners need to pay special attention to the choke and threads for cleaning, ensuring that the choke is appropriate for the load and that it is screwed tightly into place.

as proprietary chokes for shooting Hevi-Metal loads, are on the drawing board. Meanwhile, any choke that is steel-rated is adequate for Hevi-Shot.

A year ago, Hevi-Steel was introduced to increase the range of an effective shot with smaller pellets. Shells use a layer of steel beneath a layer of higher density tungsten-matrix shot. All of the pellets have the approximate same ballistic performance; there are just more of them in Hevi-Metal shells. By contrast, Hevi-Steel pellets all have the same density, about 20 percent denser than steel.

Hevi-Metal steel pellets have a density of about 10 gm/cm^3 and are coated with a thin dry-film preservative that inhibits corrosion, while the high density tungsten pellets are non-corroding. Tungsten matrix pellets cannot rust and bind together under normal circumstances. Except for certain military shotshells, the company warns, no shotshells are completely waterproof.

The company tops off its shells, by the way, with a filler of flax seed which it says helps give a solid surface for crimping. This filler is a buffer that will also suppress some of the shot's natural resonance or "bounce." Like steel shot, when the powder begins its explosive burn and presses almost instantaneously against the column of pellets, the column of hard shot does not uniformly transfer energy toward the muzzle. Individual pellets tend to transfer energy in all directions and a buffer helps cushion the effects of "stray energy."

Hevi-Steel shells cost $26/box of 25; Hevi-Metal shells are about $5 per box cheaper.

Hull

An English company dating from 1947, Hull is one of those traditional lead shot manufacturers that has dipped its toes only slightly in the non-toxic business. Consequently, it has steel in limited shot sizes in Steel Game (12-gauge #4 and #5) with full-length photo-degradable shot cup; Steel Game & Clay (20-gauge #4 and #5); and Solway Steel Magnum (12-gauge, 3-inch #1, #3 and #4). The Pro Competition steel is a #7 load of 12-gauge 7/8- or 1-ounce at 1400 fps while Steel Clay is Hull's 20-gauge #7 load (7/8-ounce moderate recoil).

Kent

Kent Cartridge was formed in 1996 when a group of U.S. sporting businessmen purchased Activ, which was located in West Virginia. Their goal from the beginning was to explore the upper ends of quality and performance in non-

Kent loads tungsten matrix in its Impact shotshells, a blend of pure tungsten powder in a sintered polymer matrix that was specifically developed to match the physical and ballistic properties of premium quality lead shot.

Kent believes that development of the photo-bio-degradable wad – it deteriorates when left exposed to the open air and sun – plus a quality steel load are superior for competition or field.

toxic shot. This they have done, and in 1998 they bought Gamebore, officially becoming Kent-Gamebore. (While they purchased the Activ facilities, they don't manufacture any Activ products nor have any Activ components.)

Like all shotshells, Kent says, its shells are not water proof, but are instead water resistant. Kent shells are made with Italian B&P wads and French Cheddite hulls.

In terms of performance, Kent claims "Speed Kills" and that shot velocity is "the single greatest advantage when shooting steel." Thus, the company produces a lineup with several options in the "Super Fast" range that waterfowlers especially demand in a premium steel shotshell.

Since Kent's original Fasteel shotshells were introduced, the lineup has grown.

• Kent notes "as more areas around the world turn to non-toxic shot for game shooting," it was time to designate some of the smaller steel loads for upland birds. Hence, Upland Fasteel has 2 ¾-inch 12- and 20-gauge loads of #5, #6 and #7.

• In Fasteel Waterfowl, Kent notes that the "only way to increase performance in a steel shotshell is with increased speed" and thus has a 1625 fps shell in the mix. There is a 20-gauge shell for sub-gauge shooters and options for all chamber lengths in #BBB - #6 shot sizes.

• With Velocity Steel Target, Kent offers 2 ¾ loads of #7 for 12- or 20-gauge and its biodegradable wad and shotcup (the same combination offered by Gamebore).

• Finally, looking for shooters in the "value conscious" group – those of us on a budget – Kent offers 12- and 20-gauge promotional All Purpose Precision steel loads.

Although it has invested heavily in tungsten and still produces lead as Diamond Shot, Kent's steel loads are comprehensive.

At 10.8 gm/cm^3 Kent's tungsten matrix loads are a blend of tungsten powder in a polymer matrix "developed to match the physical and ballistic properties of premium quality lead shot." Tungsten, Kent says, "responds to traditional choke constrictions providing optimum pattern performance at a variety of practical ranges" for waterfowl. "Just like lead, only non-toxic" in 12-, 16- and 20-gauge. Kent produces three lines of tungsten: Waterfowl, High Performance Turkey (12-gauge only) and Pheasant/Game. (For the ultimate in non-toxic – indeed, they are non-lethal – for dog or spouse training try Kent's 12-gauge Field Blanks. All of the sound, none of the fury!)

In terms of price, Kent tungsten is expensive. For 12-gauge shells, the following prices were recently quoted for a case (10 boxes with 10 shells each) at HuntStuff.com. Add shipping and you do pay a premium for these high quality shells: 3 ½-inch = $440/case; 3-inch = $319 - $407/case (1 ¼- to 1 ¾-ounce of shot); and 2 ¾-inch = $275 - $297 (1 ¼- to 1 3/8-ounce).

Lyalvale

Lichfield, England's Lyalvale steel shot cartridges is designed to approximate the performance of traditional lead cartridges, the company says: "This allows sportsmen that are required to shoot non-toxic cartridges only to enjoy their sport without any severe loss of performance."

Lyalvale's steel is manufactured in Italy and designed with a single-base fine flake powder from France to burn at the low pressure required by steel cartridges. Inside the shell, the plastic wad has very thick walls to protect barrels from shot-scrub, wad petals opening within 10 feet of the muzzle: this allows the pattern to form and ensures that barrels are protected.

Supreme Steel cartridges were developed to increase range without increasing recoil, a trick Lyalvale says it performed because of its new Vectan powders. 12-gauge Hunting Steel runs from 1- and 1 1/8-ounce in 2 ¾-inch to 1 ¼-ounce in 3-inch, and there are 20-gauge steel loads also.

Nobel Sport

Steel loads in the Nobel Sport-Italia line are manufactured for American trap shooters, though the 12- and 20-gauge 2 ¾-inch loads of #6 and #7 would be fine for grouse, woodcock and even dove. Nobel Sport is located in San Giuliano, Italy, where they have been making shotshells since 1830. Their web site states that they have built more than 3.2 billon cartridges.

Pinnacle

From the Pinnacle Ammunition Company, Magnum bismuth loads are available in 12- or 20-gauge filled with BB - #7 shot. The High Velocity line is 12-gauge only in sizes BB - #6. For upland birds and small game, however, Classic loads are made in standard 12- and 20-gauge, and also in 16- and 28-gauge and – remarkably – .410 bore, which makes this a very complete line, indeed!

Polywad

Jay Menefee incorporated Polywad in Georgia in 1985. Ten years later Polywad began loading shotgun shells on fully automated, high quality Italian loading machinery and has loaded for many of the "big names" in the industry including Hevi-Shot.

High speed photography of a Polywad GreenLite 20-gauge load exiting the barrel at distances: 8, 13 and 18 inches. The "obturating medium" that packs the shell between the powder and the steel shot in the bio-degradable paper cup shows clearly as the cup separates from the tightly-packed shot. (Photos Tom Burczynski, Experimental Research, Inc.)

Women often prefer the reduced loads now available from most manufacturers, but once they become accustomed to shooting with any load, they are deadly hunters says Tracy Blake, head guide for SwanHunting.com. (Photo T. Blake)

Better known perhaps for its Spread-R shells and shell inserts designed to disperse shot patterns quickly, Polywad's GreenLite shell line use a wad-less technology with a light load (about 3/8 ounce) of steel shot. Components from the steel shot itself to the brown paper wad – except for the shell case (or "hull") which can, though, often be reloaded – are bio- and photo-degradable.

Polywad recommends its low-recoil GreenLite soft steel loads for small birds and small game out to 35 yards and target shooting to 40 yards. The paper wad cup has no slits; it opens and falls behind the shot rapidly upon leaving the barrel. The velocity of the two steel offerings is 10467 fps three feet from the muzzle, which is quite fast, well within the range of comparable commercial loads … and these are sub-gauge shells, in both 20- and 28-gauge.

GreenLite 20-gauge 2 ¾-inch has 240 pellets per load while 28-gauge 2 ¾ loads contain 220 pellets. Compared to lead pellets, Polywad's #7 - #8 steel pellets are "are not as big as #7s and not as small as #8s" and they have a recoil energy of only 6 ½ pounds. What is even more remarkable about these loads is the price, an affordable $15 per box of 25 shells.

Menefee also developed "Squound" shot a few years ago, but said he could not interest a major shell Name Brand and has since worked with Pinnacle to market this odd-shape shot. With a dome-shaped head, straight sides and a dished bottom, Squound is neither square nor round and is coming in 2010 as AeroSteel.

Remington

Remington, one of America's oldest corporations, is moving toward embracing non-toxic shot at a glacial pace, but the change-over from lead in manufacturing, distribution, sales and promotion toward the non-toxic ideal is – paradoxically – an enormous step for such a large company.

The company's Sportsman Hi-Speed Steel offers loads in 10-, 12- and 20-gauge for 2 ¾-, 3- and 3 ½-inch chambers. In sizes from BB - #7, Remington says this brand is an "economical, high-speed steel load that is ideal for short-range high-volume shooting during early duck seasons or over decoys. Sportsman Steel works equally as well in upland situations that require the use of non-toxic shotshells." With 3- and 3 ½-inch loads of BB and #2 delivering 1550 fps, the difficulty with these shells will be trying not to vaporize a bird with its wing set coming through the swamp.

Nitro Steel Hi-Velocity brand plates the shot with zinc and seals hulls at primer and mouth to minimize corrosion due to prolonged exposure to moisture. Conscious that shotgunners are sensitive to price, Remington leads its description with: "Looking for premium performance without the premium price? Nitro-Steel delivers…. Nitro-Steel is a luxury everyone can afford." Not only are there plenty of 12-gauge shells – shot sizes T - #4 – there are a 10- (1 ¾ ounce); two 20- (¾ and one ounce); and one of the rare 16-gauge (15/16 ounce) shells in #2 and #4.

At 12.0 gm/cm3 Wingmaster HD contains a tungsten-bronze-iron shot that is 10 percent denser than lead and 16 percent softer than Premier Hevi-Shot, which makes it easier on your barrel and more responsive to conventional chokes. If that isn't good enough, its "Drop Dead Better" slogan is a real winner. Remington says that with its consistent ultra-round pellets it is superior for long range shooting, putting 60 percent of its pellets in a 30-inch circle at 60 yards. Loads are available for 10-, 12- and 20-gauge with shot sizes from T - #6.

A modern box of Remington 12-gauge, 3-inch steel shot – 1 1/8 ounces of #2 – appropriately called "Steel" should give plenty of knock-down power for waterfowl and could be used effectively for turkeys. The older generation will be impressed with the performance of new steel loads; the younger generation has grown up with them and so is perhaps more accustomed to "non-leaded" performance.

Does lead cause cancer?

According to the American Cancer Society (www.cancer.org) there is "some evidence showing that lead may cause cancer, but this evidence is weak. Still, lead has been loosely linked with cancers of the lung and stomach, and more weakly linked to brain and kidney cancers."

Lead is indestructible and like most metals, it's difficult to evaluate lead's ability to cause cancer because it is found in so many forms. Most evidence linking lead exposure and cancer comes from studies of workers in heavily lead-exposed industries where blood lead concentrations of 40 - 100 mcg/dl occur. In comparison, in 1991, the average blood lead concentration in U.S. males was a low 4 mcg/dl.

Lung cancer: Eight studies of highly exposed workers reported lung cancer. Two showed at least 50 percent higher risk. In all studies combined, the risk was 30 percent higher, but results depended heavily on one study where a threefold excess risk was found. Workers in the highest risk study may also have been exposed to arsenic, a known cause of lung cancer. Without the highest risk study, all studies combined estimate the risk at an additional 14 percent. (These studies could not determine if this increase was because of lead or because workers smoked more.)

Stomach cancer: Eight groups of lead-exposed workers showed a 34 percent stomach cancer increase, but workers with the highest exposure were no more likely to develop cancer than workers with low exposure. Studies in the general population found higher rates of stomach cancer among those in jobs with high lead exposure. Stomach cancer among people exposed to lead is a concern, but unproven.

Brain cancer: A 2006 study found that brain cancer risk was highest among people with the highest likelihood and intensity of lead exposure, further support for the link between lead and brain cancer.

Kidney cancer: In animal studies, kidney cancer is linked to lead exposure. Still, the combined results from all seven studies of lead-exposed workers showed no evidence of an increased risk. Two of the studies showed a two-fold excess of kidney cancer.

Colon and rectal cancer: A 1991 study found that workers in tetraethyl lead manufacturing industries were four times as likely to develop rectal cancer; workers with higher estimated exposure had higher risk. Less tetraethyl lead is produced today because it is no longer used as a gasoline additive.

Rio

Although its name gives it an exotic Brazilian beach flavor, Rio Ammunition has been produced near Bilbao in Northern Spain for more than a century. Rio is the explosives division of UEE or Union Espanola de Explosivos (Spanish Explosives Union) and it claims to manufacture more than 550 million shotshells a year. Rio also claims to be the only private company which actually builds all of the essential components for its cartridges including hulls, primers, powders and wads, noting that most "manufacturers" are simply assemblers of products manufactured elsewhere. This private company, one of the largest shooting sports manufacturers in the world, began planning to enter the U.S. market nearly a decade ago, a market which it estimates at a whopping 1.5 billion shells a year.

Large as it is, Rio is barely represented in the non-toxic field. Its two commercial loads in 2 ¾ are #7 for the 12- and 20-gauge and, while it shows a mallard rising from a marsh on its web site, the loads are clearly labeled Target Steel and the box shows a bursting clay.

RST

RST is the shotshell line from Classic Shotshells in Pennsylvania where all of the shells are assembled from purchased components, tested and marketed, including Nice Shot. Classic president and co-owner Alex Papp says that he and a group of investors bought the company in 2005 and specialize in building low-pressure shells for classic, vintage shotguns. (Papp only laughs when asked what RST stands for" "Really Smashing Targets," he says, as if he has been asked that question a thousand times.)

"Nice Shot" is built in China and imported for RST by California's EcoTungsten. The RST line of 10.2 gm/cm^3 Nice Shot is a tungsten-iron-tin mixture that is attracted to a magnet. It covers not only the customary 12-gauge and occasional 20-gauge, but also 10-, 16- and 28-gauge, which makes this small group of shells arguably the most comprehensive non-toxic tungsten offering in the U.S. Low pressures, modest velocities and a relatively low 10.2 gm/cm^3 shot density also make these shells compatible with most older guns and the shot's malleability means it can be shot with conventional chokes and will not scar barrels.

Pricing is steep for Nice Shot, 10-gauge coming in at $40 per box of 10 shells and all others in a $75 box of 25 shells. The 1200 fps 10-gauge in 2 7/8-inches is 1 ¼-ounce of #2, #4 or #5. The 1200 fps 12-gauge in 2 ½ inches is 1-ounce of #2, #4, #5, #6 or #7 ½. The 1225 fps 16-gauge in 2 ½ is 1-ounce #5, #6 or # 7 ½. Two 20-gauge shells are available in #5, #6 and #7 ½, with either an 1125 fps ¾-ounce or an 1150 fps 7/8-ounce. Finally, the 28-gauge is an 1175 fps 2 ¾-inch shell with ¾-ounce of #6 or #7.

Note that RST has #7 ½ which means that the shot is competitive on target ranges more accustomed to that size and #8.

Pennsylvania's Dan Tercho was instrumental in the development of Nice Shot. Tercho says he named the tungsten-tin combination for the shout he hears on those occasions when his old 10-gauge side-by-side brings down a goose: "Nice shot!"

"I was shooting steel and found a bulge near the choke tube," Tercho says, "and had it measured by a gunsmith who said it was between .015-.020. While it wouldn't terribly affect my shooting, he advised me to stay away from steel. So in about 2001 from my garage workbench I began looking around for some options and came up with Nice Shot."

Tercho says South Dakota's Precision Reloading is working on a reloading manual for Nice Shot: "It works like lead, but performs better."

Sellier & Bellot

This company name has the ring of an old British company, but its U.S. affiliate is headquartered in Missouri and the ammo has, for nearly two centuries, been built in Europe. It is now part of the Czech Republic. But that's not all. It has been acquired by CBC – Companhia Brasileira de Cartuchos, which is incorporated in Sao Paulo State, Brazil, and is one of the largest manufacturers of military and commercial ammo in the world. Small world.

S&B steel is produced for its hunting line and, the company reports, for skeet and trap shooting. The primary cartridge manufactured is lead but, should you be in the market, it also produces hard rubber shot for shotguns, too.

Winchester

This American name manufacturer has deep roots in shooting and manufacturing history as well as the psyche of outdoor men and women. In 1855 Oliver Winchester purchased stock in Volcanic Repeating Arms, helped it through the Civil War, marketed the famous Henry rifle and by 1866 bought controlling interest and changed the name to Winchester Repeating Arms. The great early hit was the 1873 lever-action rifle, the famous .44-40 "Gun That Won the West."

The Winchester brand has been through quite a few corporate restructurings and purchases, but its commitment to the shooting sports is evident in its Supreme shotshells which Winchester calls its best. These shells in 10-gauge (3 ½-inch) and 12-gauge (3- or 3 ½-) have "water-resistant, high-velocity, knock-down performance in any foul-weather hunting condition." Depending upon chamber size, a box of 25 costs between $26 and $36.

Super X is a Winchester brand with 30 shell options in 10-, 12- and 20-gauge designated as waterfowl loads because of the larger shot sizes: T-#4. The line also

The U.S. FWS says waterfowl populations are healthy and rising in the Mississippi Flyway and a great day of shooting can give your shotgun and your Labrador a workout. Hunting with Matt Kostka's Top Gun Guide Service in Minnesota, four hunters pose with a day's take of snow geese and blue wing teal. (Photo Matt Kostka)

has a Super Pheasant in steel (12-gauge, 3-inch, 1 ¼-ounce of #4 at 1400 fps, $25.05) for "pheasant hunting in areas where lead shot is not allowed."

The company's new Xpert Hi Velocity Steel Shotshells are "value priced, high performance" and "deliver a sizzling velocity of up to 1550 fps for an incredible boost in superior, bird-bagging performance." Indeed, a box of these 12-gauge, 3-inch, 1 ¼-ounce of #4 at 1400 fps is $17.26.

Xpert Steel – not the Hi Velocity line – for 12-gauge come in #6 and #7 and as 20-gauge come in #7. Winchester says it recognizes "the increasing demand for low cost non-toxic loads for upland, target and waterfowl shooting" and has thus "re-engineered the way steel loads are built and perfected a new way to manufacture corrosion resistant steel shot." Although there are only three 2 ¾-inch shells in this line now, the cost of a box is a low $11.47 (and if you scout around, might be found for about half that amount).

Winchester has reluctantly dipped its toe into the tungsten arena with Xtended Range Hi-Density shotshells. Loads combine high density shot – a 55 percent higher density than steel – with Drylok Wads. The high density shot is softer than most shotgun barrels and chokes. Waterfowl and turkey loads are in 12- and 20-gauge and the designated coyote shell is 12-gauge.

Wolf Ammunition

Imported through California, Wolf is a Russian company that sells ammo produced in factories formerly owned by the communist state – the USSR. Wolf has two steel loads, both 12-gauge and both designated as waterfowl cartridges. The 2 ¾-inch shell contains 1 1/8-ounce of BB, #2 or #4 for a velocity of 1365 fps. The 3-inch shell contains 1 ¼-ounce of BB, #2 or #4 for 1425 fps.

CHAPTER NOTES

Internet sites for companies mentioned in the text are: Ballistic Products www.ballisticproducts.com, Baschieri & Pellagri www.bandpusa.com, Clever Mirage www.clevervr.com, Estate Cartridge www.estate-cartridge.com, Federal Premium www.federalpremium.com, Fiocchi www.fiocchiusa.com, Gamebore www.kentgamebore.com, Hevi-Shot/Environ-Metal www.hevishot.com, Hull www.hullcartridge.co.uk, Lyalvale www.lyalvaleexpress.com, Nobel-Sport www.nobelsport.it/public/pages/ENG/home.asp, Pinnacle Ammunition www.pinnacleammo.com, Polywad www.polywad.com, Precision Reloading www.precisionreloading.com, Remington www.remington.com, Rio www.rioammo.com, RST Classic Shotshells www.rstshells.com, Sellier & Bellot www.sellier-bellot.cz, Winchester www.winchester.com and Wolf www.wolfammo.com.

CHAPTER 5

RELOADING NON-TOXIC SHOTSHELLS

Why reload your own shells?

There are three reasons to hand-load or reload, which of course means loading your own shells at home. Purchasing parts individually and assembling the completed cartridge on your own press (or perhaps a member-only press at the range or club) carefully following a shotshell recipe, and having everything work exactly as planned, is hugely satisfying and, since we are dealing with explosive powders and primers, can be a huge relief as well!

From what we have seen in the earlier chapter, commercial shell manufacturers have two principal objectives when developing shells … but perhaps your situation requires something different.

Hand loading either shotshells or solid cartridges is a superior way to learn more about shooting and shooting components. Loading data is not the same for lead as it is for steel or other non-toxic shot and one cannot simply substitute components. (Photo Rick Sapp)

1. First, manufacturers by and large are promoting very fast loads with heavier shot to be effective at distances of 60 yards and beyond. When they develop a new shell line – think of the buzz Federal created around Black Cloud – they must sell millions of boxes because they are driven by stockholder profitability. A niche shell doesn't get built, but perhaps a niche shell is exactly what you need. Now, 60 yards isn't all that far when you're shooting a 3 ½-inch 10-gauge or even a 3-inch 12-gauge in good weather, but at a high flying passing duck moving 50 mph that distance requires a dynamic lead, more than you typically expect. Should you take that shot? Is that the right distance for you? (The Black Cloud load PWB134 for 3 ½- inch 12-gauge contains 1 ½-ounce of #2, #4, BB or BBB and registers a muzzle velocity of 1500 fps! Very fast. The web site, by the way, has trademarked "Ducks Drop Like Rain" which has an interesting and almost poetic ring, but perhaps not for a conservationist.)

2. Second, manufacturers compare every non-toxic load to lead. About Wingmaster HD, Remington says, "At 12.0 gm/cm3, it's 10 percent denser than lead and the scientifically proven optimum density for pellet count and pattern density." And Pinnacle, the new producers of bismuth cartridges, writes, "More energy plus Bismuth's lead-like malleability means more impact on your target, and not through it." Sure lead is traditional for all kinds of shooting, but is it only habit and convenience, or the fact that lead is cheap, plentiful and easily worked that makes it so. And any missed shot for any reason leads to an immediate, "If I'd just been shooting lead …." Is there a standard that is more appropriate for your shooting?

The primary reason shooters load their own shells, and perhaps the most talked about, is the opportunity to save money if you shoot regularly – save money compared to buying individual boxes or even cases at retail. Given the volatile price of metals on the world market, this is still true – sometimes – even for non-toxic loads of steel and tungsten. As a rule, figure that after you amortize your investment in reloading equipment you may be able to cut the price of a cartridge in half and your cartridges will perform as well as if not better than the manufacturer's. If you're an avid waterfowl hunter paying $2.25 per each pull of the trigger when chasing ducks with Hevi-Shot, reloading is worth considering.

Another reason to reload is so that you can build custom loads that fit your shooting needs and perhaps for the specific way your gun patterns. This is certainly true for sporting clays shooters who take on the occasional pheasant or woodcock, or perhaps for scattergun lovers who hunt private land one day and public land the next and may shoot an occasional afternoon of trap. With so many private ranges and public wildlife lands concerned about lead shot management, the ability to reload may pay dividends by giving you the option of building half-a-dozen shells from one loading manual and then spinning out a couple hundred of another: one shell for 60-yard geese with a tail-wind and a different load for 30-yard mallards settling into your decoys.

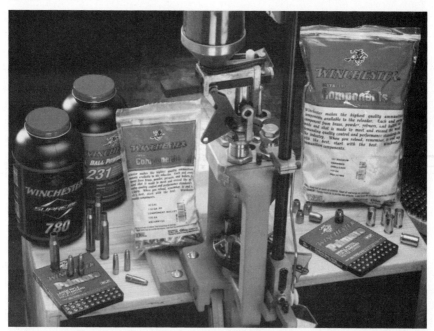

One of the most fascinating hobbies in the shooting sports is cartridge reloading. It is a combination of science and art that requires patience and attention to detail. Reloading or handloading can save money if you are more than a casual shooter. (Photo Winchester)

And of course there is the day your buddies suddenly invite you to a dove shoot and Walmart has sold out of Remington ShurShot Heavy Dove, both the #7 ½ and #8, and the local store doesn't carry the #6. If you reload, you can crank out a box of 25 – which ought to bring down at least two or three of the speedy, elusive birds – in 15 minutes. Convenience.

It is also true that shotguns pattern differently. This is acknowledged with guns that have a little pedigree, those that have knocked around the fields and ranges for a few years, more so than with new off-the-shelf shotguns. Using computer modeling and laser guided machining, modern guns from quality companies are built with extreme mechanical precision. While few gun designers today have the breadth of knowledge of Eliphalet Remington, for example, or Samuel Colt or Dan Wesson, and most are engineers instead of craftsmen in the old-school sense, 21st century products can be built on an assembly line with such quality control that experts cannot tell one gun from another except for its serial number. Sam, Dan and Eliphalet would be astonished.

So the top three reasons to consider hand loading are to cut the cost of shooting, to build custom loads and to conveniently have the right shell for the shooting task. The bonus is that extra edge that craftsmanship, a pride of accomplishment that "doing it yourself" allows.

Generally Speaking ...

If you are already familiar with the basics of reloading you probably know that non-toxic loads are a little different in composition – in the load data or recipe – and that you can never simply substitute ingredients: steel in a lead load or a different primer or hull because you have a few left-over. Switching ingredients or volumes, or something as simple as a wad type, may cause your load to perform poorly ... or even disastrously. If the load data calls for a Windjammer WJI 20078

AT INTERNATIONAL TRAINING...

When frangible and non-toxic rounds are used in training scenarios, the teaching-learning curve flattens because a much greater emphasis can be placed on realistic response techniques. Urban situations that call for building-by-building clearing operations are otherwise difficult to rehearse unless paintball markers or perhaps soft-air guns are used and neither is a best-practices substitute.

The development of fragmenting or frangible rounds allows law enforcement to conduct training in realistic scenarios which might have otherwise been extraordinarily dangerous. And if these rounds are non-toxic as well as frangible, the outdoor ranges will have less long-term difficulty with heavy metals leaching through the soil. (Photos ITI - International Training, Inc.)

and you are out of this particular wad, find another recipe. If there is one universal caution before beginning this discussion, it is to stick tight to the load data.[1]

Should you decide to hand load shotshells, be cautious about taking advice. A 12-gauge load develops barrel pressures between 6500 and 11000 psi. Rifle and handgun loads, even a .22 Hornet or a standard police-carry .40 S&W, operate at significantly higher pressures, two or three times safe shotgun levels, and one body of knowledge does not translate into another shooting medium. Beware also of individuals who are casual in their approach to loading shells. Freelance at your own risk!

Regarding loading data for non-toxic shot, adhere strictly to established loading recipes. They will most likely spell out ingredients very specifically as in these examples, randomly selected 12-gauge loads from Alliant's reloading manual for Steel Power which was formulated specifically for steel shot:

1. 2 ¾-inch steel: Remington Nitro Mag hull and Federal 209A primer filled with 29.5 gr. of Alliant Steel powder, a TUPRW12 wad from Precision Reloading, and 1 1/8-ounce of steel shot, gives 1361 fps with safe barrel pressures of about 10,400 psi.

2. 3-inch bismuth: Remington SPELV Yellow BW hull and Federal 209A primer filled with 45 gr. of Alliant Steel powder, a Rem RP12 wad, and 1 ½-ounce of bismuth shot gives 1441 fps with only slightly higher 10,700 psi.

3. 3-inch Hevi-Shot: Fed 7/16 Paper BW hull and Federal 209A primer filled with 33 gr. of Alliant Steel powder, a TUPR23 (orange) wad from Precision Reloading, and 1 ½-ounce of Hevi-Shot, gives 1274 fps with 10,500 psi. The load requires a ¼-inch thick felt spacer under the shot for additional cushion and to take up space in the shell column.

Alliant's double-base Steel powder was introduced in 1998. Although to the naked eye, even at night, the flash of a steel or lead or Hevi-Shot shell is indistinguishable, powders are said to burn, not explode, at variable rates and Steel is ballistically a slow burning powder. It's also good for a dense load of Hevi-Shot.

Because Steel burns quite slowly, it requires a greater volume to generate a load's energy curve than it would with a faster burning powder. Thus when reloading, it is sometimes necessary to compress Steel a little more firmly than, for instance, Red Dot. It is always possible then to add a felt or cork filler wad – or remove or use a thinner slice – at the base of the shotcup to create the best crimp for the shell.

That being said, reloading non-toxic shot is easy. It is essentially no different than loading lead. Tungsten and bismuth require little in the way of special adjustments to loading presses except to change powder and shot bushings, a procedure you would normally follow for different loads. Load designs use the same fundamental ingredients in shell make-up as lead: wads, primers, powders, and of course, shot. Occasionally a buffer is recommended or an extra card under or over the ingredients.

Manufactured by Continuous Metal Technology and sold exclusively through Ballistic Products, ITX is a tungsten-based cast pellet designed for density and softness similar to lead, only non-toxic. It is soft enough to crush with pliers. Like lead and bismuth, ITX registers below 27.0 on the Rockwell C scale of hardness. "Each individual pellet is a spherically formed projectile with a mid-band that enhances lethal wound channels," says Ballistic Products.

Steel shot, however, requires a slight modification of materials. The operation of the press needs greater attention to moving parts like bushings and shot bars, because steel caught in a jam does not shear off like soft lead: it is far too hard for that. Several reloading press companies compensate by offering rubber inserts which fit along the shot cavity. The soft rubber helps pellets to compress into the insert and avoid a jam. You should not load steel without the designated steel bars or bushings in place because you could damage the press.

Of course, steel shot should probably have wads that stay with the load until it is outside the barrel to prevent steel from scraping against the bore. Bore damage can occur even on new guns, but it will rarely matter if one shoots only occasional loads of steel (unless the shotgun is quite old)[2] and the industry generally has over-played the barrel damage possibilities. Still, it is better to be careful and, when hand loading, be absolutely certain not to mix shotcups. Loading its Universal powder in several 12-gauge steel loads, Hodgdon recommends the plastic CSD100 wad from Ballistic Products. The CSD100 has a recoil-absorbing cushion and barrel-protecting shotcup and comes in three sizes for specific payloads: CSD078 for 7/8-ounces, CSD100 for 1-ounce and CSD118 for 1 1/8-ounce. "We recommend using steel pellet sizes #3 or smaller with CSD wads," says Grant Fackler of Ballistic Products. "CSD wads are not pre-slit. Use the stainless steel wad snips to cut the number of petals best suited for your shooting."

Steel reloading has a less forgiving reputation and certainly requires your full attention. Neither the shot nor the wad column crush or collapse to absorb excess pressure as will lead when too much of an ingredient, either shot or power, is used. In fact, barrel and chamber pressures tend to rise faster and higher from improper assembly of steel loads than lead.

Regarding shot and powder, experienced hand loaders testify that steel is safe within +/- 25 gr. of the indicated shot charge and +/- 0.5 gr. of the indicated powder load. That's not much room for error, so if you become the least bit distracted while operating your press, it will be best to take apart an occasional shell and weigh the ingredients, matching your results against the load formula.

A powder baffle installs between the powder-bottle and charge bar helps produce evenly metered powder volume – an occasional problem with Alliant's Steel, for instance – and therefore consistent charges. (Photo Multi-Scale)

Bouncing and Blooming

While steel shot will not crush, it will bounce. After the primer explodes and as the powder begins to burn, a pressure wave hits the shot column. Individual pellets are accelerated unevenly. If they were small pellets, #8 ½ or #9, and thus densely packed inside a shot cup, this would not be a concern, but steel is not yet available in those sizes. Steel is typically shot in large #2 or #4, though you can find it as small as #6.

Bounce happens very rapidly, but that does not mean the impact on shot inside the shell column is negligible. Because a rapidly expanding gas pressure wave is more explosive with steel than with lead, effective wads for steel loads tend to be thicker. This protects the barrel from scarring because the rule of columnar loading says that force is exerted toward the sides – into the shot cup and through the slits in its sides – as well as forward toward the barrel. (Examine the inside of a spent wad and you will see a similar result, even in a light lead load).

Hard shot like steel generally performs best with more open chokes as squeezing rigid loads through a constricted, inelastic bore has been known to cause barrel blooming. Note that even an otherwise solid manufacturer like Browning struggles with hard steel shot[3]:

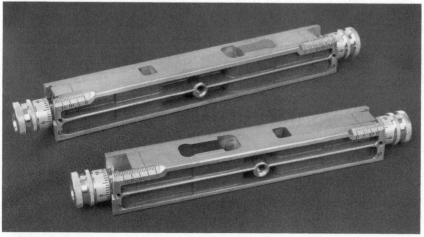

Universal Charge Bars from Multi-Scale (Shooting Chrony) replace all the standard charge bars and bushings used in MEC reloaders.

The single-stage MEC Steelmaster is the only shotshell reloader specifically equipped to load steel or lead shotshells. The Steelmaster's resize station handles brass or steel heads in either high or low base. The E-Z Prime auto primer feed, which dispenses primers automatically, is standard equipment.

"In not all, but a number of instances, a very slight ring will develop about 1 1/2" to 3" rearward of the muzzle. This ring is about .005 of an inch above the plane of the barrel, completely encircling the barrel. From our tests we could determine no adverse effect on pattern or shot velocity because of this ring. Our conclusion is that the most significant objection, the slight ring, is entirely cosmetic. This ring effect does not affect the function or safety of the firearm. The damage to your gun is purely cosmetic, but the bulge can be a factor in resale, especially with collector-grade shotguns."

Basic Gear for Reloading

You will find that a dedicated area for reloading works best: a place that is quiet, humidity controlled and perhaps off-limits to the smaller members of the family. Youngsters will be naturally – though inappropriately – curious and no good can come from having children or animals among your reloading components.

Your first acquisition, other than a few good books about reloading, will be a shotshell press. Here are three examples: a single-stage press from MEC, and progressive presses from Ponsness/Warren and RCBS.

Mayville Engineering has manufactured shotshell reloaders under the MEC name since 1956. It says the single-stage MEC Steelmaster is "the only shotshell reloader that comes specifically equipped to load steel shotshells" ... even though it also works perfectly well with lead.

For beginners, a single stage reloading press like the Steelmaster is the best first step. A single stage reloader is a simple one-step-at-a-time operation. It is difficult to screw up a shell by going slowly and thoughtfully through your load.

MEC's E-Z Prime auto primer feed, which dispenses primers automatically, is standard and the resize station handles brass or steel heads in either high or low base. Separate presses are available for 12-gauge ($261 for 2 ¾- or 3-inch; $274 for 3 ½-) and 10-gauge ($274 for 3 ½-). MEC presses are sold with one charge bar and three powder bushings.[4]

Ponsness/Warren has built reloading gear for 40 years. Its L/S-1000 is the only fully progressive reloader that loads lead, steel and bismuth without requiring a conversion kit. A quiet indexing system automatically aligns each shell at every station. With each cycle of the operating handle, the L/S-1000 automatically indexes, de-primes, final crimps and ejects a completed shell. Primers are filled in the primer feed tray and then slide down a track into the primer feed assembly. There are no primer tubes to fill, and you can count the remaining primers at any time.

The shell holders and primer knockout/resizing assembly ensures that low or high brass shells are easily resized to factory specifications. This means re-sized shells will always feed and chamber in any shotgun. The LS-1000 drops any shot size, up to and including BB, and now comes with a semi-crystalline nylon (called grivory) die removal system. The 12-gauge ($829.95) model loads 2 ¾- and 3-inch shells while the $879.95 10-gauge model loads 3 ½-inch.

Once you become proficient loading shells with RCBS' The Grand progressive reloader for 12- or 20-gauge, a shell is completed each time you pull the handle. The case-activated power system will not drop powder or shot unless a case is in position to receive it, which can eliminate a tricky mess if ingredients spill over your press or loading table. Both powder and shot bushings are easy to change and are available in all popular loads. The press is also compatible with Hornaday shot bushings.

The Grand is $966.95 and, if you shoot multiple gauges, a conversion kit is $461.95 – cheaper than buying another press – or if you get hooked on one of the clay games such as trap or if you load for friends you are going to need a lot of shells, an $899.95 hydraulic kit will save hours while helping you build great loads.

As you set up a reloading station, invest in a quality scale, one that will measure at least 1000 gr. which, because there are 437.5 grains in one ounce, is little more than two ounces. In a hobby that requires as much precision and attention as reloading shotshells, you ought to check your load manually every 50 or 100 shells, depending upon how many you are loading. It is easy to put in the incorrect bushing for instance, if you are new to loading or you are setting up multiple loads or become the least bit distracted, and it is not unheard-of for a progressive reloader to malfunction.

A scale such as the Classic Pro 1000 from Lyman measures both powder and shot. This older style scale, however, while it is inexpensive at $75.95 and certainly better than nothing, uses balance weights and a measuring arm that you read by eye.

Especially with older shotguns and older chokes, steel shot has required use of specialty reloading components, such as shot cups or wads that fully encapsulate the hard pellets. (Photo Ballistic Products)

Far better and easier to use is Lyman's 1000 XP Compact Electronic scale. Accurate to within 1/10-grain, this scale operates on a 9V battery or can be plugged into a wall socket (AC adapter included). At $144.95, it costs twice the beam-arm Classic Pro, but the ease of operation and digital read-out are worth the additional cost.

Standing CW on its Head

Ballistics Products (BPI) is the exclusive source of ITX shot which is manufactured by Continuous Metal Technology of Pennsylvania, a specialist in molding powdered metals.

ITX is a soft tungsten/iron compound that is approved for use by the U.S. Fish & Wildlife Service. It is engineered, says BPI, "for density, softness and near perfect spherical formation," but this shot, like Federal's Flitestopper steel, is designed to not be a perfect sphere. In fact, ITX shot has a flat side that circumscribes each pellet like a 360-degree belt or band.

Disputing the conventional wisdom developed over centuries of scattergun shooting, both BPI and Federal now claim that their unusual shot styles actually give tighter patterns and increase penetration. Unlike Federal's cartridge composition, however, BPI does not mix this new shot with true spherical shot in a load.

Because it is denser than steel, this tungsten/iron mix carries the knock-down energy of lead – without, it appears, the nasty side-effects of that metal. Like lead, ITX is soft enough to crush with pliers and thus is easy on barrels. It is not brittle like bismuth though and won't break up or fracture during ignition setback.

BPI's ballistic lab is developing shotshell loading data for this new pellet. BPI loads will be buffered with a new ITX Buffer Blend to promote pattern density by preventing damage from setback and evenly distribute the force from burning powder. What's more, BPI says the shot is affordable and balances cost versus performance. A 7-pound bag of ITX BB, #2, #4, #6 or #00 buckshot is currently $129.50.

A Bit About Bismuth

Bismuth is different and it loads different. Bismuth shot cannot be used with lead or steel load recipes or proportions, because it has unique characteristics and ballistic reactions. To substitute recipes or pellet types is to sacrifice the advantage of using bismuth and thereby waste time and money as well as jeopardize one's own safety. Use only bismuth-specific load recipes and components no matter how insignificant the differences may seem.

Interestingly, given the same amount by weight, bismuth shot produces higher chamber pressures in a given load than does lead. You also cannot use steel or lead shot bushings to load bismuth in loading presses. Specialized bismuth shot bushings or charge bars (they are not expensive) are the only accurate volumetric way to measure bismuth pellets for loads – except as noted for the

Multi-Scale charge bar for MEC loaders. Otherwise, if you do not have specialized bars or bushings, you must weigh the shot charge on an accurate, calibrated scale or count the pellets individually.

Since bismuth loads can be used in a range of hunting and shooting applications, there is a wide disparity of volume between various loads. Applications of filler wads will be less specific than you may have become accustomed to with steel shot loading. Use cork or felt filler wads as necessary to produce the proper shot column height for a good crimp. Filler wads are the only optional components in a load. Carefully follow the formulas for all components, including wad/shotcup and when buffering.

Reloading specialists Ballistic Products recommend careful selection of wads and also adding buffers to bismuth loads because the shot is relatively brittle or frangible and pellets often break during the firing process. A buffer helps absorb some of the shock of the initial explosive burn of the powder and cushions pellet setback. This of course means that just any shotcup won't do....

To achieve good patterns, bismuth loads require larger payloads and the care provided by larger payloads and the care provided by a specialized wad. Larger loads need extra room and this often necessitates hunting-style wads that do not have cushioned sections. Without a cushion, load formulas often offer buffering options, but unless you have excellent shooting form expect your shoulder to take a pounding.

Bismuth is the only non-toxic shot that has been available in all bore sizes from 10-gauge to .410 bore. Still, loads tend to end at #7 and clay target shooters need shot sized from #7 1/3 to #9 for competition.

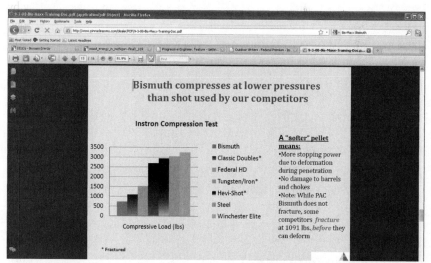

New loaded bismuth shells are produced and imported under the Bis-Maxx brand for Pinnacle Ammunition of St. Louis. Note that Pinnacle addresses the common fault rumored about bismuth shot, that it fractures or splinters during passage down the gun's bore.

Shot Reloads – Cost Comparison Table (shot only)[a]

Shot Type	Shipping amt	Cost+Shipping[b]	Cost/lb	Cost/shot[c]
Lead (2% Sb)[d]	25-pound bag #4	$38.58+$17.31	$2.24	$0.17
Steel	10-pound bag #4	$18.99+$10.96	$3.00	$0.24
Copper-plated lead (3% Sb)	10-pound bag #4	$34.39+$10.96	$ 4.53	$0.35
Nickel-plated lead (2.5% Sb)	11-pound bag #4	$37.81+$11.25	$ 4.46	$0.35
BPI ITX	7-pound bag #4	$129.95+$12.17	$20.30	$1.59
Tungsten/Iron	5-pound bag #4	$98.50+$10.10	$21.72	$1.70
Hevi-Shot	7-pound bag	$158.95+$12.17	$24.45	$1.91

[a] All purchases from Ballistic Products in Minnesota.
[b] Shipping estimated with FedEx residential ground.
[c] Cost per shot estimated at 1 ¼-ounce of shot per shell.
[d] Sb is the chemical sign for antimony.

CHAPTER NOTES

1. In *Reloading for Shotgunners* (Gun Digest, Krause: 5th Edition, 2005) the repeated caution is: "Follow load recipes exactly: do not substitute components, exceed listed maximums or load less than listed minimums."

2. One does hear stories, though…. In 2000 Pennsylvania's Dan Tercho discovered a .015 - .020 bulge near the muzzle of his shotgun after firing steel loads. Tercho says he was shooting his favorite, vintage 10-gauge side-by-side. He went on to develop eco-friendly Nice Shot which is now loaded by RST.

3. www.browning.com/faq/detail.asp?ID=128

4. If you load multiple recipes and use a MEC reloader, it is a good idea to check out the versatile Universal Charge Bar from Multi Scale. MEC bushings are currently $4.17 and charge bars are $18.40. The Multi Scale Bar is infinitely adjustable and handles both shot (lead, steel and bismuth) … and powder (12 gr. to 55 gr.) in all gauges, both for field and clay targets. The $38.95 Model C/CS replaces all of the standard charge bars and bushings used in MEC single-stage reloading machines such as the Sizemaster 77 and the Mark 5, while the D/DS replaces all of the standard charge bars and bushings used in MEC progressive reloaders such as the MEC 9000.

Internet sites for companies mentioned in the text and not formerly noted are: Alliant Powder www.alliantpowder.com, Federal Premium Black Cloud www.blackcloudammo.com, Mayville Engineering (MEC) www.mecreloaders.com, Multi Scale http://multiscalecharge.com, Ponsness/Warren www.reloaders.com

CHAPTER 6

SHOTGUNS R US

On-Line Chat, November 2006[1]
– We See It Coming

"I'm still not decided but I'm beginning to feel that lead shot just isn't friendly to the environment. Not to the water supplies, nor to non-game birds that may ingest lead shot while feeding in upland bird feed or cover areas or to predators such as the variety of raptors that routinely takes cripples.

"I'm not sure that, with all the other alternatives to steel available, it would really be a major inconvenience to switch. It might cost a few dollars more per box of shells but the increase in gas prices from last season to this hasn't slowed anyone I know from enjoying the sport. There seems to be a lot of good that could come of it, and not too much on the negative side.

"After talking to several other hunters, I'm becoming convinced that something other than lead shot will be the way I go in future seasons. All of my input to date is favorable. It just appears that non-lead shot will kill as cleanly, and the left-over shot is not toxic to other parts of the environment."

Forum Moderator –GameBirdHunts.com

◄ The original idea for non-toxic shooting began with waterfowl hunters and shotshell suppliers.

HUNTING

Lead can be toxic, but whether shooting it outdoors from shotguns, rifles and handguns causes a problem or not, even in heavily hunted areas, will be debated for many years. The answer may not be as obvious as a child swallowing lead-based paint chips, either. In complex systems – and hunting and shooting are parts of complex social, economic and ecological systems – the obvious answer is often wrong or correct only with many caveats and exemptions.

When asked about lead, hunters typically respond that lead is a mineral; a metal that is dug out of the ground and that they are simply returning it to the ground. This is true, of course, but as a pure metal lead is extremely rare in nature. It is commonly found in ores and must be extracted and processed to be used in products like shot pellets or bullets.

Still, while there are examples of lead shot causing the poisoning death of waterfowl in certain areas of the U.S., whether it is a statistically significant problem for any other genus or species is an open question. And of course, the new loads using tungsten matrix shot are not above toxic suspicion, having proved that they can decompose on firing ranges – where deposits admittedly become thick – and leach into the underlying aquifer.

Lee Sowers' first swan. Hunting these great birds is a means of balancing healthy populations with available supportive resources.
(Photo T. Blake, SwanHunting.com)

Although the wetlands and waterfowl issue seems to be settled, the debate about non-toxic shooting elsewhere is not over. In fact, it is spreading and may be long and contentious. It is probably also true that all of the lead shot expended by sport hunters and shooters (and all of the lead used by fishermen) will never amount to the quantity of lead toxins spewed into the atmosphere – where it is unquestionably highly poisonous to every living thing on earth, animals and plants – from the exhaust and lead-acid battery disposal of one year of automobiles.[2]

Waterfowl

The U.S. nixed lead for waterfowl in 1991 and Canada followed in 1999. A FWS study in the mid-1990s found that the nationwide ban on the use of lead shot for waterfowl hunting was a remarkable success. Six years after the ban, researchers estimated a 64 percent reduction in lead poisoning deaths among surveyed mallards and a 78 percent decline on ingestion of lead pellets.

While the non-toxic movement began with concerns about waterfowl, that is a general category rather than a specific animal. Mammals versus whitetails. Bears, as opposed to the one climbing your treestand.

Waterfowl range in size from diminutive buffleheads (13 – 15 ½ inches, one pound), the smallest wild duck flying over the U.S., to great tundra swans (a 6- to 7-foot wingspan, weighing more than 20 pounds). Unless you are a crack shot and limit your blasting to within 40 yards, stick with 12- and 16- or even 20-gauge guns; 10-gauge is only excellent for small birds if you are shooting at extreme range or you enjoy seeing them vaporize. And most experienced waterfowl hunters prefer having the greater number of pellets in 3- and even 3 ½-inch shells than the 2 ¾. For pass-shooting ducks and geese, you need #2, BB, T and possibly on up, depending on range, wind and the size of the birds.

Oregon's Tom Roster has spent years conducting ballistic research in the field and the laboratory. He believes that a load of #3 steel has the best-all-around performance qualities for taking ducks and that BBB is generally best for geese. Roster says an improved cylinder choke generally gives the best steel patterns for waterfowl out to 35 yards; more choke is needed for shots past that distance. On large geese over decoys, which is closer than pass-shooting the high flyers along the Missouri River, for instance, his data suggests that modified chokes give decent steel shot patterns out to 50 yards. For small ducks like teal at close range over decoys, smaller shot – steel #4 or #6 – in a light modified or modified choke will give satisfactory results in most guns.

Steve Johnson has been guiding duck hunters out of Port Aransas, Texas for Texas Gulf Duck Hunting[3a] for more than a decade, says most of his clients shoot a 3-inch 12-gauge load of #2 steel or tungsten. Johnson prefers a Remington cartridge on those rare occasions when he gets to shoot. For clients, he recommends anything except a cheap shell, because in the salt water environment of the Gulf of Mexico, cheaper shells quickly corrode around their metallic base.

At the farthest extreme from the tiny bufflehead, hunters along the southeastern Atlantic flyway have an opportunity to take a tundra swan. Swans are hunted as a method of population control because when they move, they move by the thousands and can become serious predators in farm fields.

This beautiful white bird has an impressive 7-foot wingspan and can weigh 25 pounds. When a swan settles into decoys and others are winging overhead says Tracy Blake, owner of SwanHunting.com[3b], a nice November morning along Pamlico Sound and adjoining wheat fields quickly becomes an unforgettable day. A guide with 20 years experience, Blake recommends a 10- or 12-gauge with 3- or 3 ½-inch chamber and a #2 box of Hevi-Shot or tungsten.

Even though the swan is much larger than a duck, #2, #3 or even #4 shot works fine, says Blake, because a hunter aims for the head (which is about the size of a dove) and neck; and shots are close, so greater pellet count wins. A hunter who shoots for the body risks hearing his shot bounce off the swan's densely layered feathers.

Matt Kostka has operated Top Gun Guide Service[3c] for 11 years and likes BBB shot for big Canada geese. After all, this wild bird can grow to 14 pounds with a 6-foot wingspan.

Kostka's company[3d] employs guides from Saskatchewan to Missouri, following the migrations and taking advantage of the longer waterfowl seasons to hunt right through the turkey spring. Clients hunt from pit blinds located near agricultural fields. "The use of non-toxic shot is required for hunting migratory game birds in Canada. Non-toxic shot includes steel, bismuth, tin and tungsten-iron/matrix/nickel-iron/polymer combinations. Lead shot can still be used for all upland game birds except in national wildlife areas."

For hunting geese in North Dakota, Brad Finneman of Honker Down Guide Service[3e] bundles his hunters under ghillie blankets and lets them load up with Hevi-Shot #2 or BB for Canada geese. When his clients hunt near water for ducks, he recommends loading down from #2 all the way to #6.

"The new, heavier shot patterns well out to 60 yards and kills effectively to 70 yards," Finneman says. The guide has hunted since he could lift a gun and, with his wife Dianne, has been guiding hunters full-time for almost a decade.

Migratory ducks are divided loosely into two categories, divers and dabblers. The wigeon represents the dabbling and grazing clan. While its numbers are down slightly this is thought to be a result of habitat degradation and the use of poisonous agricultural chemicals – not poisoning from shotgun pellets. (Photo Donna Dewhurst, U.S. FWS)

"I've kind of fallen in love with Kent Fasteel," Finneman says, "and Hevi-Shot Dead Coyote is a bunch of ugly shot, but it's pretty effective if you can afford it. Federal Black Cloud is a killer, too, but it leaves your barrel dirty after a couple of shots." (Kent offers a 3 ½-inch 1 ¼-ounce load of BB, #1, #2 or #3 that is rated at a smokin' 1625 fps.)

Finneman urged waterfowl hunters to check their gun's choke prior to flying to North Dakota. "I've seen a lot of people have trouble with choke tubes when they were shooting the new brands of hard shot. I recommend stainless steel Pattern-master[3f] chokes when people ask, because I've seen them give great results in long distance shooting." (Patternmaster chokes are built with five small studs to very slightly retard the wad, helping it separate from the shot column. Like all things relating to developing the best shooting cartridge, this is a hotly debated point, but it, in theory, gives a hunter better patterns and a more compact shot string because the lightweight wad is not fired through the heavier shot column.)

Table: Non-Toxic Shotshell Game Bird & Small Game Guide for the 12-Gauge*

Game	Examples of Commercial Loads	Gauge	Choke	Shot Size
Geese, Swans	Estate High Velocity Magnum Steel: 1 3/8 oz. BBB, BB, 1, 2, 3 or 4: 1375 fps	10, 12	F, M, IM	T, BBB, BB, 1, 2
Ducks	Hevi-Shot Duck: 1 ¼ oz. B, 2, 4, 6: 1550 fps	10, 12, 20	F, IC, M, IM	1, 2, 3, 4, 6
Turkey	Remington Wingmaster HD: 1 3/8 oz. 2, 4, 6: 1450 fps	10, 12, 16, 20	F	4, 5, 6
Pheasant	Winchester Super Pheasant Steel: 1 ¼ oz. #4: 1400 fps	2, 16, 20	F, IC, M, IM	4, 5, 6, 7 ½
Grouse, Partridge	B&P High Velocity Steel: 1 1/8-oz. #7: 1350 fps	12, 16, 20, 28	IC, M	5, 6, 7, 7 ½, 8
Woodcock, Snipe, Rail	Fiocchi Speed Steel: 1 oz. 6, 7: 1400 fps	12, 16, 20, 28	IC, M	6, 7 ½, 8
Dove, Quail	Pinnacle Bis-Maxx Bismuth Classic: 1 oz. #7 ½: 1300 fps	12, 16, 20, 28	IC, M, IM	7 ½, 8
Rabbit	RST Nice Shot: 1 oz. 2, 4, 5, 6, 7 ½: 1200 fps	12, 16, 20, 28, .410	IC, M	4, 5, 6, 7 ½
Squirrel	Hull Steel Game: 1 1/8 oz 4, 5: 1400 fps	12, 16, 20, 28, .410	M, IM, F	4, 5, 6

* The 12-gauge is the most popular shotgun size in the U.S.

Small Game and Upland Game Birds

Small pellets are superbly effective on lightweight upland game, especially when you use an open choke for a wider dispersal – for upland hunting you are walking, whereas for waterfowl you are typically seated or even lying down before rising to fire. For rabbits or pheasants, grouse or even for smaller ducks flaring and settling into your decoys, #6 or #7 is a fine choice for excellent patterns with plenty of close-range knock-down power – although we tend to use the term "power" loosely.[4]

Manufacturers generally have not explored smaller shot sizes in non-toxic loads – the force of law apparently drives the issue – and they can be hard to find. The initial requirement for non-toxic shooting was for big balls for waterfowl, #2 to BBB. So over the next few years, expect a raft of smaller shot options – #7 ½, #8, #9 – to become available. This is important for small game and upland birds – except of course for pheasant which, when kicked up flies directly away from the hunter and his dog, and thus requires a sturdier pellet than #8; and also for clay target shooting as more ranges are pressured to switch from conventional lead-based shot. So if you are looking for a good 12-gauge load of #8 in a non-toxic spreader load for walking-up woodcock, you will still have to build your own.

Classic Shotshells produces the RST line of low pressure shells for vintage shotguns: neither their lead nor their "Nice Shot" will scar the barrels and are safe for older guns. (Photo Alex Papp, RST)

Hunters who might be required to use non-toxic ammunition for upland game hunting will find options are few in small shot. Still, the manufacturing industry can gear up quickly and the next few years should witness an explosion of shells in all gauges. (Photo Lee Karney, U.S. FWS)

Of course rabbits, squirrels, pigeon and dove are often the path whereby young people or novices are introduced to hunting. If small shot isn't sold nearby, it is helpful to know that non-toxic shot is available in reduced recoil loads, and if that isn't readily obtainable in the neighborhood, dropping to a smaller gauge is a good option. In fact, most small game and upland birds can readily be taken with a 16- or 20- or 28-gauge. A 49-inch 12-gauge 2 ¾ Remington 1100 with a 28-inch barrel, one of the most popular and affordable semi-autos ever produced, weighs more than eight pounds when fully loaded; a 20-gauge with the same specifications weighs at least a pound less, and for a young person that pound is important by the end of the day.

Hull Cartridge has a 20-gauge 7/8-ounce shell (Steel Game 20) that loads #4 (166 pellets) and #5 (198 pellets) steel. This is an acceptable load for birds as big as pheasant and, by calling them close, a careful hunter who aims for head and neck, perhaps calling them close to a blind with decoys, can get away with this 20-gauge load on turkeys as well.

England's Lyalvale Cartridge has several steel loads that illustrate a reduced load. If you were shooting a 1 ¼-ounce load of 3-inch High Performance #4 at 1400 fps, about 28 ft-lb, you could significantly lower the felt recoil by changing to a 7/8-ounce 2 ¾-inch Game Load of #4 while maintaining shot speed of 1400 fps, about 13 ft-lb. The difference is a slightly smaller shell, less shot in the load and a slightly different Vectan powder: A1-36 in the 2 ¾- shell and A0 in the 3-inch.[5]

The best solution for sub-gauge shooting on small game and upland birds is currently offered by Polywad's GreenLite 2 ¾ shells, available in both 20- and 28-gauge. This soft steel shot is offered in a special proprietary size of #7-#8 (240 pellets in the 20-gauge load and 220 in the 28-gauge), which the Georgia company says is "Not as big as #7; not as small as #8." These shells are produced with "wad-less technology" – using a simple paper cup to hold the shot – that is both eco-friendly and effective.

Polywad owner Jay Menefee rates his shot at 1,000 mph three feet from the muzzle and says that each pellet carries a foot-pound of energy – all of which is an unusual albeit refreshing way of discussing shotshell speed and energy in an international manufacturing atmosphere attuned to faster and farther. Still, Polywad also presents ratings for recoil and that, too, is different than the standard manufacturer discussion of shooting, which rarely or never backs up such statements as "reduced recoil" with numbers. Menefee says that a load of his 20-gauge GreenLite steel produces 6.5 ft-lb of recoil in a 7-pound gun while the 28-gauge gives the same recoil in a 6-pound gun.[3g]

Recoil and its effects present interesting questions for all shooters, but are especially critical for novice gun handlers or people with slender frames, and steel shot has a reputation for producing heavier recoil. All shooters experience recoil, of course, because for every action there is an equal and opposite reaction, but all experience "felt or subjective or perceived recoil" differently. While "absolute recoil" can be determined mathematically, felt recoil is what you complain about to the guy next to you when you fail to get the gun properly mounted on your shoulder after a couple stray shots on an abruptly flying grouse.

Steel shot has had greater felt recoil because, size-for-size, steel is less dense, less heavy. To achieve down range effectiveness, companies have – as noted earlier – raced for the highest speeds possible without blowing up barrels, 1500 to 1600 fps. Federal Black Cloud 12-gauge is 1450-1500 fps; its Ultra-Shok High Velocity Steel is 1550 fps. A 1 1/8-ounce load of Remington Nitro-Steel is 1550 fps. A good many of Winchester's Xpert Hi-Velocity Steel and several Hevi-Shot Duck loads chronograph at 1550 fps. All of which means that any shot taken at close range with these products is going to vaporize your quail.

A few simple non-shot accessories will help tame recoil, as well as dropping down in gauge and shot volume. A shoulder pad inside a shooting vest or shirt is a good first step although if it becomes a bit too thick or too loose, it can interfere with bringing the gun to your shoulder. A cheek protector on the stock may help if young shooters have difficulty consistently levering the gun to proper position, often because they are peeking to see if they hit the target rather than focusing on proper execution, and end up with a bruise. Finally, a few shooting sessions with a coach – someone who is not a parent is usually best – and if the youngster shows interest and/or promise perhaps a special stock fitting session as well.

A Note About Turkeys

There's no reason non-toxic shot should be restricted to waterfowl. Many established loads will kill a wild turkey, either hunting from inside an enclosed blind or with your back against an oak tree and your camo in place, just as easily as they will a migrating Canada goose.

A wild turkey can be formidable – 20 pounds is average for an Eastern male bird, but the National Wild Turkey Federation says it has registered one bird that weighed a whopping 37 pounds.[6] The wingspan can approach five feet and a wild bird can fly for short distances at up to 55 miles per hour. Also fast on the ground, they can sprint at speeds to 25 mph. Still, these big birds spend their daylight hours poking along in the woods and typically fly only when threatened by a predator, when a member of the flock is at shot or when they are flapping up and down from their overnight roost in a tree.

Classic shot size is #4 to #6 and not only do almost all companies that sell non-toxic shot have these loads, but reloading recipes for turkey are available from multiple sources. Remember as you pattern your gun that shotgun pellets shed energy rapidly and smaller, lighter pellets shed them faster than heavier pellets. Plan accordingly.

Steel shot is frankly a bit light for turkeys unless you are calling them to within 30 to 35 yards. Even loads that are labeled "Turkey" may not pattern well beyond that distance through the full chokes generally required to hit the big bird hard enough to knock it down.

We tend to understand that non-toxic shot is for waterfowl, but many states are gradually changing the rules for upland hunting – especially in ecologically sensitive areas – toward U.S. FWS-approved shot and shell only.

Tungsten, including or especially Hevi-Shot, is a preferred material for turkeys, even preferred to lead. Tungsten matrix will pattern well to 50 yards, putting sufficient pellets in a 3-foot circle to kill a bird at half a football field distance … recognizing that the special thrill of hunting turkeys is calling them close, making the wild bird hunt you.

In that respect, Craig Endicott, the Northeast Wildlife Supervisor for the Oklahoma Wildlife Department and an outdoorsman who has spent considerable time studying turkey loads, suggests the following – and I agree: "My analysis of the maximum effective ranges for pellets comprised of different metal types is: #6 tungsten, #5 lead or #4 steel to 45 yards and #5 tungsten, #4 lead or #3 steel to 55 yards."

Non-toxic for Big Game: Slugs and Sabots

"Would you point that somewhere else … please?"

Momma always said "please" was a magic word. It was an unusual moment, but not frightening; a little irritating at the instant I looked into the barrel of a scoped shotgun. After all, I was bowhunting an archery-only area. The camouflaged shotgunner was either confused or just taking a chance, and that day he took a chance with my life.

Since then, I have often wondered about that man and his set-up, but it was the '80s and I imagine he had a Brenneke slug in the chamber and four more in the magazine. Enough to pulverize my body and its every attachment.[7]

Shotgun slugs are often used for big game hunting near heavily populated areas and in tactical loads by law enforcement. Slugs can be fired

Barnes' Spit-Fire T-EZ muzzleloader saboted bullets reduce the ramrod pressure needed to load and seat these .50-caliber (.451-inch), 250-gr. flat-base bullets. A polymer tip enhances expansion and boosts BC. The T-EZ expands at both close and extended range with six razor-edge cutting petals to maximize shock and penetration.

Winchester's XP3 Sabot Shotgun Slug is 300-grains of power with polycarbonate tip and fully-encased sabot sleeve.

through any properly gauged shotgun whether a smoothbore (grooved or self-stabilizing slugs) or a barrel manufactured with land-and-groove rifling (slugs or sabots are spin-stabilized). Think of slugs as an intermediate step between a handful of BBs and a bullet. Actually, something akin to a firing sledge hammers at a target.

The first widely recognized slug that wasn't a simply ball of lead slightly smaller than the barrel of the gun was made by Wilhelm Brenneke in 1898. Brenneke's slug was a cylindrical solid with a bit of a nose, and until 1931 when Karl Foster developed his hollow-base, weight-forward slug there were few commercial options. Barrel fouling, muzzle or choke wear, speed, accuracy and distance were problematic with these early slugs until sabots (saboted slugs) came along in the latter half of the 20th century.

A sabot is a slug with a base and perhaps a partial side sleeve, usually of plastic, that acts as a gas seal and engages the barrel rifling, imparting true spin stabilization to the slug. The sabot slug itself need not come in contact with the barrel at all, and as it exits the muzzle, the choke strips the plastic or sabot material away. Whereas a sharpshooter might shoot a ball slug accurately to 50 or 75 yards, an early Foster slug could double that distance and a modern sabot might again double the distance for accurate, lethal impacts to 200+ yards or beyond when shooting a scoped shotgun with a rifled barrel. Another beauty of a sabot is that it will not damage a screw-in choke.

Here is a look at some of the 12-gauge non-toxic slugs and sabots on the market now. Several well-known slug manufacturers do not offer non-toxic slugs: Hornaday, Hastings, Lightfield and Wolf. In the near future, you can expect that these offerings will dramatically increase:

Brenneke

Today, 90 percent of Brenneke's product is lead, but the 1 1/8-ounce (492.2 gr.) 12-gauge .63-inch diameter Super Sabot in 2 ¾- or 3-inch lengths is lead-free. "Frankly," Brenneke writes, citing loss of knockdown power, "we never believed in sabots. Sure, they are capable of very good accuracy. But …." And yet, here they are and Brenneke rates its Super Sabot ($15.98 - $17.79, box of five) for accuracy at "less than 2 ½-inches (five rounds) at 100 yards" and for expansion from .63 to 1.0 inch.

3-inch
- muzzle velocity 1526 fps with 2536 ft-lb energy
- at 100 yards 1065 fps with 1236 ft-lb energy

2 ¾-inch
- muzzle velocity 1407 fps with 2157 ft-lb energy
- at 100 yards 1017 fps with 1127 ft-lb energy

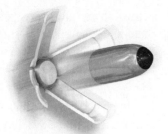

Anyone who does not fully appreciate the raw power of a shotgun slug such as this Barnes Tipped Slug from Federal has not hunted with one lately. Visit www.theboxotruth.com to see slugs in action versus typical handgun and rifle rounds and a number of target mediums.

Federal Premium

The basis of this slug line is the copper Barnes Expander, and Federal uses it in its tipped or non-tipped Vital-Shok loads. "It's designed for use in fully-rifled barrels only," says Federal, and provides accurate shooting to 200-yards. Federal offers both 12- (1-ounce and ¾-ounce: $16.99 box of five) and 20-gauge (5/8-ounce) Vital-Shok copper sabots.

2 ¾-inch, 1-ounce (437.5 gr.)
- muzzle velocity 1450 fps with 2042 ft-lb energy
- at 100 yards 1211 fps with 1423 ft-lb energy

2 ¾-inch, ¾-ounce (328.1 gr.)
- muzzle velocity 1900 fps with 2630 ft-lb energy
- at 100 yards 1492 fps with 1621 ft-lb energy

3-inch, 1-ounce (437.5 gr.)
- muzzle velocity 1530 fps with 2274 ft-lb energy
- at 100 yards 1274 fps with 1577 ft-lb energy

Fiocchi

Fiocchi's EMB non-toxic full-bore slugs are designed as expanding copper with elements of tungsten composite. Its two new 12-gauge slugs are 2 ¾ at 1 oz. and 3-inch at 1 1/8 oz.

Remington

Copper Solid sabot slugs from Remington, the company says, combine "the angled petal score design of the Copper Solid muzzleloader bullet with the ballistic coefficient of a deep penetrating slug round" for 100 percent weight retention, 2X controlled expansion and groups of 2 ½ inches or less from fully-rifled slug barrels. Copper Solids come in 12-gauge (2 ¾- 1 oz., 1450 fps: 1 oz. managed recoil, 1200 fps: 3-inch 1 oz., 1550 fps) and 20-gauge (2 ¾-inch 5/8-ounce, 1500 fps). The cost is $13.99 - $16.99 for a box of five shells.

SinterFire

A specialist in copper/tin composite, SinterFire builds a single 12-gauge 325-gr. shotgun slug (#SF12-325), RHSS or reduced hazard shotgun slug.

Because of the volume of lead deposited on traditional trap and skeet fields, it is critical that outdoor ranges have an environmental plan which includes documenting their efforts. (Photo Browning)

Winchester

Tin core, lead-free alloy Supreme Elite XP 3-inch, 12-gauge slugs from Winchester feature one-piece, 300-grain (.69 oz.), plastic-tipped sabots. Winchester has achieved a high velocity with this lightweight deer-killer, an unusually high 2100 fps. According to the web site, "Winchester developed the slug "to extend consistent, ethical and lethal big game hunting ranges beyond 175 yards in 12-gauge rifled barrel slug guns." Cost is $11.99 for a box of five.

2 ¾-inch
- muzzle velocity 2000 fps with 2665 ft-lb energy
- at 100 yards 1622 fps with 1753 ft-lb energy

3-inch
- muzzle velocity 2100 fps with 2937 ft-lb energy
- at 100 yards 1708 fps with 1944 ft-lb energy

NON-TOXIC FOR COMPETITION

Sanctioned or Tournament Shooting

Notice as we check in with each of the three common American clay target games – trap, skeet and sporting clays – how few cartridges and how few commercially available small pellets are being manufactured that meet the requirements for sanctioned or tournament shooting. There are two reasons:

1. First, when the lead-poisoning phenomenon began to get press in waterfowl circles in the '70s and '80s, it would have been the rare soul who predicted the migration of the concept into sportsmen's target ranges. That's curious, because while there may be more licensed waterfowl hunters (one million) than registered clay shooters (paid membership in the major organizations may be 200,000, tops), ten times as many shots are taken at clay birds than at live birds each year.[9]

2. Second, even though millions of rounds are fired in these disciplines annually, there is a heavy presence of reloading, and this fact may make the machining, packaging and marketing of specialty pellets too expensive at this time.

Discussing the possibility of non-toxic shooting with officials of the three governing organizations – the Amateur Trapshooting Association (ATA), the National Skeet Shooting Association (NSSA) and the National Sporting Clays Association (NSCA) – it quickly becomes apparent that they are practically oblivious to the possibility of a coming revolution in their shooting sport.[8] It is a classic example of the ostrich phenomenon at work: if we don't look at it and don't acknowledge it, it either isn't real or will go away without bothering us. Nevertheless, here are the three disciplines and their cartridge requirements.

Trap

The heaviest loads allowable for shooting sanctioned ATA[10] targets are 12-gauge, 1 1/8-ounce of #7 ½ (.950-inch diameter). The maximum allowable velocity is 1290 fps with the 1 1/8-ounce shot charge; 1325 fps with the lighter 1-ounce charge; and 1350 with a 7/8-ounce or lighter shell. Competitive or handicap trap shooting is a 12-gauge game; you have to be an excellent trap shooter to consistently score behind the 16-yard line with the sub-gauges.

This formula has become such a standard that loads in this combination are invariably referred to as "trap loads," and every ammunition manufacturer offers them. At the 16-yard line, good shooters can score with #8 ½ (.850-inch diameter).

ATA vice president John Hiter says there have been some changes at clubs which traditionally shot over water, but as long as your shell has the proper size shot – allowing for #7 steel – and velocity, you're good to go.

Skeet

Skeet is a close-range game and sanctioned target shooting is governed by NSSA[11] rules. Skeet does not require a diverse selection of loads. The 12-gauge is allowed a maximum of 1 1/8-ounce; the 20-gauge a maximum of 7/8-ounce; the 28-gauge ¾-ounce; and the .410-bore only ½-ounce.

Since #9 (.080-inch diameter) can reliably break any target inside 25 yards, it has become the almost universal choice for skeet. With a pellet count of about 585 per ounce (Winchester standard shot size), that gives 1 1/8-ounce 12-gauge loads about 650 pellets. A few shooters prefer #8 ½ for the second shot in doubles or in the challenging .410.

Sporting Clays

According to the NSCA[12], loads for registered tournaments must conform to shot weight standards by gauge. The maximum gun size is 12-gauge and the maximum 12-gauge load is 1 1/8-ounce; 20-gauge 7/8-ounce; 28-gauge ¾-ounce; and .410, ½-ounce. While lead shot must be no larger than #7 ½ and no smaller than #9, the steel shot range is wider: #6 to #9 (or .110- to .080-inch diameter). Plated shot is allowed, but (at this time) neither bismuth nor tungsten are accepted in official shooting.

• A single Bismuth cartridge in the Pinnacle Classic line is available for the 12- and the small gauges in these sizes. It will be useful for fun shooting but not for registered clays that count for national or regional ATA standings.

• B&P has one 12-gauge, 2 ¾-inch, 1 1/8-ounce load of #7 steel – 1350 fps as F2 Mach Professional Steel.

• Clever Mirage has three 12-gauge 2 ¾-inch loads: ¾-, 7/8- and 1 ounce.

• Estate has one 12- (1 1/8) and one 20-gauge (3/4), both 2 ¾ loads of #6 steel.

• Federal's Steel Game & Target has one 12-gauge steel is 1 ounce of #6 or #7 – 1375 fps – and two 20-gauge loads (Game & Target and Top Gun Steel).

• Fiocchi has both 12- and 20-gauge loads.

• Kent has two 12- and a single 20-gauge shell in #7 Upland Fasteel and several 12- and 20-gauge #7 cartridges in its Velocity Steel with biodegradable wad.

• Hull loads #7 12-gauge in Pro Steel and a 20-gauge in Game & Clay.

• Lyalvale #6 steel for the 12-gauge.

• Remington's Hi-Speed Steel has a 12-gauge in #6 or #7 and a 20-gauge in #7. The HD series offers several loads in #6 steel.

• Winchester offers steel shooting for sporting clays in its Xpert Steel line. All gauges except the 10- and 16- are covered with shot in the #6 and #7 size.

When non-toxic loads other than steel are eventually encouraged, they will become available. These are two current options:

• Polywad has its tungsten composite loads available only for the 20- and 28-gauge: not as big as #7 and not as small as $8, it says.

• Nice Shot from RST has its proprietary tungsten composite loads of #6 and #7 ½ in 12-, 16-, 20- (two in this sub-gauge, the 2 ½- and 2 ¾-inch) and 28-gauge.

SELF- AND HOME-DEFENSE

Non-toxic for hunting is one thing. Non-toxic for self-defense on the other hand, sounds ridiculous. It isn't ... or not entirely

ICC

The Green Elite shotgun line from International Cartridge (ICC)[3j] was developed for frangible characteristics, but has the additional advantage of being lead-free. The ammo is a copper-tin composite and ICC says it is safe for use on ¼-inch AR 500 steel, with reduced splash-back, and little or no damage to targets. Hence, law enforcement and private citizens can train in close quarters and then use this ammo in a critical situation at home, if necessary, without killing the neighbors.

Green Elite frangible, lead-free Duty & Training ammo for the 12-gauge is loaded to minimize recoil. Buckshot cartridges hold 270 gr. of shot in 9-pellet wads and even the 325-gr. Shotgun Slug can be used on steel.

ICC 325-gr. Slug
• muzzle velocity 1450 fps with 1700 ft-lb energy
• at 50 yards 1175 fps with 1250 ft-lb energy

ICC 270-gr. Buckshot
• muzzle velocity 1425 fps with 1325 ft-lb energy
• at 50 yards 1175 fps with 900 ft-lb energy

Remington

Remington[3k] is capitalizing on the rise in public uncertainty and has begun marketing a line of shotguns and ammunition for home defense.[13] The shotguns are, of course, non-glare black from their tactical line-up and the brochure features an appropriately hooded man breaking into what appears to be a home, with a crowbar and a flashlight held precariously in his left hand. What is surprising though is that Remington HD Ultimate Home Defense ammo is non-toxic in composition.

Ultimate Home Defense shotgun ammo uses the same tungsten-bronze matrix pellet material as Wingmaster HD. Remington says you can choose from a load of BB's for "the highest terminal energy" or a duplex mixture of #2 and #4 for "excellent pattern density and outstanding stopping power with a reduced chance

Non-toxic shotgun loads (or handgun loads classified as RRLF or "reduced recoil, lead-free") may be ideal for home- or self-defense situations. The objective is to stop the attacker immediately without causing harm to neighbors. (Photo by Rick Sapp)

of over-penetration." And in a sleepy community with neighbors just on the other side of a couple sheets of drywall, that is surely something to keep in mind. Both loads are 12-gauge, 2 ¾-inch with 1 ¼ ounces of shot rated at 1250 fps.

Remington's idea of a tight pattern for "one-shot confidence" with whatever load is extremely debatable. Awakened at night by a thug breaking through your back door, the pinpoint accuracy required when firing at high-flying ducks is not the best program for survival. You want a gun and load that gives you maximum spread because, unless he or she is chemically pumped, only a few pellets in the face will be enough to drive the intruder back out the door in search of a hospital or his momma.

Winchester

The Supreme Elite XP3 is a one-piece lead-free 300-gr. tipped sabot, which to date is only available for the 12-gauge. With a tin core and plastic tip (for improved down-range ballistics, Winchester says – not just because it looks good), the slug is supposed to give deeper penetration at longer ranges says Winchester Shotshell Product Manager Brad Criner, "near-centerfire rifle distances" or beyond 175 yards with a rifled barrel slug gun.

Winchester introduced the 2 ¾-inch saboted, lead-free slug two years earlier than its roll-out of the 3-inch version. With the same BC (0.189), bullet dynamics at the muzzle for the two slugs is similar: 2 ¾-inch = 2000 fps with 2665 ft lb of energy and 3-inch = 2100 fps with 2937 ft lb.

CHAPTER NOTES

1. From the forum on www.gamebirdhunts.com.

2. According to Jared Saylor blogging for EarthJustice, founded as the Sierra Club legal defense fund in 1971 and available through http://communities.justicetalking.org, the U.S. EPA "has identified 58 lead acid battery manufacturers as major sources of lead pollution – emitting more than 26 tons of lead and 47 tons of other hazardous pollutants each year."

3. Internet sites for companies mentioned in the text are:

a. Texas Gulf Duck Hunting www.texasgulfduckhunting.com

b. SwanHunting.com www.swanhunting.com

c. Top Gun Guide Service www.topgunguideservice.com

d. 2009 Saskatchewan Hunter's and Trapper's Guide, Ministry of the Environment www.environment. gov.sk.ca

e. Honker Down Professional Guide Service www.honkerdown.com

f. Patternmaster Chokes www.patternmaster.com

g. Polywad www.polywad.com

h. Brenneke USA www.brennekeusa.com

i. Federal Premium www.federalpremium.com

j. International Cartridge www.iccammo.com

k. Remington www.remington.com

4. By "power," we usually mean energy. When something is still – a book on the edge of a shelf, a shotshell loaded in the chamber with the safety off – it has potential energy, but when something is in motion, it is said to have kinetic energy. The question of whether traditional lead carries more energy than new non-toxic loads (or bullets) is easily answered.

It's easy to compute the kinetic energy of a shotgun shell with the equation: kinetic energy equals one-half of the mass of the object times the square of the speed of the object. In symbols KE = (1/2) mv2 which requires a bit of conversion, but it would be wrong to allow the formula to intimidate and so we calculate this manner in our antiquated English/American system: KE = (velocity in fps) x (velocity in fps) x (total weight in grains) ÷ (450,240).

Here's an example (and yes, I cheated and checked most of these formulas and conversions via the Internet):

Winchester Xpert Steel (WE127) is a 12-gauge, 2 ¾-inch shell with one ounce (437.5 gr.) of #7 shot measured three feet from the muzzle for a velocity of 1300 fps = 1,621 ft-lb. (This load we believe to be adequate for woodcock and squirrels.)

To put this in perspective, let's take two hunting examples, an arrow and a bullet:

A. A Carbon Express Aramid KV hunting arrow tipped with a Muzzy MX-3 might weigh a total of 425-grains. Shot out of a Mathews Z7 bow at 280 fps = 74 ft-lb. (Bowhunters tackle brown bears and African big game with this set-up.)

B. Second, a 95-gr. Winchester Supreme Elite XP3 fired from your .243 deer rifle has a muzzle velocity of 3100 fps = 2,028 ft-lb. The design or composition of the bullet has no influence on this rating although its down range performance may change dramatically if these elements change.

5. There are quite a few web sites that offer approximate recoil calculators and I used the one at www.10xshooters.com/calculators/Shotgun_Recoil_Calculator.htm although www.gunnersden.com/index. htm.shotgun-recoil.html uses the same formula; it just makes you do the calculations yourself:

a. Add the weight of powder, shot and wad together, expressed in grains.

b. Multiply this number by the weight of the powder.

c. Multiply the weight of your shotgun in pounds (a decimal as in 8.2, not 8 lb. 1 oz.) by the number 80.

d. Divide the number from step "b" by the number from step "c" and the answer is expressed in foot pounds (ft-lb) of recoil.

6. www.nwtf.org/all_about_turkeys/new_turkey_look.html

7. Anyone who does not fully appreciate the raw power of a shotgun slug has not hunted with them and ought to visit our shooting friends at www.theboxotruth.com. If you're reading this book, you will find that web site informative and entertaining because the maestro of shooting shows bullets, shotgun slugs and shotshells in action attacking drywall, bricks, plywood and car widows. You will understand that, as the Texas owner of this site says, the walls of your home provide concealment, but not cover.

8. A regional director of one of the major shooting associations complained that his headquarters could spend a week arguing about proper footwear for a tournament, but was completely bewildered by something as potentially serious as using non-toxic shot for sanctioned tournaments. "Can't even talk about it," he said. Nevertheless, he acknowledged that because of the cost differential there was little interest in moving toward bismuth or tungsten loads except at those ranges with shot-fall zones near water, in which case the range was forced to consider closing (several in the northeast U.S. have been forced to close); working with a range designer to re-structure the shooting (expensive and not always possible); or considering non toxic shooting options (resisted by most of the membership).

9. Author estimates.

10. www.shootata.com

11. www.mynssa.com

12. www.mynsca.com

13. Experts are not at all in agreement because this varies by each personal situation, but a shotgun can be excellent for those extremely rare cases where defense of one's home from intruders is required. A shotgun is more unwieldy than a handgun (8 pounds loaded and about 40-inches long versus 1 pound and maybe 8 inches long). And of course we believe that because a shotgun has a short barrel, shot disperses like an umbrella opening, but this is not so. At the very close ranges involved in non-military self-defense situations, a shot pattern may be no more than two or three inches – which is, however, a whole lot more than a .45 or .357. For home defense possibilities, go with what makes you comfortable. (In the author's home state of Florida and, thankfully, in many states, the homeowner may now legally presume that an intruder in such situations is there to cause harm and may, without fear of retribution in the courts, fire in self-defense.)

SECTION III:
THE GREEN HANDGUNNER

Secondary effects of lead poisoning have reportedly been discovered in bald eagles and other omnivorous raptors that feed off the carcass of non-recovered waterfowl. (Photo Tom Barnes, U.S. FWS)

Photo Carl Chapman Phoenix, AZ

CHAPTER 7

LEAD AMMO – THE TRUTH IS OUT THERE ... SOMEWHERE

"**W**ho you gonna believe, me or your lying eyes?"

If you think the past couple of decades were a roller coaster for hunters and shooters, buckle your seat belt. You ain't seen nothing yet. Part of our problem is knowing who to trust to tell us the truth. Remember what we learned from Watergate?

"Follow the money."

Here is the non-toxic argument that is affecting the way we shoot, and may perhaps change the nature of shooting in America.

First, however, how much lead is safe in the human body? The U.S. Centers for Disease Control and Prevention states that a blood lead level of 10 micrograms per deciliter (usually abbreviated as μg/dl) or greater in children is cause for concern; 25 μg/dl in adults.

Lead is not radioactive, but in the bloodstream it has a half-life of approximately 30 days. Eat a fragment of a lead bullet that causes your blood-lead level to rise to 10 μg/dl and, if you are not further exposed, in about 30 days it will be back down to 5 μg/dl, then down to normal 30 days after that. Unfortunately, the damage will have been done.

How much is 10 μg/dl? It is 2.96 μg or about three millionths of a gram per ounce. Put that much on the tip of your finger and you couldn't see it with a laboratory microscope.[1]

The CDC says that when it comes to lead there is no known safe exposure level.

AND THE LAST SHALL BE FIRST . . .

The Players

- Arizona Game and Fish Dept. [www.azgfd.gov]: Since 1996, six to 10 condors – a giant, carrion-feeding vulture, the largest flying bird in the Western Hemisphere, a bird which may live more than 60 years – per year have been released in the vicinity of the Grand Canyon. Each carries two radio transmitters and is monitored by as many as 10 biologists. Lead poisoning is the leading cause of condor death and the main obstacle to a self-sustaining population. All-copper bullets have superior knock-down power on big game, are less toxic, and do not fragment like lead. In their first questionnaire, 93 percent of hunters respond that non-lead bullets perform as well as or better than lead.

Table: North American Condor Numbers July 2009

Total	356
Captive	176
Wild	180
Arizona	75
California	89
Baja	16

Source: www.azgfd.gov/w_c/california_condor.shtml

- California Dept. of Fish and Game [www.dfg.ca.gov]: Most causes of condor death for 200 years have been from human activities: lead fragments in carcasses, poison bait and environmental pollutants. Past use of the pesticide DDT may have prevented some eggs from hatching – condor chicks take as much as a week to break out of an egg – and human activity is followed by growing numbers of ravens, which threaten eggs and nestlings. Fish and Game says accidental collision with wires and structures is also a risk. "There have been so many problems facing the condor for so long that the species was not going to survive in the wild without help from people."

- Center for Biological Diversity [www.biologicaldiversity.org]: Headquartered in Arizona and now 20 years old, CBD says it "work(s) to secure a future for all species, great and small, hovering on the brink of extinction. We do so through science, law, and creative media, with a focus on protecting the lands, waters, and climate that species need to survive."

- Individuals: Bill Cornatzer, MD (dermatology), Bismarck, ND: member Peregrine Fund Board of Directors, falconer, conservationist, hunter; and Ted Fogarty, MD (radiology), Medcenter One, Bismarck, ND: golfer and sailor.

- Iowa Dept. of Natural Resources [www.iowadnr.gov]: Responsible for maintaining state parks and forests, protecting the environment, and managing energy, fish, wildlife, and land and water resources.

- University of Iowa Hygienic Laboratory [www.uhl.uiowa.edu]: "The lab tests water, air, soil and just about anything else that may affect the health of our neighbors." Laboratory facilities in Iowa City and Ankeny.

- Minnesota Dept. of Natural Resources [www.dnr.state.mn.us]: X-rays from a study by Lou Cornicelli, DNR big game program coordinator, showed that lead fragments travel inside a body far beyond the bullet's primary wound channel. "It never dawned on me that it might be an issue," said Cornicelli. "Copper bullets leave no lead."

- Missouri Dept. of Conservation [www.mdc.mo.gov]: The departments of Conservation, Health and Senior Services (DHSS) and Agriculture meet with representatives of the Conservation Federation of Missouri. They discuss appropriate responses to a growing awareness of the potential presence of lead bullet fragments in hunter-killed deer. Missouri officials also attend a meeting of conservation, health and agriculture officials from five other Midwestern states. "People who eat venison can reduce the risk of exposure to lead bullet fragments by careful handling of the meat."

- National Institute for Occupational Safety and Health (NIOSH) is a part of the Centers for Disease Control and Prevention [www.cdc.gov]

- National Rifle Association [www.nra.org, www.nrahuntersrights.org]: Calling itself "America's oldest civil rights organization," the NRA's mission is to preserve and defend the U.S. Constitution, especially the inalienable right to keep and bear arms guaranteed by the Second Amendment. The NRA's Institute for Legislative Action says organization membership is around four million.

- National Shooting Sports Foundation [www.nssf.org]: Formed in 1961, the Foundation (NSSF) is the trade association for the shooting, hunting and firearms industry. NSSF is a not-for-profit organization with a membership of more than 4,000 shooting sports businesses. The mission is to promote, protect and preserve hunting and the shooting sports.

- North Dakota Dept. of Health, Terry Dwelle, MD (epidemiology), State Health Officer [www.ndhealth.gov]

- The Peregrine Fund [www.peregrinefund.org]: Established in 1970 and headquartered in Idaho, the fund (TPF) works internationally through about 100 staff to conserve birds of prey by restoring species, conserving habitat, educating students, training conservationists, providing factual information and accomplishing "good science." TPF says, "Condors present a warning that fragments from lead bullets fired from a rifle are an environmental danger to scavenging wildlife, and also to humans."

- Fish & Wildlife Service [www.fws.gov]

- National Park Service [www.nps.gov]

- Wisconsin Dept. of Health Services [http://dhs.wisconsin.gov]

- Wisconsin Dept. of Natural Resources [http://dnr.wi.gov]: "Avoid consuming internal organs, as they can contain extra lead from heart-lung shots."

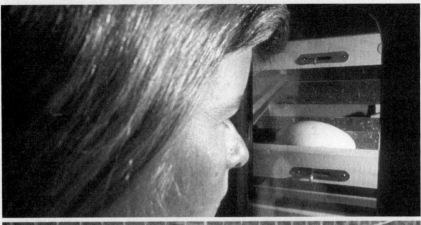

THE CONDOR CONTROVERSY – A great deal of the current debate about non-toxic rifle bullets centers on fragmenting lead bullets which may be consumed by vultures like the endangered California condor. The world's largest carrion-eater, the condor is released in California and Arizona, a cooperative effort between the states, the federal government and private non-

profit organizations. First, eggs are incubated. Birds that have been injured are nursed back to health. Remote areas of the U.S. Southwest are selected for release of young and healthy birds. Naturally laid eggs perch precariously on an open nest near the Grand Canyon. Once they hatch and can fly on their own, birds are tagged and released, but are continually monitored. (Photos Ron Garrison, John and Karen Hollingsworth, Rob Miles and U.S. FWS)

The Time Line

July 1987

In April 1986, the Federal Reserve Bank of Cincinnati asks the National Institute for Occupational Safety and Health (NIOSH) to evaluate airborne lead at their indoor firing range.[2]

In May, "breathing-zone" air sampling was conducted during the firing of standard lead target bullets.

Hoping to reduce lead exposure, the bank bought copper dip-plated lead target bullets and NIOSH sampled the air again in April 1987.

Lead exposures were 89 ug/m3 shooting the standard lead bullets; 79 ug/m3 shooting the copper-coated lead bullets. Permissible lead exposure is 50 ug/m3.

"It was concluded," wrote NIOSH Investigator Stephen Lee, "that there was little or no difference between air lead emissions from the two bullet types. It appeared likely that the copper-coating was too thin to effectively isolate the lead portion of the bullet from the firing process."

Previous firing range studies showed that airborne lead exposure could be reduced to less than four µg/m3 when jacketed lead or zinc bullets were used. The disadvantages were the greater cost and the tendency for the harder zinc bullets to damage the range.

An evaluation of airflow patterns revealed that insufficient bullet-trap exhaust caused the unbalanced ventilation system to deliver turbulent airflow at the firing line.

NIOSH investigators determined that a hazard from overexposure to lead existed at the Federal Reserve Bank's Indoor Firing Range at the time of the investigation. They recommended that jacketed bullets be used until the ventilation system could be repaired.

1991

Concluding a long and contentious debate, the U.S. implements a nation-wide ban on lead shot for all waterfowl hunting. "Waterfowl can ingest expended lead shot and many then die from lead poisoning."[3]

1999

After September 1, 1999, non-toxic shot is required throughout Canada for migratory game birds, except for American woodcock, band-tailed pigeons and mourning doves. "Non-toxic shot is defined as bismuth, steel, tin, tungsten-iron, tungsten-matrix or tungsten polymer shot, in which the concentration of lead and other materials must not exceed one percent. This limit, which is the same as the limit for non-toxic shot under American federal wildlife legislation, permits the use of metals, such as tin, that normally have some lead content."[4]

Big game hunting has been allowed on most lands in the National Wildlife Refuge System since the days of their founding. Here, a 1953 photo shows Alaskan hunters with Dahl sheep and ptarmigan. Like many public agencies, the U.S. Fish & Wildlife Service is considering the merits of requiring big game hunters to use non-toxic rounds. (Photo U.S. FWS)

Fall 2005

To reduce lead exposure in condors, Arizona Game and Fish offers free non-lead rifle ammunition to big game hunters in Units 12A and 12B, the area condors most frequent. Paid for by the Arizona Heritage Fund, 65 percent – two-thirds of 3600 hunters participate – participate; condor lead exposure rates decline by 40 percent, the first decline since testing began in 2000. Post-hunt surveys indicate 93 percent of successful hunters who used non-lead ammunition say it performed as well as or better than lead. The free non-lead ammunition program continues in 2006.

The Peregrine Fund, the state's partner in condor reintroduction, is still not appeased: "these rates of hunter participation are insufficient..." it writes. "Given the extensive evidence that lead exposure from spent ammunition is harmful to wildlife it now appears obvious that responsible society will end the use of lead for hunting throughout much of the world."[5]

March 2007

According to the Missouri Conservation Commission, it has resisted calls from environmentalists for a ban on lead shot for years, even when nearby states such as South Dakota banned lead on state game production areas (1998).

A month before turkey season 2007, the Conservation Dept. implements a ban on lead shot in 21 heavily hunted conservation areas. Assistant director John Smith says the change comes after years of studying how lead affects bird populations. Lead shot is already banned on most of the 4,300-acre Columbia Bottom Conservation Area in St. Louis.

"[Lead is] a widely recognized toxic substance and it's something that can be harmful biologically if it's ingested," Smith said. "Even one (pellet) would probably result in incapacitation and death."

Waterfowl and mourning doves "seem to be" the birds most susceptible to lead shot poisoning. As many as 6.5 percent of mourning doves eat lead shot, which kills almost as many doves each year as hunters." [6]

May 2007

Bill Cornatzer attends a Peregrine Fund staff presentation. One of The Fund's stated missions is to eliminate lead ammo where endangered condors have been re-introduced into the wild. Staff argues that condors in northern Arizona feed on the remains of hunter-killed animals, and that lead fragments in the gut piles cause condors to die. They also suggest that spent ammunition fragments contaminate game meat eaten by humans.

August 2007

A press release from the Peregrine Fund insists that to establish a self-sustaining population, it has released condors in northern Arizona since 1996. Slow to reproduce, the birds number only about 60. Lead poisoning, principally from eating gut piles that contain spent bullets/shotgun pellets, is the most frequent cause of death.

A "radiographic [X-ray] study of rifle bullet fragmentation shows the presence of hundreds of lead particles in whole deer and gut piles."

The Fund claims that 15 condors have bullet fragments or pellets in their digestive systems and that five birds died of lead poisoning in 2006 alone. The release concludes, "Lead exposure is currently so prevalent that the population cannot maintain itself by natural reproduction unless lead incidence in the wild food supply is greatly reduced."

Scientific evidence, says the Fund, indicates lead is more serious than formerly believed. Most rifle-killed gut piles, known to contain lots of lead, are eaten by scavengers: condors, bald and golden eagles and ravens. In addition, it suggests that more than 50 other bird species including mourning doves and many upland game birds, are poisoned by bullet fragments and shotgun pellets.

"Indeed," the Fund writes, "carcasses contain so much lead that hunters must seriously consider whether human consumers of deer meat are not also at risk.

"We trust in the long-standing tradition of hunters to take a proactive role in wildlife conservation and management, and we recognize the beneficial role they already have in helping condors thrive in the wild. We invite other hunters and hunting organizations to join with us in providing factual information … that best serves the interest of hunters and the wildlife they help conserve and manage."[7]

Fall 2007

Cornatzer recruits Ted Fogarty, a Bismarck radiologist with access to a CT scanner, a sophisticated computer aided X-ray machine, to assist him and then collects 95 packages – more than 100 pounds – of ground venison donated by hunters to area food pantries. With Fogarty, he X-rays the packages and takes his findings to the ND Dept. of Health. Of the 95 samples, 53 appear to contain metal fragments.

October 2007

Governor Arnold Schwarzenegger signs a bill passed by the California Legislature to create a "non-lead" zone for hunting in the range of the California condor. The purpose is to reduce the risk of indirect lead poisoning to the condor and other scavenging birds from hunting activities and to facilitate the management and recovery of this listed endangered species. (California's Fish and Game Commission adopted regulations in December 2007 to implement this law.)

November 2007

In a cooperative study paid for primarily by the Peregrine Fund, nine hunters shoot 30 whitetails with centerfire rifles using lead-core copper jacketed 150-gr. Remington 7 mm Magnum ammo in Sheridan County, Wyoming. The average range of shots is 127 yards.

Field dressed carcasses are taken to Washington Animal Disease Diagnostic Laboratory at Washington State University, Pullman, where wound channels are X-rayed.

Back in Wyoming, each deer is commercially processed at a different location and the meat packages are again X-rayed.

Study authors test "the bioavailability of ingested bullet fragments" by feeding the processed venison to pigs. The eight pigs are all female, young (less than 90 days) and small (less than 67 pounds); four additional pigs are used as controls – they are not fed meat with lead-fragments. Blood samples are taken from all pigs multiple times before and after they eat.

"All the pigs consumed all the venison provided to them within two hours. None of the experimental animals showed any signs of lead toxicosis or other illness for the duration of the experiment; none exhibited vomiting or diarrhea which might have affected gastrointestinal physiology or retention times in the stomach or intestines."[8]

December 2007

Following a year of public testimony, discussion and environmental analyses, the California Fish and Game Commission prohibits "the use of projectiles containing lead for hunting deer, bear, wild pig, elk and pronghorn antelope – plus coyotes, ground squirrels and other non-game wildlife – in areas designated as California condor range." Rules take effect on July 1, 2008.

While hunting these species in these areas hunters "may not possess any lead projectiles/ammunition and a firearm capable of firing it." Lead is still legal for hunting upland game species, however, within the non-lead zone.[9]

Winter 2008

North Dakota DOH takes five ground venison samples, targeting some with metal, and sends them to University of Iowa's Iowa Hygienic Laboratory. Results indicate that the contaminating metal is indeed lead.[10]

March 2008

In media interviews, Cornatzer says he is shocked at the amount and distribution of lead found in sampled venison. Describing himself as a "big hunter," he recommends avoiding lead bullets altogether, and says he has already purchased four boxes of copper bullets for his next hunting season. He says that lead from spent ammo is a national problem.

"The truth is," writes the Peregrine Fund, "that Dr. Cornatzer's study was motivated by a presentation by Peregrine Fund staff to the Board in May 2007 showing that lead fragments in the remains of hunter-killed animals are respon-

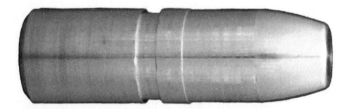

Nosler's non-toxic Solids like this 500-grain .458 are designed to be stoppers on big, dangerous game.

sible for the death of condors, and are the most important obstacle impeding recovery of condors in northern Arizona."

ND departments of Health, Agriculture and Game and Fish advise food pantries not to distribute or use donated ground venison because of contamination with lead fragments. It is no different, they note, from the precautions they would take when any food, beef to spinach, is contaminated.[11]

April 2008

Food pantries in Iowa may resume serving venison to the needy. Sampling of the ground meat for lead indicated only trace amounts, the Iowa Dept. of Natural Resources (IDNR) reports.

Testing was performed by the Iowa Hygienic Laboratory on 10 samples of ground venison from a central Iowa food pantry. All samples had less than one part per million of lead; eight had no detectable amounts; and two had only trace amounts.

Distribution of venison donated to food pantries by hunters was temporarily halted in late March 2008 until the ground meat could be sampled for lead.

Samples were tested in the Ankeny Sample Prep section and laboratory technicians also conducted ion chromatography (IC) and mass spectrometry (MS) testing, which provides greater sensitivity and can detect metals at lower levels.

"Based on the samples that were analyzed and the extensive data currently available through blood testing of Iowans by our department, no additional tests of the venison are necessary," says Ken Sharp, director of the environmental health division of the Iowa Dept. of Public Health. "When we look at the results of this testing and the blood data that has been collected over the years, the venison provided through the HUSH (Help Us Stop Hunger) program presents no recognized risk for lead exposure."[12]

Note: In five years, more than 25,000 deer have been donated through the DNR-administered HUSH program; this amounts to four million meal servings. Program goals include reducing the deer population while providing high quality, red meat to the needy.

Since 1992, more than 500,000 children and 25,000 adults in Iowa have been tested for lead poisoning. Not one case of lead poisoning identified from this testing was caused from ingestion of venison, according to Iowa DPH. Based on these results and on Food and Drug Administration guidelines, DPH says people can safely consume the following amounts of ground venison:

- Children under the age of 6 years: two 4-ounce servings per week
- Pregnant women: one 4-ounce serving per day
- All other adults: three 4-ounce servings per day

May 2008

The Peregrine Fund hosts a well-intentioned but poorly attended "international conference" on lead in bullets. A paper submitted to the conference by The Fund's Dominique Avery and Richard Watson says, "A timeline demonstrates the momentum with which this issue is gaining ground with most of the regulations taking place in the past 15 years and further regulations under discussion in many areas. An accumulating body of evidence shows that a reduction in the use of lead for hunting also benefits wildlife and humans who consume wild game."

The November 2007 experiment in which 30 wild deer were shot with a rifle in Wyoming (see Time Line reference) results in a paper titled "Lead Bullet Fragments in Venison from Rifle-Killed Deer: Potential for Human Dietary Exposure" and it is read at this conference.

"Our findings show that people risk exposure to lead when they eat venison from deer killed with standard lead-based rifle bullets and processed under normal commercial procedures."

Based on results from analysis of pig blood, "we infer that human consumption of venison processed under prevailing standards of commerce results in increased blood lead concentrations."

Referring to data presented elsewhere by others, the authors claim the body does not rid itself of lead in waste, but rather stores "a substantial proportion in soft tissues and ultimately in bone from which it may eventually be mobilized, as during pregnancy or in old age." (The authors have not designed their test to prove or disprove this point, but present it nevertheless as established fact.)

"The observed elevations in blood lead concentrations, while not considered overtly toxic, would nevertheless contribute to cumulative lead burdens, and would be additive with further meals of contaminated venison.

"Factors that may influence dietary lead exposure from spent lead bullets include the frequency and amount of venison consumption, degree of bullet fragmentation, anatomical path of the bullet, the care with which meat surrounding the bullet wound is removed, and any acidic treatments of the meat that would dissolve lead, i.e., coating the hanging carcass with vinegar or the use of acidic marinades in cooking.

"Exposure to lead from spent bullets is easily preventable if health-minded hunters use lead-free copper bullets now widely available and generally regarded as fully comparable to lead-based bullets for use in hunting. The potential for toxic exposure to copper from these bullets is presumably insignificant because little or no fragmentation occurs, and there is no meat wastage from having to discard tissue suspected of contamination."[13]

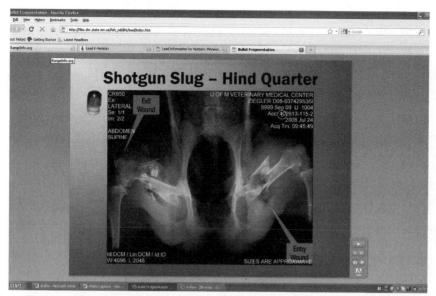

Screen capture of radiograph by Lou Cornicelli, Minnesota Department of Natural Resources big game program coordinator, showing the relative lack of fragmentation of a shotgun slug, even when it hits bone. (http://files.dnr.state.mn.us/fish_wildlife/lead/index.htm)

May 2008

North Dakota DOH and the U.S. Centers for Disease Control and Prevention (CDC) ask whether people who eat wild game have higher blood lead levels than people who do not: 738 state government employees volunteer to have their blood tested.

June 2008

In a preliminary letter to food pantry managers, Wisconsin Dept. of Health and Family Services Bureau of Environmental and Occupational Health employees Chuck Warzecha and Rob Thiboldeaux write: "We recommend that remaining venison from food pantries not be consumed or distributed unless the meat has been tested. If it is not possible to test the meat, pantries have the discretion to discard it."

They also note, "The number of samples with lead present was fairly low, about 4% …. Although lead in venison does not rival lead paint in older homes as a health risk for Wisconsin children, the risk is not low enough to ignore."

July 2008

To study bullet fragmentation and lead deposition, Lou Cornicelli, Big Game Program Coordinator, Minnesota DNR, selects 72 "previously euthanized" domestic sheep as surrogates for white-tailed deer. "We selected bullets based on their advertised performance and consumer availability."[14]

Each carcass was propped up in a wooden frame broadside position and shot in the chest from 50 meters. A chronograph recorded velocity and bullets were recovered from a sand-filled box behind the target.

Guns and ammo used included:

- .308 centerfire rifle shooting 150-gr. bullets and five different bullet designs: rapid expansion (ballistic tip, soft point), controlled expansion (exposed lead core, non-exposed lead core) and non-lead (copper);

- 50 caliber muzzleloader firing 100 gr. of powder (2-50 grain Hodgdon 777 pellets) and two different bullet designs: 245- and 300-gr.; and

- 12-gauge shotgun and a 1-ounce Foster-style slug.

Three carcasses were shot in the pelvic region using a ballistic tip, soft point, and slug to document dispersion of lead in animals shot poorly.

X-Rays and CT scans were taken at the Univ. of Minnesota Small Animal Hospital and lead analysis was completed by the university Veterinary Diagnostic Laboratory.

Results – bullet type, average number of fragments, and average maximum distance from the wound channel:

- Bullets with no exposed lead (a copper case completely surrounds the lead core) or entirely copper significantly reduce (or eliminate) lead exposure: nine copper fragments seven inches from the wound channel. "Overall, both of these bullet designs fragmented very little and left no lead."

- Ballistic tip bullets (rapid expansion) had the highest fragmentation rate: 141 fragments 11 inches from the wound channel. "In one carcass, a fragment was found 14 inches from the exit wound."

- Soft point bullets (rapid expansion): 86 fragments 11 inches from the wound channel.

- Bonded lead-core bullets (controlled expansion, exposed lead core): 82 fragments nine inches from the wound channel.

- Shotgun slugs: 28 fragments five inches from the wound channel.

- Muzzleloader bullets (245-gr.): three fragments one inch from the wound channel.

- Muzzleloader bullets (300-gr.): 34 fragments six inches from the wound channel.

"A key take away message from the study," Cornicelli writes, "is that given fragments were found so far from the exit wound, routine trimming likely will not remove all of the fragments and DNR cannot make a recommendation as to how far out trimming should occur.

"In counting fragments, only about 30 percent were within two inches of the exit wound. The vast majority was dispersed further from the carcass. In some cases, researchers found low levels of lead as far away as 18 inches from the bullet exit hole. The DNR also learned that rinsing a carcass produced mixed results.

While rinsing tends to reduce lead around the wound channel it also transports lead away from the wound.

"The research also showed that a shot to the hindquarters of a deer – where heavy bones are found – will result in extensive fragmentation. Fragmentation was so pronounced that a hunter would likely not want to utilize this meat as there would be no way to remove all the fragments."

July 2008

Andrea Grondahl, DVM, State Meat and Poultry Inspection Director, ND Dept. of Agriculture, writes to venison processors.[15] "Recent studies in ND and other Mid-western states, she says, found lead fragments in venison. There is currently no evidence linking venison consumption to lead poisoning in humans."

Nevertheless, lead was found in "some venison samples." Indeed there is a "high likelihood" that deer shot with lead bullets contain lead particles. Lead bullets may disintegrate into fragments too small to see on impact and spread, even during processing and grinding.

Effective July 1, 2008, ammunition for hunting big game and small game within the range of the California condor in California must use a projectile which has been certified to contain less than one percent lead by weight. (Photo Don Friberg and Joshua)

Manufacturers of copper and tungsten-compound bullets have received a great deal of resistance from the shooting sports establishment. In spite of this, performance of non-leaded cartridges and clean primers is now equal to and in some cases exceeds traditional ammunition.

Grondahl cites a small sample (10 wild boars and 10 red deer), but peer-reviewed study from Poland which noted that greater contamination is caused when bullets hit vertebrae. Elevated lead levels were found four to six inches from the bullet path. Even six to 10 inches away, about half the animals still had a detectable lead level and the researchers concluded: "Careless removal of tissues from around the bullet pathway in the animal body results in elevated lead doses being ingested by humans."

Lead poisoning "could potentially occur in people who consume venison shot with lead ammunition." The risk depends on how much lead is consumed and how often. Therefore, limiting lead limits risk.

Grondahl made these recommendations for processing:

• Determine a bullet's path, especially if it contacted bone.

• Trim and discard meat generously around the wound channel. "You may need to discard complete legs, shoulders, or back strap [as] it may not be possible to determine if there is lead contamination in a piece of venison by looking at it."

• Ground venison has a higher rate of contamination than non-ground product, 26 percent to two percent.

• Check grinders for fragments "at least once per hour or between each batch."

• Avoid or minimize batching of multiple deer to avoid cross-contamination.

• Develop Standard Operating Procedures for employees.

• Post information for customers.

July 2008

Effective July 1, ammunition for hunting big game and non-game species within the range of the California condor must use a projectile which has been certified to contain less than or equal to one percent lead by weight. Projectiles are "any bullet, ball, sabot, slug, buckshot or other device which is expelled from a firearm through a barrel by force." Fish and Game estimates this regulation change will affect between 30,000 and 50,000 hunters, primarily of deer, wild pigs, and non-game species.

The law also requires the commission and department to implement a certification process to identify legal projectiles for hunting in the area.

August 2008

ND develops guidance for hunters and processors regarding cleaning and dressing wild game to reduce the chances of lead fragments in game harvested with lead bullets.[16]

It is estimated that this cost the Sportsmen Against Hunger venison donation program, administered by the ND Community Action Partnership, more than 4,000 pounds of what was remaining from about 17,000 pounds donated by hunters during the 2007 hunting season.

September 2008

The CDC sends results to study participants, finding, "Although a high percentage of people who were tested had lead in their blood, none had levels higher than 10 µg/dl. A lead level of zero is preferred for health reasons, but it is not unusual to see lead levels of up to 2 µg/dl in people across the U.S."[17]

September 2008

Missouri Conservation Dept. Assistant Director Dave Erickson says health officials in several states have concluded that lead in venison is not a human health crisis. They note that millions of deer and other big game animals are taken by hunters each year and eaten.

"There are no known cases of lead poisoning from this type of exposure," says Erickson. "It simply is not something that has been encountered over many years of dealing with lead and human health. Still, lead is a toxic substance, and efforts to reduce exposure are prudent. Health officials recommend an approach that emphasizes risk management."

Missouri State Veterinarian Taylor Woods says, "We have never had an illness or case of lead poisoning by consumers eating deer, quail or pheasant, but we recommend that meat be trimmed around the wound channel to get rid of more than 98 percent of the lead."

Lead particles in hunter-harvested venison have not been linked to any human illness. However, most lead particles that have been found in venison are too small to be seen or felt. This makes careful processing important to reduce the risk of lead exposure.[18]

October 2008

A Minnesota Dept. of Natural Resources study (see above) indicates that lead particles commonly are found farther from a wound channel than previously thought; that the number of lead fragments varies widely by bullet type; and that most lead particles in venison are too small to see, feel or sense when chewing.

Wisconsin's Dept. of Health Services notes, "Although lead in venison does not rival lead paint in older homes as a health risk for the public, the risk is not low enough to ignore."[19]

November 2008

The ND/CDC study results are released to the public[20]: "People who eat wild game harvested with lead bullets appear to have higher levels of lead in their blood than people who don't," writes Stephen Pickard, MD, DOH epidemiologist. On the other hand, "some individuals with substantial wild game consumption may have lower blood lead levels than some other individuals with little or no wild game consumption."

ND issues wild game guidelines for food pantries:

• Shot with lead bullets, accept only whole cuts, not ground meat. (Whole cuts appear to contain fewer lead bullet fragments than ground venison.)

• Shot with bows and arrows, accept whole cuts or ground meat.

November 2008

The Wisconsin Dept. of Health Services asks food pantries to hold venison pending an "initial assessment of risks." Investigators collect 183 one-pound samples from freezer stocks and from commercial meat processors. Samples are X-rayed, finding 46 "radiopaque fragments." These samples are submitted to the Wisconsin State Laboratory of Hygiene along with 114 additional samples volunteered by DNR employees who hunt. Recognizing that data is still incomplete, the Department writes, ". . . it is clear that many venison samples contained unhealthy levels of lead."

Lead is detected in 15 percent of commercially processed samples and eight percent of hunter samples. (Seven of the eight positives are from ground meat; one is from a whole cut.)

Note: The 2006 Wisconsin deer harvest was approximately 500,000. From these, about 400,000 pounds of venison were donated to food pantries via 126 meat processors.[21]

November 2008

In a press release, Iowa's Dept.s of Natural Resources and Public Health write, "Recent concerns over the safety of venison harvested by hunters using lead ammunition prompted the Centers for Disease Control and Prevention to conduct a study in North Dakota. The study compared the blood lead levels of people who consumed venison and other wild game with those who didn't. While the CDC study indicated a slight increase in blood lead levels for those who consumed wild game, they did not make any national recommendations for consumption of wild game harvested by hunters using lead ammunition.

"Hunters may choose to avoid the potential for lead exposure by using non-lead ammunition....

"According to the Iowa Dept. of Public Health, the greatest lead-related risk in Iowa continues to be deteriorating lead paint in homes."[22]

November 2008 – February 2009

ND inspectors collect 404 samples of ground venison (deer taken only by rifle) from 54 processors. Samples are X-rayed at the Lewis and Clark Veterinary Clinic in Bismarck: 49 (12 percent) are found to contain "metal, bone, plastic or any other material that is not ground meat product." The samples, plus two clean controls, are sent to Iowa Hygienic Laboratory for analysis.[23]

January 2009

The Center for Biological Diversity (CBD) files suit against the U.S. Bureau of Land Management (BLM) and FWS. The lawsuit alleges that federal agencies mismanage federal lands in Arizona because those agencies failed to consider the potential impact on local wildlife resulting from authorizing activities such as off-road vehicle use and livestock grazing.

CBD's lawsuit also claims condors are becoming sick and dying from eating lead in scavenged game shot by hunters using lead shot or bullets. Thus, the government is violating the Endangered Species Act by allowing hunters to use of lead shot and bullets.[24]

March 2009

Without seeking public comment, the U.S. National Park Service (NPS) announces a plan to ban lead ammunition and lead fishing sinkers from all of the lands it manages: "Our goal is to eliminate the use of lead ammunition and fishing tackle in parks by 2010," says Acting Park Service Director Dan Wenk.

Criticism from the NRA is instantaneous. The Park Service soon relents, applying the ban only to its employees and authorized agents, but leaves open the possibility of banning use by the general public on a park-by-park basis.[25]

August 2009

Managers at Grand Teton National Park and National Elk Refuge ask elk and bison hunters to voluntarily use non-lead ammunition. Elk Refuge manager Steve Kallin says a recent study shows a compelling link between elevated blood levels in ravens and eagles with the beginning and end of hunting season on the refuge.

Kallin admits there have been no "population-level" impacts but some individual birds "may be" suffering. Kallin says he has used non-lead ammo and has been satisfied with its performance.[26]

September 2009

Iowa laboratory tests report that of 51 of the submitted North Dakota samples, 24 (5.94 percent) show measurable amounts of lead.

Noting that most lead is removed during processing, DOH says, "There is still a chance some pieces will remain," and warns that pregnant women and children under six should not eat venison harvested with lead bullets. Others should "minimize their potential exposure" and "use their judgment about consuming game that was shot with lead-based ammunition."[27]

November 2009

To preserve the ability of hunters to use lead ammunition, the NRA asks the U.S. District Court of Arizona to be allowed to join defendants in the CBD lawsuit.[28] It says "there is no guarantee that either BLM or FWS will vigorously challenge the unproven assertions CBD is making about lead-based ammunition."

The NRA says the theory that condors die from consuming lead bullet fragments in gut piles junk science and that the organization "most recently worked with experts, researchers, and attorneys in California to defeat proposed state hunting regulations based on the unproven condor/lead bullets link [legislation to broaden the area in which non-lead bullets would be required]. That success was based in large part on meticulous scientific reports prepared by experts working with NRA that exposed the deficiencies in the science."

Barnes says its MPG (Multi-Purpose Green) copper-based loads are "ideal for shooting steel targets, competition, plinking, hunting and home defense," which pretty much covers the shooting spectrum. Not sintered (oven hardened with no jacket), MPGs have a copper jacket (for feed reliability) with an open tip. The core is compressed powdered metal. MPGs do not disintegrate unless they hit hard objects such as steel or concrete. They penetrate clothing, sheetrock, plywood and other intermediate barriers, but will usually not get through windshields or heavy commercial glass.

December 2009

North Dakota DOH says, "The most certain way of avoiding lead bullet frag-ments in wild game is to hunt with non-lead bullets."

Sandra Washek, DOH Lead Based Paint Program Coordinator and Environ-mental Scientist, says she shoots an old fashioned .30-30 in the thick willows and a .243 in open country. "We've issued some voluntary guidelines," she says, "but we're not interested in regulating this thing. At the present time, this is as far as it goes."[29]

THE BITTER AND NEVER-ENDING ARGUMENT?

When the Cornatzer-Fogarty CT scans were made public, some government burcaus were either forced by law or chose because of personal or political prefer-ence to take action, the National Shooting Sports Foundation and The Peregrine Fund began a vicious war of words. The NRA attacked the studies as non-science and sneered at the groups or agencies that developed it. For its part, The Fund responded in an insufferably elitist manner and, in the finest of American tradi-tions, the Center for Biological Diversity looked for someone to sue. The NSSF was petulant and unreasonable; the NRA, pompous as a dinosaur. The Fund posi-tioned itself between untrustworthy and cunning; and the CBD – "saving species for 20 years" – disingenuously says that solving difficult problems is as easy as writing them a check …

All of these organizations are, of course, using the issue of lead bullets. All of them understand "the secret," which is that once lead was conclusively demonstrated in the bellies of gut pile-feeding endangered species, federal and state agencies by law had to act. The elementary school recess-level blustering, name calling, refusal to recognize one-another's reasonable interests and inten-tions, and adamant repudiation of cooperation is satisfying on an emotional level, but organizationally, it is a magnificent way to boost a group's financial profile among its members, both on the political left and the right. Dredging up emotions rather than calling for collaboration becomes a cash windfall for Greenpeace when its activists are attacked. Following the publicity surrounding Kenya's closing its borders to big game hunters, Safari Club International lifetime memberships skyrocket.

We rally the faithful, preach to the choir and it is successful. It is also hu-man nature.

Of course, there is always the slim chance that the politicians, the bureau-crats and even the courts will exceed our expectations and get it right for the long term. Take, for example, a portion of the U.S. Environmental Protection Agency's warning about lead[30]:

> *If you work in construction, demolition, painting, with batteries, in a radiator repair shop or lead factory, or your hobby involves lead, you may unknowingly bring lead into your home on your hands or clothes.*
>
> *You may also be tracking in lead from soil around your home. Soil very close to homes may be contaminated from lead paint on the outside of the building. Soil by roads and highways may be contaminated from years of exhaust fumes from cars and trucks that used leaded gas.*
>
> *• Use door mats to wipe your feet before entering the home.*
>
> *• If you work with lead in your job or a hobby, change your clothes before you go home and wash these clothes separately.*
>
> *• Encourage your children to play in sand and grassy areas instead of dirt which sticks to fingers and toys.*
>
> *• Try to keep your children from eating dirt, and make sure they wash their hands when they come inside.*

There are valid reasons to question our governmental agencies (as well as non-governmental agencies that feed off public monies, from the Peregrine Fund to the Red Cross), their personnel and findings, so much so that to make a list would defy a book of this size. Nevertheless, for the state of North Dakota to quickly and publicly cast a mountain of suspicion from a molehill of findings, however well-intentioned, in a non-vetted manner as it did with the Cornatzer-Fogarty X-rays, was, at a minimum, indiscreet and, from the position of public policy, rather careless.

If the issue of toxic or non-toxic shooting were not so serious, did not have implications that might change the habits and pocketbooks of millions of sportsmen, law enforcement officers and even the military – not to mention the international manufacturing infrastructure that supports shooting – it could all be a little silly, although to think of it in those terms is to overlook the gravity of the issue.

The Man Who Started It All[31]

Of course, that's a little misleading. North Dakota's Bill Cornatzer did not "start it all." He was simply in the right place at the right time and acting in the finest of American conservation traditions ... or, from a different perspective, was a meddling fool with an agenda who was operating out of his professional element, a man who has almost single-handedly upset our proud American traditions.

The practice of medicine runs deep in the Cornatzer family. Bill's medical specialty is dermatology. His father was an award-winning biochemist, and his son is aiming for a medical degree as well.

It was his son's third year medical project, in fact, that threw the national non-toxic shooting debate into high gear. The fact that it also coincided with Bill's interests – hunting, medicine, falconry and conservation – was sufficient to merit the dad's involvement.

Thus, when Ted Fogarty, a Bismarck radiologist, assisted with the venison sample X-rays and the results showed so many lead bullet fragments, Cornatzer says he was stunned by the results and believed he ought to quickly make them public.

Cornatzer insists that every step in the research project was taken in absolute good faith, but is quick to point out that there is still much to learn

Dr. William Cornatzer brought the lead fragmentation to the attention of North Dakota health and wildlife specialists. On his 2009 Kodiak Island hunt, he shot a Benelli R1 chambered for 300 Win. Short Mag with Barnes Triple X loaded by Federal and topped with a Swarovski 3x-9x scope. (Photo W. and E. Cornatzer and E. Fogarty)

about the issue. "The CDC has never done a study on children over the age of six," he says, "and the more I read the less I feel that any child of any age should eat wild game that may contain lead fragments. And sure, the work we did has definitely affected the way I personally hunt and process deer," he says.

One of the heroes of Bill Cornatzer's youth – other than his father – was the writer Jack O'Connor and Cornatzer well remembers O'Connor's thrilling adventures printed in Outdoor Life magazine. "I'm a big, big hunter," he recalls. "I still hunt by the magazine's statement of ethics that I read as a kid in 1962."

A member of Safari Club International and former NRA member, at the time of our interview Cornatzer had only recently returned from a deer hunt in Tennessee and was excited that he would soon be headed north on an Alaskan hunt. (The doctor is also a bowhunter and not long ago took a record book musk ox.)

Has media attention since his famous X-rays changed him?

"I don't think so," he says, "but it hurt a little bit that the NSSF and the NRA have called my motives into question. Sure, I raise and hunt with falcons; I'm a member of the Peregrine Fund and I'm a conservationist. But isn't what we actually do to back up the term conservationist more important than what we just say?

"It seems to me they should have taken what we did in a different way, maybe embraced it as a couple of average guys out here on the prairie trying to make things better, not as people trying to harm hunting and shooting."

So what is Bill Cornatzer taking to Alaska? "I bought some Barnes Triple-Shock X-Bullets for my .270," he says. "It's an all-copper bullet."

Relying on his Leica rangefinder, Dr. William Cornatzer of North Dakota took this Kodiak Island buck with a single shot at 400 yards. The only one in his group to take a buck, Cornatzer says it was a tough hunt: "We had four days of rain before arriving and the deer moved up to 1,200 feet. This buck's antlers fell off when he went down." (Photo Dr. William Cornatzer)

CHAPTER NOTES

1. The CDC says "Approximately 250,000 U.S. children aged 1-5 years have blood lead levels greater than 10 micrograms of lead per deciliter [µg/dl] of blood, the level at which CDC recommends public health actions be initiated. Lead poisoning can affect nearly every system in the body. Because lead poisoning often occurs with no obvious symptoms, it frequently goes unrecognized." General information about lead, for we non-scientists, is readily available through many trustworthy sources on the Internet, among them www.cpsc.gov/cpscpub/pubs/5054.html, www.epa.gov/lead/ and even http://en.wikipedia.org/wiki/Lead.

2. Centers for Disease Control and Prevention www.cdc.gov/niosh/hhe/reports/pdfs/1986-0269-1812.pdf

3. Fish and Wildlife Service www.fws.gov/hunting/whatres.html

4. Health Canada www.hc-sc.gc.ca/cps-spc/pubs/cons/lead-plomb/appendix-g-annexe-eng.php

5. The Peregrine Fund www.peregrinefund.org/pdfs/Commentaries/PositionLeadAmmunition2007.pdf

(According to an affidavit filed with the Florida Dept. of Agriculture and Consumer Affairs "Gift Giver's Guide" http://app1.800helpfla.com/giftgiversguide/, as a charitable fund The Peregrine Fund has total annual revenues of $5,815,975 of which 87 percent are dedicated to programs, 7 percent to administration and 5 percent to fund raising.)

6. Missouri Conservation Commission www.mdn.org/2007/stories/shot.htm

7. The Peregrine Fund www.peregrinefund.org

8. The Peregrine Fund (These findings are presented at the May 2008 Peregrine Fund Ingestion of Spent Ammunition: Implications for Wildlife and Humans conference in a paper titled "Lead Bullet Fragments in Venison from Rifle-Killed Deer: Potential for Human Dietary Exposure.") www.peregrinefund.org/Lead_conference/default.htm

9. California Dept. of Fish and Game www.dfg.ca.gov/wildlife/hunting/condor/

10. North Dakota Dept. of Health www.ndhealth.gov/lead/Venison/

11. James Macpherson, Associated Press in USA Today March 29,2008

12. University of Iowa Hygienic Laboratory www.uhl.uiowa.edu/aboutuhl/news/archive/deermeat/index.xml

13. Study authors were: Peregrine Fund (W. Grainger Hunt, Richard Watson, Chris Parish and Kurt Burnham), Boise State Univ. (James Belthoff), Washington State Univ. – Pullman (Russell Tucker, Dept. of Veterinary Clinical Sciences, and Garret Hart, School of Earth & Environmental Sciences) and Washington Animal Disease Diagnostic Laboratory – Pullman (Lindsay Oaks). Funding was obtained by: "The data were collected as part of The Peregrine Fund's California Condor Restoration Project, which is supported by" a host of agencies, bureaus, funds, trusts, foundations and donors. www.peregrinefund.org/lead_conference/PDF/0112%20Hunt.pdf

14. Minnesota DNR http://files.dnr.state.mn.us/fish_wildlife/lead/bulletstudy/resources/shortsummary.pdf

15. North Dakota DOH www.ndhealth.gov/lead/venison/LeadVenisonGuidelinesForProcessors.pdf Dr. Grondahl cites a paper in the European Journal of Wildlife Research by A. Dobrowolska and M. Melosik. Received in January 2007 and published that year in September, "Bullet-derived lead in tissues of the wild boar and red deer" can be found in its entirety at www.springerlink.com/content/cgn3m6j87731u322/.

16. North Dakota DOH www.ndhealth.gov/lead/venison/2008-2009LeadFragmentsInGroundVenison-ProcessorsStudy.pdf

17. Results are reported at: www.peregrinefund.org/lead_conference/2008%20CDC%20ND_Final_TripReport_5NOV08.pdf

18. Missouri Conservation Dept. http://mdc.mo.gov/cgi-bin/news/news_search.cgi?item=1221842978,44563

19. Wisconsin DHS http://dhs.wisconsin.gov/eh/HlthHaz/pdf/foodpantryltr2008.pdf

20. North Dakota DOH www.ndhealth.gov/lead/Venison/

21. Wisconsin DHS www.atsdr.cdc.gov/HAC/pha/LeadFragmentsinVenison/Venison and Lead HC 110408.pdf

22. Iowa DNR www.iowadnr.gov/other/hush/files/iowadnr_lead.pdf

23. North Dakota DOH http://www.ndhealth.gov/lead/venison/2008-2009LeadFragmentsInGroundVenisonProcessorsStudy.pdf

24. Center for Biological Diversity www.biologicaldiversity.org/news/press_releases/2009/arizona-strip-01-27-2009.html

(According to an affidavit filed with the Florida Dept. of Agriculture and Consumer Affairs http://app1.800helpfla.com/giftgiversguide/, as a charitable fund The Center for Biological Diversity has total revenues of $5,974,407 of which only 34 percent are dedicated to programs while 19 percent go to administration and an astonishing 47 percent to fund-raising.)

25. National Park Service http://home.nps.gov/applications/release/Detail.cfm?ID=855

26. Grand Teton National Park and National Elk Refuge http://gtnpnews.blogspot.com/2009/08/volun-tary-use-of-non-lead-ammunition.html

27. North Dakota DOH (University of Iowa Hygienic Laboratory) http://www.ndhealth.gov/lead/veni-son/2008-2009LeadFragmentsInGroundVenisonProcessorsStudy.pdf

28. National Rifle Assn., Institute for Legislative Action www.nraila.org/Legislation/Read.aspx?id=5197

29. Personal communication

30. U.S. Environmental Protection Agency www.epa.gov/iaq/lead.html

31. Personal communication

CHAPTER 8

NON-TOXIC – WHAT'S AVAILABLE AND WHAT'S COMING

The shooting sports industry has invested billions of dollars in infrastructure, highly competent personnel and internationally recognized brands. It is not possible or desirable to require sudden change in an industry that is as fundamental as ammunition. Still, we do hold a double standard on this point, for we as a nation are justifiably proud of our flexibility, the agility of our entrepreneurs (in a business sense smaller is better for agility, adaptability) in times of crisis. Yet no one reasonably calls the need to study and move toward lead alternatives for big and small game or upland birds a crisis. Pressing, perhaps, even serious – but not crisis.

Ballistics is the science of the billions of dollars invested in ammunition infrastructure and its products. That is primarily lead-based ammo, and this product has been designed, examined and debated for centuries. Everything in our present cartridge models, from primer to powder, cannelure to case, has been fought over – sometimes quite literally – and is now generally understood by shooting enthusiasts.

Although some organizations would prefer that shooters world-wide give up lead and switch to other bullet or shotshell ingredients now, it will not happen quickly, and perhaps not at all.

Nevertheless, who in 1960 would have imagined that only 50 years later they would not be able to shoot their traditional 12-gauge lead shells for the annual father-son duck hunt? Who in that seemingly distant past cared whether North America's biggest buzzard, the California condor, survived or slipped into extinction? Who had then heard RRLF, reduced ricochet and lead free?

Times indeed change. Now there is widespread acceptance, although it is gradual and grudging, of copper, tungsten and other non-toxic shooting loads. Here is a sample of bullets for handgun and rifle (and muzzleloader) on the market today.

Cut-away of a Barnes MRX 4x4 copper bullet and a bullet after firing into ballistic gel with the four wide petals open. The purpose of the petals is to create a wider wound channel and to ensure delivery of maximum energy to a target.

A Step Ahead: Barnes Bullets

In the depression days of 1932, a Colorado man named Fred Barnes began building bullets in his basement. Eventually Barnes discovered that he could expect deeper penetration and more controlled expansion with a soft lead bullet encased in 99 percent pure copper tubing which he pressure-formed around the molded lead core.

Barnes began selling copper-jacketed bullets from his home, becoming the first custom supplier of bullets to handloaders. Still, in the spirit of "don't give up your day job," Barnes Bullets did not officially come into being for seven years.

Thirty-three years later, Barnes sold his company to the Burford Corporation of Maysville, Oklahoma. Instead of moving the company east, the new owners moved to Colorado and changed the name to "Colorado Custom Bullets." CCB did not thrive however and in 1974 Randy and Coni Brooks, both of whom are active big game hunters, purchased the company, moved it to Utah and reintroduced the Barnes name.

Searching for a business niche, the Brooks introduced Barnes Solids in 1979. Designed for deep, consistent penetration on dangerous game, these lead-free bullets were constructed of a solid copper/zinc alloy.

Then in 1985, while hunting brown bears in Alaska, Randy "got to thinking about" an expanding, solid copper one-piece bullet and "immediately began designing and testing." Brooks believed he could cut a bullet's tip into an "X" so that upon impact the four sections would peel backward explosively, doubling the size of the wound cavity, but not separating from the body of the bullet.

Federal has made CCI's TNT Green available for small game in 17 HMR rimfire. The cartridge features clean-burning propellants behind a 16-grain TNT hollow point at 2500 fps.

"Because this bullet would hold together and not fragment," Brooks believed, "it ought to retain most of its original weight yielding deeper penetration and a larger wound channel." The result was the Barnes X-bullet.

With its hollow nose cavity and four sharp, pre-engineered copper jacket petals, this heat-treated bullet expands into an X-shaped silhouette on impact. In addition, unitary construction eliminates separation of the jacket from the lead core, the primary engineering dilemma of more traditional bullets.

The X-bullet was quickly followed by Barnes Burners, jacketed rifle and handgun bullets designed for target-grade accuracy and varmint shooting.

A hallmark of acceptance was realized in 1991 when PMC began loading Barnes X-bullets in PMC factory ammunition. PMC was soon followed by Weatherby, ICC, Cor-Bon/Glaser, Sako, Lazzeroni, Taurus, Federal Premium ("Regular-Unleaded") and Black Hills. The U.S. military got in line, too. And in Fred Barnes' own tradition, Barnes bullets are also used by thousands of handloaders who closely followed edition after edition of company reloading manuals.

The expanding non-toxic discussion seems custom-tailored to increase Barnes business, yet the Utah company has eschewed any involvement – with funding or support – in the lead ban issue in California or elsewhere. "Nor will we ever do so," Coni Brooks says, recognizing the tightrope their company walks over the shark tank of huge ammo manufacturers and the business and sportsmen's organizations those companies sponsor. "We're bullet manufacturers, not biologists and we don't have any expertise in this field; however, it is our position that legislation further restricting hunters and shooters in their freedom of choice of products is a threat and is devastating to the hunting and shooting industry and community.

"Bullet performance drives Barnes' designs. Whether a Barnes bullet contains a lead core or not depends on the desired terminal performance. We have several lines of products manufactured from lead-free materials that were developed for their performance. These happen to meet the criteria set forth under the Condor Preservation Act, but we still manufacture the premium Original line of jacketed, lead-cored bullets. A lead ban would remove the very foundation on which our company was built.

"Copper bullets are more difficult to manufacture than lead-core bullets. Copper requires advanced technology and tooling, and increased testing during production to produce a high quality product. In the 'impact extrusion' manufacturing process, lead flows like water compared to copper. Copper is hard on the equipment, but the results are a bullet that we believe delivers the best terminal performance on game."

The Barnes product line is no longer anchored on lead, but it still makes use of that metal in at least one bullet.

• Triple-Shock X Bullet – 100-percent copper, lead-free rifle bullet for fast expansion. Multiple versions have a blue polymer tip that, Barnes says, boosts ballistic coefficient, and improves accuracy. Rings cut into the shank relieve pressures and eliminate copper fouling. When dug out of targets and weighed, the bullet retains nearly 100 percent of its original mass.

• MRX – Barnes calls the ultra-dense lead-free core of this copper-jacketed green rifle bullet "Silvex." It is a tungsten matrix material and rings cut into the bearing surface of the bullet "increase accuracy and reduce fouling."

• XPB – All-copper XPB pistol bullets offer dramatically increased penetration and energy transfer, plus superior expansion and weight retention over conventional jacketed lead-core bullets. Neither do they leave any harmful air-borne residue behind in practice environments. "These lead-free bullets are ideal for use in environmentally restrictive areas," Barnes' catalog summarizes. "They're in full compliance with California game laws, and should be acceptable in other states considering lead bullet bans."

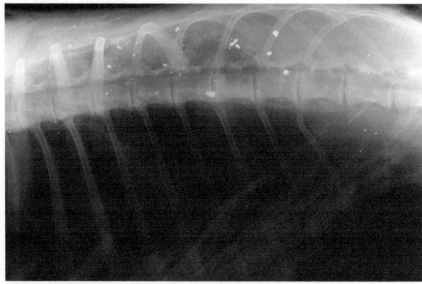

CT scans indicate that traditional lead rifle bullets fragment when they hit a big game animal. Fragmentation is especially severe when a bullet hits heavy bone vertebrae or shoulder, and lead fragments may end up 12 to 18 inches from the wound cavity. (Photo Minnesota DNR)

- MPG (Multi-Purpose Green) – These open tip flat base bullets have a compressed copper-tin powder core surrounded by a thin, guilding metal jacket. "They meet lead-free requirements at environmentally restrictive practice ranges," writes Barnes. The protective jacket allows these frangible[1] rounds to remain intact when less durable bullets might disintegrate on feeding and firing. Because they are RRLP (reduced ricochet, limited penetration), they are recommended for steel shooting, competition, plinking, hunting and home defense. (Jessica Brooks says Barnes MPGs meet the lead-free requirements at environmentally restrictive practice ranges. "We don't talk environmental requirements," she says. "We talk improved performance.")

- M/LE Tactical – Classified as RRLP for rifles and handguns these lead-free military/law enforcement bullets are also excellent for training and home-defense.

- Varmint Grenade – A highly frangible, hollow-cavity bullet with a copper-tin composite core and copper jacket, the Grenade is designed to remain intact at ultra-high velocities, yet fragment explosively upon impact.

- Banded Solids – Made from "virgin brass alloy," don't expect these ultimate penetrators to deform. They can be interchanged with the TSX without varying point of impact, Barnes claims. Because they are solid brass, they won't deflect on heavy bone at distance as they lose energy and speed. Spitzers or blunt tip.

- Originals – Copper jacketed and cannelured, Originals have a soft lead interior. These heavy-for-caliber bullets are designed for penetration without fragmentation for rifles or handguns.

Green is Go for Muzzleloaders

Barnes Spit-Fire 100 percent copper muzzleloader sabots load easily, the Utah manufacturer says, even in tight bores. A new sabot reduces the ramrod pressure required to seat them, too.

The .50-caliber, flat-base T-EZ bullets have a polymer tip that enhances expansion and boosts ballistic coefficient for better long-range ballistics. They expand at both close and extended range, creating six razor-edge cutting petals that maximize shock and penetration.

Actual T-EZ bullet diameter is .451 in both the 250-grain (.195 BC) and 290-grain (.223 BC) models. (Ballistic coefficient or BC measures a bullet's ability to overcome air resistance in flight. You might say that it is a measure of drag or a bullet's streamlined profile. BC is inversely proportional to the deceleration – the faster it slows down and the more it drops, the lower its BC – and thus the BC of the 250-grain bullet is different than that of the 290-grain bullet. Bullets with a high BC travel farther than those with a lower BC because they retain their velocity better as they fly downrange. This is a function of wind resistance and thus they have a flatter trajectory.)

The Spit-Fire MZ comes in 245-gr. and 285-gr. The Tipped MZ or T-MZ is available in 250-gr. and 290-gr. Both are shaped with a boat-tail base for higher ballistic coefficient.

The Expander MZ is an all-copper muzzleloader sabot bullet with a 6-petal hollow cavity that expands on impact, doubling the bullet's original diameter. The purpose of the sabot is to prevent gas blow-by, ensure consistent shot velocity and therefore tighter groups with a given ammo. Expander MZs are available in .45-caliber (195 gr.), .50 caliber (250 and 300 gr.) and .54 caliber (275 and 325 gr.).

The muzzleloading fraternity – even including those who shoot the new style in-line black powder guns – is tight, but small. If the force of social change dictates that all recreational shooting will "go green," and this may not entirely be a bad thing, muzzleloading hunters will be swept along in the current of change. (Photo National Wild Turkey Federation)

Cleaning Copper-Fouled Bores

If you choose copper or copper-jacketed bullets, a bore cleaning solvent such as Barnes' CR-10 effectively removes copper and powder fouling. (While it may be lead-free, it still leaves efficiency-impeding residue in the bore.) Barnes calls it an "aggressive" solvent that quickly loosens and lifts heavy copper deposits left in the bore by jacketed bullets. CR-10 is non-corrosive, Barnes says, and won't harm barrels.

CR-10, along with most other copper cleaning solvents and most household cleaners, contains ammonia. Ammonia helps remove the copper but attracts moisture. This can cause the cleaned steel to quickly rust.

"We've tested barrels by submerging them in CR-10 for up to 18 months without any obvious damage to the barrel," Barnes says, but of course it is not the submerging that causes a barrel to corrode. That's caused by removing it from submersion, in the same way that it isn't the fall out of an airplane that kills, but the landing. An oil patch is recommended after cleaning to prevent rusting.

The ammonia in CR-10 reacts with the copper in a barrel and creates the blue discoloration seen on patches. Barnes suggests running CR-10 soaked patches through a barrel until they come out clean – just one stroke is not be sufficient to remove copper or lead.

For heavy fouling, alternate soaked patches with a CR-10 soaked bronze brush to increase scrubbing intensity – remembering to run the brush or patch only in one direction, chamber to muzzle to prevent pushing gunk into the receiver. Finally, run a dry patch through the bore to wipe away as much of the CR-10 as possible. Then remove any excess CR-10 left in the bore with a non-chlorinated cleaner-soaked patch. Repeat until all CR-10 is removed from the bore. Remember to follow the directions and don't leave the CR-10 in the bore for more than 15 minutes.

Even non-toxic cartridges will foul a barrel. The essentials of gun cleaning are no different when shooting copper or tungsten or lead. Barnes calls their non-corrosive CR-10 an "aggressive" solvent that for heavy copper deposits left in the bore by jacketed bullets.

Barnes-Brooks Patents

Randy Brooks has two patents of special interest. U.S. Patent No. 5,131,123 relates to "Methods of manufacturing a bullet," and No. 5,259,320 is a refinement of the method.

Here Brooks describes the method of producing an expanding X-Bullet with an interior cavity such as the Tactical Bullets in the Barnes Military/Law Enforcement Line. Let's look in detail at something we shooters usually take for granted, because the machining (and the description) are painstaking:

1. A bullet is manufactured by providing a slug of metal having an end face and applying an axial force against the end face of sufficient magnitude to form an axially outwardly opening first cavity.

2. Thereafter a force is applied against the first cavity to reform it into

a. a second cavity having a peripheral edge of a generally scalloped configuration, and

b. an interior surface defining tears of alternating triangular flat faces set-off by edges converging toward a blind end of the cavity.

3. The end portion is then contoured into a generally convex curvature which

a. constricts the scalloped peripheral edge and

b. transforms the triangular faces into

i. radially inwardly directed ribs and

ii. alternating lines of weakness which, upon bullet impact, control radial expansion and axial tearing of petals formed during impact which creates maximum hydraulic shock in the absence of fragmentation which in turn ensures humane killing of game.

The Specialist: Black Hills Ammunition

Jeff Hoffman says that when he started making remanufactured ammunition for local law enforcement officers and a few dealers 25 years ago he was still a young cop "too ignorant and inexperienced in business to know how badly the odds were against us, but too stubborn to accept the possibility of failure."

Today Black Hills has 65,000 sq/ft of space and supplies thousands of dealers and all branches of the U.S. military. Black Hills is popular among cowboy action shooters, Hoffman says, because the company produces trustworthy ammo in some of the obsolete 19th century calibers, such as .44 Russian, .38 Long Colt and .44-40.

A Black Hills specialty is loading .223 Remington. Rifles in .223 have a wide range of rifling twist rates, from one twist in seven inches (1:7) to 1:12. (The Remington Model 700 has a 1:9 twist in .223, but when stepped up to the .308 has a 1:12 twist.)

A Black Hills specialty is loading .223 Remington. Here, 20+ foot berms keep bullets from leaving the Orange County Sheriff's Department shooting range near Orlando, Florida.

Bullets larger than 60 gr. in this caliber require fast twists for greatest stability and accuracy. As a general rule, bolt action rifles have a 1:12 twist and shoot best with bullet weights of 60 gr. or less. Semi-automatic rifles – at least those produced since 1985 – generally have a faster twist and can stabilize the heavier bullets, but may not perform well with the lightest bullets. Hoffman says his 60 gr. are good choices for agencies or individuals who need a single bullet weight to work in a variety of rifles with different twist rates.

Although Black Hills works with many calibers and weights, they load two non-toxic Barnes bullets for the .223. The 36 gr. Varmint Grenade with powdered copper-tin composite core and copper jacket has a muzzle velocity of 3750 fps with 1124 ft/lb of energy. The heavier .55 gr. Barnes TSX has a 3200 fps muzzle velocity and 1250 ft/lb of energy. (The powdered metal open tip copper-tin bullets are "certified for use on appropriate non-game species only," says California's Dept. of Fish & Game.)

Dakota Ammo

Peter Pi, Sr. founded Dakota Ammunition, manufacturer of Cor-Bon/Glaser products. An American family owned and operated corporation with a staff of nearly 20 people, it has been in business for more than 28 years.

The company is recognized, among other things, for the development of the 400 CorBon cartridge, essentially a .45 ACP case necked-down to accept .40 caliber bullets, to which many guns chambered in .45 ACP can relatively easily be converted.

Dakota also builds loads with the +P designation indicating the brass is loaded to above-standard pressure, although still within a standard deviation for safety set by SAAMI[2]. As an example, the .45 ACP may reach 18,000 psi in standard loads, but climb to 22,000 psi in +P. With a 230 gr. bullet, a standard load in .45 ACP can be clocked at 850 fps while a heavy +P load can run as high as 920 fps, increasing the bullet's smack-down power in the meantime. This increase in velocity can also encourage hollow point bullet upset.

Cor-Bon handgun ammunition runs the gamut from rounds with exceptional penetrating abilities to those that will not over-penetrate or ricochet.

- The Glaser Safety Slug is a good choice for in-home use because it should not over-penetrate – always a danger when a gun goes off in a house – and endanger others behind the intended target. It will pierce three to eight inches in soft targets but will not go through interior walls or defeat hard barriers. It is however extremely effective on soft target hits. Cor-Bon suggests a self-defense strategy that includes using a magazine or speed loader of Glaser Safety Slugs inside the home; and then switching to a higher penetrating load such as Pow'R Ball or DPX if carried outside the home.

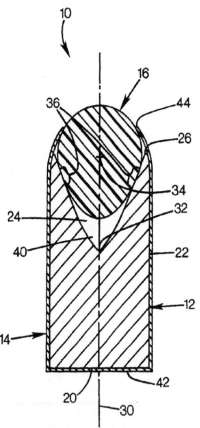

Detail from Peter Pi's September 2004 Patent No. 6,792,869 for an "expanding soft point bullet."

- On the other hand, standard self-defense JHP bullets and Pow'R Ball loads will still penetrate seven to 15 inches of ballistic gelatin after passing through four layers of denim. These rounds are a reasonable choice for outdoor carry. Pow'R Ball ammo is also designed to eliminate feed problems in semi-autos.

- Finally, DPX gives deepest penetration in most pistol calibers. It is capable of blowing through 18 inches of ballistic gelatin. It will defeat hard barriers including one layer of automotive steel or glass, and still stay on a straight course. Obviously, it's a good choice for law enforcement. The DPX is a 115 gr. load using the Barnes X-bullet, solid copper with a long "bearing surface" for accuracy. This round's nose expands in a sweeping 4-petal formation when it hits its target. While the body remains solid when splashing at 1240 fps, the long shank allows for tearing and expansion. Cor-Bon says it is an excellent all around choice in 9 mm for police work or personal defense.

Regarding the DPX, Peter Pi, president of Cor-Bon/Glaser says, "An effective self-defense load must deliver two basic fundamentals, bullet expansion and penetration. They are the critical elements to stopping a fight instantly.

"The construction of a bullet is one crucial factor of its performance. With traditional hollow points, they must have a soft lead core and a thin jacket, along with a hollow point that is large enough for material to get inside and push outward on the walls to enhance its expansion. If the hollow point is too small or perhaps the lead is too hard then it will not expand enough to perform well. It also must have adequate penetration without over penetrating. This is the key to a better bullet. DPX construction is all copper and has a large enough hollow point to exceed all traditional expansion expectations."

The renowned Thunder Ranch training center in Oregon works with Peter Pi's business to brand label Thunder Ranch Defensive Ammunition. This DPX round is built and packaged specifically for head tactics trainer, Clint Smith.

Thunder Ranch Oregon is a frangible bullet and lead free range. A typical handgun course requires "a nominal 850 rounds" for revolver or urban rifle, and typical gun owners have never put this many rounds through their weapon ... hence the value of a course at The Ranch. The unique "Integrated Handgun and Urban Rifle" training requires "a nominal 1,000 rounds rifle and 1,000 pistol" ... which reinforces the need to hand load your own ammo because from retail sources the ammo for this $1,200 course could run in the neighborhood of a thousand bucks. (Don't think of that expense as a cost; think of it as an investment!)

Don't show up in Oregon with standard lead core bullets, though. "If you bring the wrong ammo," says Ranch director and principal instructor Clint Smith, "you will not be allowed to shoot. We strongly suggest you purchase ammunition for your class as soon as possible."

Frangible and Green: Extreme Shock

Virginia's Extreme Shock is one of those All-American businesses that got a start because its founders saw an un-met need and because our nation encourages entrepreneurs. CEO Jeff Mullins recalls that by 1995 he and a group of friends had become frustrated with ammunition presented as frangible and a year later they went into the ammo business, specifically into the green ammo business.

"We wanted to develop frangible ammo that would meet modern needs for home-defense and law enforcement," Mullins says, "and I think we've done that. Still, for years Extreme Shock has been the red headed step child of the ammo industry."

No respect? Mullins admits there was some push back from entrenched industry. "It's been a pretty hard road. When we got part of the FBI contract, we became a credible, though still thought of in industry circles as a niche, supplier. Still, in the beginning we didn't have a thought about non-toxic or green shooting."

Extreme Shock sets up for the non-toxic shot of a lifetime. Front row: Air Freedom rounds are engineered for home defense, tactical entry teams and aircraft applications where it is crucial to contain rounds fired inside a structure. Back row: The Extreme Shock line-up has diversified and now includes – among other offerings – 12-gauge Shotshells, 7.62 x 39 mm, .308 and .300 Winchester Magnum.

Frangible and green may be their niche, but Extreme Shock is still a small company compared to the giants: Federal, Remington and Winchester. "It isn't the green part that sells us," Mullins says. "Performance sells our bullets. We're a little expensive right now, but the cost of lead today is a quarter a pound; copper is $5 a pound and tungsten is $20 a pound. Still, how often do you need to shoot in self defense or get a shot at a trophy deer? For the average guy, it's pretty rare."

Of course, there's the performance Mullins talks about plus the high costs of toxic clean-up at shooting ranges, higher bills for liability insurance, health screening, new state regulations....

Mullins' group examined the tungsten compounds entering the market in the '90s, primarily for waterfowl hunting, and realized they could use the metallic material to develop effective handgun and rifle rounds: it was frangible and effective ... it was also green. Not only that, but their cartridges are manufactured, packaged and marketed, like most of the small companies in this chapter, entirely in the U.S.; and by 2010 they will become a brass case manufacturer also.

Because Extreme Shock bullets are lead-free and frangible, there is no ricochet and no shoot-through. Mullins says they are the ideal choice for self and home defense. A miss will not penetrate several walls and over-penetration is minimized as the projectile's complete energy, including the self-shattering bullet itself, are typically contained within the target. Extreme Shock advertises that it's bullets "transfer 100 percent" of their energy to the target through massive fragmentation, causing shock trauma, shutting down the central nervous system and resulting in instant stopping power.

The key to making any bullet perform, Mullins says, is its ability to expand when it hits fluid. Typically, organic targets are at least two-thirds water. Once an Extreme Shock bullet penetrates into soft tissue and impacts fluid, its defractor plate acts as a piston, forcing bullet fragments out into tissue at 90 degree angles to the entry channel. The compressed tungsten composite – Extreme Shock calls their version "NyTrilium" – blows apart upon impact, leaving a catastrophic wound channel. The expansive fragmentation transfers the bullet's energy far faster than conventional hollow points.

"It's similar to a shaped charge used against tanks," Extreme Shock's CEO says. And it's all green.

Finding a Niche: International Cartridge

International Cartridge (ICC) found green at the end of their rainbow. Searching for the best frangible design and material, they discovered a non-lead alternative, a copper/tin bullet.

ICC also loads a variety of cartridges with Barnes copper in their Green Elite Hunting Ammo line which is "California Department of Fish and Game Approved."

Vice President Dan Smith says ICC is the first U.S. manufacturer to dedicate its facility entirely to lead-free frangible ammunition: "Conventional ammunition has a significant hazard associated with close range fire, ricochet and over

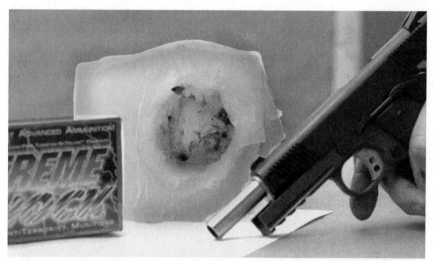

The Air Freedom Round from Extreme Shock is a good example of new bullets designed for the RRLF – reduced ricochet, lead free – niche. This bullet is designed to not penetrate the skin of conventional aircraft, thus causing cabin decompression. It is also designed to not penetrate the aluminum backs of most airline seats, reducing potential collateral damage in the event of a shootout at 30,000 feet. Unlike rounds made of polymers that can generate lethal ricochet, Extreme Shock says, its AFR round turns to "harmless powder" if it misses its intended target and hits a hard surface.

penetration. Our round is built for controlled fragmentation while maintaining lethal penetration. It is a unique performance that reduces hazards for shooters without compromising firepower.

Standard lead-based law enforcement hollow-point duty rounds expand, but cause a single wound channel. ICC's Green Elite HP Duty, however, splinters massively creating multiple wound channels. This gives an officer – or a private citizen attacked in her home or car – a better chance for a one-shot

In Williamsport, Pennsylvania, Frank Tripoli's Tripoli Triggers is founded on Tripoli's 45 years of competition shooting. Because it is an independent family business, Tripoli decides who he will sell a gun to … and who he won't. And he won't sell to someone who doesn't seem know anything about guns or shooting.

Tripoli founded his business in 1999, and opened his shooting lanes four years ago. He is justifiably proud that he is the "only NASR 5-Star non-toxic lead- and heavy-metal-free indoor range in Pennsylvania open to the public."

Tripoli says "We shoot a lot of ICC ammo on my eight lanes. Not only is it non-toxic, it's frangible, so in a firefight there shouldn't be any deflection problems. There's almost no possibility of a deflection or accident at our range, either."

A copper-alloy bullet that expands within inches of impact answers the increased law enforcement need for both frangibility and stopping power. Fired inside the typical urban apartment, however, these bullets will penetrate multiple layers of sheetrock and the 2x4 studs supporting them.

stop. Plus, their bullet's disintegration at speed in the wound channel reduces the potential for damage or injury from ricochet and pass-through into other rooms or buildings.

"We were shooting with the Homer City, Pennsylvania, Police Department not long ago," Smith recalls, "practicing with ICC frangibles all morning without any problem. With one exercise left, someone opened a case of (bullets from another manufacturer). Homer City Chief Louis Sacco was 40 yards behind the shooting line and was hit when one of these bullets ricocheted. I took it out of his arm with my Leatherman tool."

RUAG AmmoTech (formerly Precision Ammunition)

Begun in 1997, Precision Ammunition has already been swallowed by a huge international corporation – and had its name changed to RUAG AmmoTech. The parent corporation is RUAG Holding, and 100 percent of its shares are owned by Switzerland (the Swiss Confederation). The parent corporation is involved not only in ammunition manufacturing (it may be the fourth largest in the world behind America's "Big Three") – also owning RWS, Rottweil, Norma and others – but aircraft production and satellite launches.

From its beginning in 1997, Precision focused on frangible, lead-free shooting. Founder and president Dan Powers was an accountant by profession who, at a gun show in Florida, saw a man selling bullets in bags and "it started the wheels turning."

Powers believed that the shooting sports market would eventually shift toward lead-free shooting. He began the business in the same manner that so many American companies begin, while working his full time job and building the new company in his garage. "I existed for years on about five hours sleep a night."

Subsequently, Powers put together a financial team and negotiated to purchase the copper-matrix patent owned by Oklahoma's John Mullins. Powers and Mullins (who is now involved in product sales and is not related to the Mullins family involved with Extreme Shock Ammo) believed that this design had specific applications for military, law enforcement and civilian self-defense training.

With patent in hand, Powers put together a variety of cartridges to address those needs. Precision says, "We are the only SAAMI member today that solely manufactures frangible ammunition."

It took six years of struggle with the U.S. ammo market to realize that deep pockets would help his fledgling company grow, and in 2009 Powers reached a deal with RUAG. That corporation made capital available for automation and precision manufacturing. "We can now deliver as much as we can sell," Powers says.

Today, RUAG AmmoTech's Copper-Matrix NTF – non-toxic (completely lead-free), frangible – enables shooters to engage steel or other hard targets at virtually point-blank range without personal or environmental risk. It eliminates 90 percent of airborne particles; neither is there is any ricochet, splatter or backsplash.

Because this bullet disintegrates upon impact with a surface harder than itself, collateral damage to range structures is drastically reduced. Bullet residue is completely recyclable, too. If Copper-Matrix NTF is used exclusively on a range, the residue can be collected and resold since the only metal in the bullet is copper.

"We have virtually eliminated damage to steel targets," Powers says. "That decreases the costs of operating a shooting range. 'Shoot houses' can now be constructed from steel plate, as opposed to the expensive, heavy armored steel/rubber anti-ricochet panel/plywood construction, which is common in the industry."

The ammunition is produced using a bullet made of copper and a polyester polymer, which is then loaded to SAAMI specifications. Copper-Matrix NTF is well-suited for use in tactical training. Because it is frangible, tactical teams may train safely and effectively with maximum realism. Shooters may engage targets at much closer range without the risk of dangerous splash-back or ricochet, and without environmental breathing hazards.

The company's Copper-Matrix NTF 8-pellet 00-Buck works for police qualifications, too. According to Powers, five shots at 15 yards using a Remington 870 Police shotgun with an 18-inch barrel and improved cylinder choke produced a spread of 10 inches. RUAG says this makes it ideal for breaching applications as there are no attachments or "stand off" devices needed on the barrel.

"It can be used four inches to four feet from the door," says Powers. "It functions perfectly in pump, gas-operated or recoil operated shotguns without modifications – and works on hinges and on locks. It disintegrates on impact but the force of the shot may propel parts of the hinges, locks or even the door into the room, much like any other breaching round."

Copper-Matrix NTF Rifle ammo is a totally lead-free bullet equivalent to standard ammunition but with felt recoil equivalence and no-ricochet performance.

"Of course we exclusively use RUAG lead-free primers," Powers says. "It is the only NATO certified lead-free primer in the world and we're the only company in the U.S. that can use this primer. That means no more light strikes or misfires." These primers eliminate airborne lead and reduce barrel fouling. Range operators have no hazardous breathing problems because it meets or exceeds all OSHA and EPA standards.

"Green shooting is growing at a rate of about 20 percent a year," Powers says, perhaps optimistically, "and we're going to be in the forefront of that growth."

But if the costs associated with his ammunition are higher, why would ranges and individuals choose to go non-toxic?

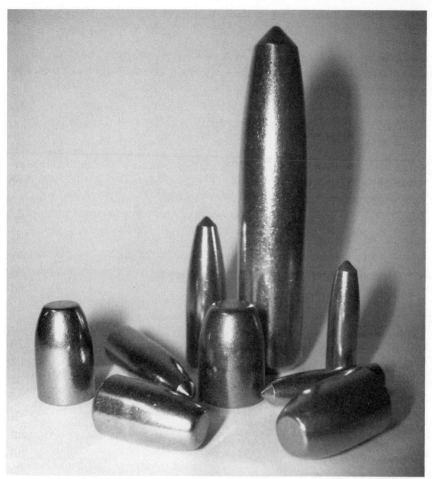

According to Sinterfire's Keith Porco, the company blends non-toxic metal composites and then compresses them while heating to a temperature that induces a metallurgical change. The heating process is done in a controlled inert atmosphere.

"For a local shooting range, the up-front cost is going to be a little more expensive than traditional ammo, but when range clean-up and health insurance savings are considered, the exposure of range personnel to airborne lead, the costs are much less as they don't have to worry about blood work.

Mullins, Powers and The Powdered Metal Bullet Patent

U.S. Patent No. 5,616,642 was published in April 1997 (www.freepatentsonline.com). The patent originators were Harley West of Yukon, Oklahoma and John Mullins of Burns Flat, Oklahoma. RUAG's John Powers says that living in a motel in Oklahoma while he and Mullins negotiated about the patent took three months.

The West-Mullins invention relates to "lead-free frangible ammunition [generally practice ammo] wherein the bullets are made of from 85% to 93% by weight of powders of copper, tungsten, ceramic, bismuth, stainless steel or bronze, or blends/alloys of the identified materials, the powder present in a polyester matrix with a small amount of ionomer.

"The bullets are injection molded under pressure to produce a projectile of appropriate size and weight and comparable to similarly sized live ammunition. The consistency of the bullet is such that it is frangible and will break upon impact with any hard surface, such as sheet steel.

"Polyester is a preferred polymeric matrix material in that it is a far more dense polymer than previously used nylons. The specific gravity of polyesters is about 1.30, as compared with about 1.02 for nylons. This enables the fabrication of a bullet with a greatly increased weight, for while the copper/polymer ratio remains at approximately the 90/10 range, the increased density allows for more actual copper by weight."

Patent – Background of the Invention

"Lead pollution at firing ranges has been a problem for a number of years. Because of current interest in the reduction of lead pollution, correction of this problem has become more important....

"There are several sources of lead at these firing ranges.

• Ordinary primers which are used in conventional ammunition to activate the ammunition's explosive charge or propellant, contain lead styphnate which is propelled into the air as a particulate.

Much of the RRLF research in the past two decades has concentrated on the sometimes conflicting law enforcement need to shoot through a hard surface like a car window and the home defense need to not injure the neighbors.

- The lead bullet or projectile itself also contributes significantly to lead pollution from several mechanisms inherent in the firing process.

  ○ The heat created from the explosion of the ammunition's propellant upon firing, melts minute quantities of the lead in the bullet or projectile which is propelled out of the barrel of the gun and solidifies into microscopic particulates.

  ○ The friction between the lead bullet or projectile and the gun barrel creates additional lead particulate through abrasion.

  ○ When the bullet or projectile strikes the back stop or other restraining mechanism at the firing range, the bullet or projectile is broken or otherwise disintegrates from the impact, resulting in additional lead particulate accumulation.

"The United States government, particularly the agencies involved in monitoring safety conditions, has set extremely restrictive standards governing the amount of airborne lead particulate which can be generated at firing ranges.

"As a result of the imposition of these standards, many ranges have been forced to install expensive ventilation and filtration systems, or to cease operations entirely.

"Restrictive standards have also been implemented governing the presence of lead in earthen butts typically associated with outdoor firing ranges. Through exposure to rain, lead can leach into underground water tables, thereby causing drinking water problems. As a result, outdoor ranges are being forced to excavate this lead and dispose it as well as all of the lead-contaminated earth disposed of in accordance with regulations dealing with the safe handling, transportation and disposal of hazardous materials.

"Prior attempts have been made to solve this problem through the use of non-lead alternative metals, e.g., copper, bismuth etc., and loading the ammunition with lead-free primers. This solution however creates its own problems. Typically, the solid copper rounds cause more damage to the back stop of the range, and also have a greater tendency to ricochet and splash back, with attendant safety hazards. In the case of bismuth, the high costs of the material makes it a viable alterative only when the substantially higher cost of the round is no object."

After a summary of prior patents mixing a metal powder with a matrix, the Mullins/West patent continues: "Such prior art techniques have, in some cases, reduced lead pollution at ranges. Others have eliminated lead pollution, but have created other problems such as excessive wear and safety hazards from splash back and ricochet.

"While the solutions of SFM, Booth and Belanger have eliminated lead in the projectile, their resulting projectiles have far less weight and mass than that of the conventional ammunition they are intended to mimic. This factor causes two significant problems.

- First, the weight of this prior art frangible ammunition is insufficient to cycle properly in the autoloaders used by many shooters.
- Second, the insufficient weight contributes to a projectile trajectory which is significantly different than conventional ammunition of similar caliber, making the practice ammunition an inadequate substitute for the live round.

"To compensate for the lack of weight and/or mass, manufacturers have attempted to increase the amount of propellant contained in each round in an effort to propel the projectile at a higher speed, thereby producing a trajectory path more closely matching the counterpart live round. However, a consequence of these higher propellant loadings is an increased chamber pressure in the firearm which can, in some cases, come dangerously close to the maximum limitation allowable under SAAMI (Sporting Arms and Ammunition Manufacturers' Institute) guidelines, creating potential hazards in weapons that may be worn or stressed and, thus, susceptible to rupture and fragmentation from these higher chamber pressures.

"In light of the deficiencies noted in the prior part, a new alternative frangible practice ammunition is presented which more closely approximates the firing characteristics of live ammunition than has heretofore been possible."

Not Afraid to Say "Environmentally Aware": SinterFire

"With an ever-growing environmental awareness and concern for reduced hazard and safer ammunition products…"

In business since 1998 – an era, apparently of great ammunition innovation – SinterFire only manufactures lead-free, frangible bullets … not completed cartridges and thus you will not see their name in large letters on your gun retailer's aisles. You will see their bullets in use, however, in cartridges used by the Office of the Inspector General – Security, CIA; NSA and NCIS – Dept. of Defense; Border Patrol, Secret Service and TSA – Dept. of Homeland Security; Office of Inspector Genera, NASA; NPS and FWS, Dept. of the Interior; FBI, ATF, Marshals Service – Dept. of Justice; the Criminal Investigations Division, IRS: U.S. Mint, Supreme Court and Library of Congress Police ….

Getting a running start on the growing market for green and frangible, the company completed a 2007 expansion that now gives it 22,000 sq/ft and an annual production capacity of more than 400 million components.

"We design and manufacturer all of our ammunition components in house," says President Joe Benini, an IDPA[3] competitor who built the first SinterFire .45 bullet in the kitchen of his Pennsylvania home, "and all projectiles are a non-toxic composite of 90 percent copper and 10 percent tin powders. Having everything right here, design to computer programming to manufacturing, gives us complete control of all products and operations once the raw materials come in the door."

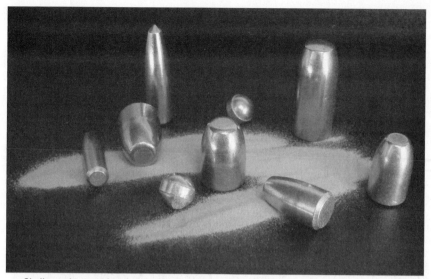

Challenged to get ahead of the non-toxic curve, individuals and companies have responded with a multitude of bullet types, compositions and processes for manufacturing. Innovation may have been spurred primarily by harassment from anti-gun factions and driven through America's legal labyrinth, but the eventual result could very well be a diversity of bullets with increased performance options … and a safer shooting environment as well.

Benini says SinterFire is the only manufacturer of heat-treated, copper/tin composite ammunition components approved by the ATF and in compliance with Federal Firearms Regulations.

In the SinterFire manufacturing process metal materials are blended and compressed under tonnage and heat treated to a temperature that induces a metallurgical change. Heat treatment is performed in a controlled, inert atmosphere with strict and redundant controls. Benini says SinterFire originated the process for building bullets from metal powders and holds patents for both the product and manufacturing processes.

SinterFire bullets are full-bodied one-piece designs with no jacketing, plating or surface treatment. Materials are 100 percent certified, fully traceable (by paper trail) and virgin, meaning there is no chance that extraneous recycled materials will be inside a bullet to reduce its performance. That way, Benini says, the company can control the fragmentation properties of the projectile upon impact with hard surfaces. Bullets literally crumble to dust on impact with surfaces harder than themselves.

The bullets are washed in a proprietary lubricant. "This results in projectiles that have superb properties for reduced hazard, no ricochet shooting. The bullets have increased velocity and inherent accuracy while guns have reduced chamber pressures and decreased bore fouling and wear."

"Our bullets were initially developed for law enforcement and military training," says Keith Porco, SinterFire's New Product Development and Technical Services chief. "Actually, they were Joe Benini's brainchild because IDPA and other competitive handgunners got tired of being whacked by bullet fragments bouncing off targets during live-fire competition. Because of their reduced hazard performance, competitive shooters have become a strong group of SinterFire users. Competitors or people in training can engage steel targets up-close with no bounce back or ricochet. (We still recommend that they wear ballistic eyewear, of course, because when you're involved in such a dynamic activity as shooting, lots of unexpected things can happen.)

"A few years ago, law enforcement officers would take their H&K MP5 to a shooting range and fire at stationery targets from 25 yards, which isn't very good training for a house-clearing operation where a long shot is going to be 10 feet and happen very quickly. Now they can load up our ammo and enter an obstacle course firing as they go … safely. That's going to be effective training!

"Trainees have to exercise all the standard precautions though because although our bullets are frangible, they won't shatter unless they hit something harder than they are – at which point they virtually evaporate into dust. It isn't legal everywhere, but I've taken deer and small game with our rounds.

"In addition, with copper/tin bullets, there're no airborne lead gas or bullet trap lead contaminants, which have become a serious issue for indoor ranges. A range like the Gun Store in Las Vegas can do their environmental clean-up with a push broom and a shop vac. When properly loaded our projectiles do not damage shoot steel targets and range officials don't have to get their blood tested every six months for lead. All in all, switching to non-leaded may actually save money and if a range sweeps up and recycles the spent materials, they might make money.

Porco says that today's movement toward green shooting is half law driven and half training driven. "On the legal side, lead is bad. We've taken it out of glass and batteries and paint, and now we are faced with this growing movement to ban it from shooting.

"Government agencies and even the Department of Defense are switching to lead-free shooting. Using our bullets, duty projectiles react just like training projectiles, and training can be much more aggressive. It just makes range operation so much easier and training so much more practical and effective."

So why are the NSSF and the NRA so adamant in their opposition?

"If you ask me," says Porco, "they have backed themselves into a bit of a corner by claiming that every move like this is backdoor gun control. I also think it is because the 'Big 3' buy so much of their stuff from us. But there are going to be applications for lead bullets for hundreds of years. During that time, though, concerns about the environment, and the need for effective training scenarios are going to drive the green and frangible bullet movement much larger."

SinterFire Says ... Component Reloading

Handloading compressed powder metal bullets is a relatively new adaptation of a time-honored tradition. To ensure success and safety, SinterFire has a few reloading tips for proper crimping:

1. Adjustment of the bell/expander die: The case mouth should be belled/expanded the minimum amount to permit proper lead-in of the bullet.

2. Bullet Seating: SinterFire projectiles are designed with a tapered length to accept a taper crimp at a pre-determined depth. They should always be loaded to the suggested OAL (overall length).

3. Final Crimping (always taper crimp): Very little taper crimp is required, less than cast, jacketed or plated bullets.

a. Prior to finalizing your loading set-up, the bullets of several loaded rounds should be pulled from their cases and inspected for crimp compression. A properly crimped bullet should not show signs of crimp compression or indentation by-or-at the case mouth. Over crimping will result in a compression and/or stress fracture at the case mouth. This will cause the bullet to break off.

b. Handloading should be done in a safe manner and by individuals knowledgeable of ammunition components, the loading process and the associated hazards. Safety is always a priority when loading or handling ammunition and components and individuals not knowledgeable of the process or hazards should seek professional assistance.

Benini's Patent – Background

SinterFire products are based on Joe Benini's July 2000 U.S. Patent No. 6,090,178 which is titled "Frangible metal bullets, ammunition and method of making such articles."

This patent specifies a "frangible metal bullet," which, practically speaking, means non-lead. It also deals with the method for manufacturing it.

For we non-engineers, the frangible metal bullet is formed from a mixture of metal particles and a metallic glue or binder. The material is first compacted into the desired bullet's shape; it is then heated to a temperature high enough that the metals will adhere, but just below the point at which they would fuse; and finally it is cooled. "Such bullets have sufficient strength to maintain their integrity during firing but disintegrate into powder on impact and can be formulated to be lead-free."

Benini's patent says, "Conventional, full-density, cast, swaged, copper plated or copper jacketed lead bullets are also used in indoor firing ranges and for training. In order to protect the shooters from ricochets, a 'bullet trap' is normally required to stop the projectile and any resulting fragments from injuring shooters. Furthermore, the walls of the firing range or training facility may be covered with rubber or some other projectile absorbing material to stop occasional ricocheting bullet fragments. Thus, the cost of constructing and maintaining indoor target/training ranges is substantial. Moreover, even using bullet traps and ricochet absorbing materials on the walls, occasionally a ricochet will somehow defeat such systems and injure a shooter.

"Shooting lead bullets causes the emission of airborne lead dust that is introduced into the atmosphere. This requires the implementation of elaborate ventilation systems and may require individuals working in such facilities to undergo blood monitoring programs to determine the amount of lead in their bloodstream. The accumulation of spent lead bullets and bullet fragments must be properly disposed of and regulations concerning the disposal of lead waste are becoming increasingly complex. Thus, the generation of lead dust and the accumulation of spent lead bullets and fragments causes environmental concerns and poses the potential for serious health problems.

"There has been a long-standing search for a material to use as a bullet that does not contain lead. One problem in replacing lead in ammunition is that the replacement material must be sufficiently heavy such that ammunition using such bullets, when used in automatic or semi-automatic weapons, will be able to cycle the weapon properly.

"The main criteria for the ability of a round to cycle automatic or semi-automatic weapons is the amount of energy that the ammunition delivers to the cycling mechanism. For some types of weapons, this energy is delivered by the expanding gases pushing back the cartridge case. For some others, the recoil is used and for still others high-pressure gases are connected, through a port inside the barrel, to a mechanism that cycles the firearm.

"All firearms, are designed to function with bullets and propellants (gunpowder) that produce certain pressure-vs-time characteristics. Using a lighter bullet may cause problems in operation of a semi-automatic or automatic weapon

Winchester has three lead-free rimfire cartridges: round nose, truncated hollow point and magnum.

if there is too low an energy transfer to give the mechanism the needed energy to cycle. While the energy can be increased by the use of additional propellant or different types of propellants, this is not desirable because the characteristics of such a training round would be significantly different from the ammunition having conventional bullets and propellants.

"In addition, in order to replace lead in a bullet, the selected material should have a large enough specific gravity so that the resulting bullet mass is compatible with commercially available propellants. It is not economically feasible to develop a lead-free round where a special propellant or other component would need to be developed.

"Further, a lead-free, training round should break up into small particles when it hits a hard surface. The individual particles are then too light to carry enough energy to be dangerous. On the other hand, such bullets should be sufficiently strong to withstand the high accelerations that occur on firing, ductile enough to engage the barrel rifling and durable enough to retain the identifying engraving from the rifling as required by government agencies.

"Practice and training rounds employing combinations of resinous binders and metallic powders have generally not proven satisfactory because of uncontrollable frangibility characteristics, insufficient strength, increased fouling of the barrel of the weapon, decreased barrel longevity and inability to retain or receive engraving from the rifling of the barrel through which it is fired."

Winchester

Curiously, the company that fought lead shot for waterfowl the hardest – continually going political and denying the science and medical reports – has expanded its lead-free rifle and handgun line the fastest. And of the "Big 3" – with Remington and Federal – Winchester is opening its line to green shooting the fastest.

Rifle

In its Super-X rifle line, Winchester has made an effort to satisfy the current black gun or AR-15 shooting phenomenon with green bullets, two .55-gr. bullets with tin cores: the .223 (3050 fps) and a 5.56mm (BC .147 3090 fps, 1161 ft/lb). It designates them as LF or lead-free. "Increased customer demand and regional lead-free regulation combined with the growth of varmint hunting have resulted in the need for a new lead-free bullet, the .223 Rem," said Glen Weeks, Centerfire Product Manager. "Our goal with the .223 Rem, as well as all of our lead-free offerings, is to make sure that shooters have a wide range of Winchester lead-free products available."

Winchester has developed its lead-free, copper alloy offerings primarily in the Supreme product line. There it features E-Tip rounds, an E-Tip being an energy "expansion cavity" (a cylindrically-shaped hollow space) behind the plastic tip which Winchester suggests "improves expansion at long and short ranges." The plastic or polycarbonate tip "prevents deformation in the magazine, boosts aerodynamic efficiency and initiates expansion."

Winchester credits Nosler for development of the E-Tip and energy expansion cavity. The bullet is made of a copper alloy instead of pure copper, which helps prevent barrel fouling and provides a high-performance, lead-free sporting bullet.

High weight retention, copper alloy Winchester boattail bullets reduce drag and provide a more efficient flight profile for higher retained energy at long range. In addition, coated with Lubalox, they have the added feature of reducing barrel fouling. They are available – and remember that these offerings will almost certainly grow in number and caliber because consumer demand, the company acknowledges "is growing among big-game hunters in states that have lead-free regulations" – for the following:

Rifle Cartridge – Super X	Weight (grains)	Ballistic Coefficient	Muzzle Velocity (fps)	Muzzle Energy (ft/lb)
.270 Winchester	130	.459	3050	2685
.270 WSM	130	.459	3275	3096
.30-06 Springfield	150	.469	2900	2801
.30-06 Springfield	180	.523	2750	3022
.300 WSM	150	.469	3300	3626
.300 WSM	180	.523	3010	3621
.300 Win Mag	150	.469	3260	3539
.300 Win Mag	180	.523	2950	3478
.308 Winchester	150	.469	2810	2629
7mm WSM	140	.498	3150	3304
7mm Rem Mag	140	.498	3100	3200

Two versions of Winchester's new Safari series ammo are offered with Nosler bullets. Nosler Partitions have copper alloy jackets but lead alloy cores; it is the Nosler Solids that are totally lead-free. According to a press release from Glen Weeks, Winchester Centerfire Product Manager, "The Safari line was developed to meet the most demanding hunting needs. Each cartridge provides the energy and knockdown power needed for the largest and most dangerous game. Partition offerings are ideal for dangerous or large thinner skin game, while the Solids will give you maximum penetration on the toughest hide and bone." Winchester Safari Ammunition features nickel-plated cartridge cases and is packaged in reusable 20-round plastic boxes.

Winchester's Super Clean NT handgun ammo is "indoor-range-friendly from the base up," says outdoor products merchant Cabelas.com. That begins with a lead- and heavy-metal-free priming mix and boxer-type primers with nickel-plated cups. The powder is clean-burning with minimal flash. These brass-cased 9mm Luger rounds are 105-gr., tin-core, jacketed lead free soft points. From Cabelas, a box of 50 costs $42.99 - $48.99 plus shipping.

Here are the ballistics of this line, including a comparison of the non-toxic Solids with the copper-jacketed lead Partitions.

Rifle Cartridge – Safari Series	Bullet Type	Weight (grains)	Ballistic Coefficient	Muzzle Velocity (fps)	Muzzle Energy (ft/lb)
.375 H&H	Partition	300	.398	2605	4520
.375 H&H	Solid	300	.198	2605	4520
.416 Rem Mag	Partition	400	.390	2400	5115
.416 Rem Mag	Solid	400	.263	2400	5115
.416 Rigby	Partition	400	.390	2370	4988
.416 Rigby	Solid	400	.263	2370	4988
.458 Win Mag	Partition	500	.330	2240	5570
.458 Win Mag	Solid	500	.272	2240	5570

Handgun

Super Clean NT means lead-free and non-toxic. Winchester says this applies not only to the 100 percent lead free tin core bullet, but to the lead and heavy-metal free primer, also. Nevertheless, in a sign of the transition from lead to non-lead, the company notes that each of these cartridge/bullet combinations "performs like lead" which means it must be good ....

Pistol Cartridge – Super Clean NT	Bullet Type	Weight (grains)	Muzzle Velocity (fps)	Muzzle Energy (ft/lb)
.357 Magnum	JFP	110	1275	397
.357 Sig	JFP	105	1370	438
.38 special	JFP	110	975	232
.40 S&W	JFP	140	1155	415
.45 Auto	JFP	170	1050	416
9mm Luger	JFP	105	1200	336

Federal Premium TNT Green is part of the V-Shok varmint hunting line. The lead-free bullet includes .222, .22-250 and .223. "Environmentally friendly" Federal suggests. "Varmint hunters need accurate, flat-shooting and explosive rounds," said Federal's Drew Goodlin.

NOT SPECIALISTS, BUT AVAILABLE

ATK Alliant: Federal, CCI, Speer

This major U.S. holding company, at this point, offers a minimum of loads for handguns and rifles.

When asked about green cartridges, the international corporation provided the following statement from Federal Premium: "We manufacture the widest selection of ammunition in the industry and take pride in offering a full compliment (sic) of offerings to shooters and hunters. We have several non-lead hunting options like the Barnes Triple-Shock X-Bullet and TNT Green, as well as a variety of non-lead target options across several shooting disciplines."

In 2009, sister company CCI released TNT Green in .22 Magnum. The lead-free round featured a pressed-powder core that, the PR department says, "releases violently on impact."

What Allied's companies have done for non-toxic shooting is to reduce the pollutants in their ammo by changing the ammo's name to sound clean and green and work to diminish primer toxicity.

Here is the example from Speer, a well-known precision cartridge manufacturer in Idaho that was acquired by Allied not long ago.

"If air quality in indoor ranges concerns you," Speer says, "Speer has the ammunition to set your mind at ease. Lawman Clean-Fire is loaded like regular Lawman except for the primer and bullet. The ignition power comes from the patented Clean-Fire primer that contains no lead, barium or antimony."

A cleaner shot is the result, Speer says, of using a low-flash, clean-burning propellant and CCI Clean-Fire primers. Note the final claim that using this combination "Virtually eliminates lead, barium and antimony at the firing point."

"Speer loads Lawman Clean-Fire with Speer TMJ. The lead core is completely and seamlessly encased in jacket material so powder gases can't burn lead off the bullet base. This design is superior to other 'base cap' bullets where the caps can loosen, leaking lead and destroying accuracy.

"Lawman Clean-Fire leaves the range air and your firearm cleaner. Fired cases don't show the usual soot coating you see in most regular ammunition. Velocities and bullet weights are the same as most Gold Dot products for realistic practice."

So what is the performance difference between traditionally leaded Lawman and Lawman Clean-Fire? Here is a muzzle comparison with a .40 S&W 200 gr. bullet (BC 0.167):

- Lawman Training: 915 fps velocity with KE of 372 ft/lb and BC of .167

- At 50 yards with a 4-inch barrel when the .40 caliber was sighted-in at 25 yards, the bullet drops 1.8 inches.

For Lawman Clean-Fire, the ballistic elements are identical.

But what is a "base cap" bullet?

From U.S. Patent #5,880,398 (filed 1997, published 1999), "A dual-purpose bullet is provided consisting of a thermoplastic body, a base cap, and a pressed powder core. The bullet in the preferred embodiment can either penetrate destroying and disrupting large volumes of human tissue or not penetrate the human tissue delivering a strong shock event and creating a thermal nuisance. The lethal mode is achieved by a high-velocity launch of the bullet without ignition of the igniter mixture and pressed powder core. The less-than-lethal mode is achieved by a low-velocity launch with ignition of first the pressed powder core and softening of the plastic projectile body."

Hornady

With more than 200 employees and 70,000 sq/ft of production area, Hornady says, "We continue to be the largest independent producer of bullets in the world."

The GMX (Gilding Metal eXpanding) line debuted in the spring of 2009 and was expanded for 2010 to include four new calibers. A benefit found in using gilding metal is that it reduces the pressure and fouling that is often associated with all-copper bullets. Hornady says its GMX consistently delivers more than 95 percent weight retention and 1.5x original diameter expansion. Streamlined design, gilding metal construction and double cannelures reduce fouling. Look for the red tip with an interior hollow to promote expansion. These bullets are compatible with conventional reloading data, and deliver the same external ballistics as SST bullets of the same weight. (Gilding metal is a slightly harder jacket than the core.)

Lapua

Lapua, or more officially Nammo Lapua Oy, is part of the large Nordic Nammo Group a major defense contractor headquartered in Finland. The principal products are small caliber cartridges and components for civilian and professional use. Lapua's cartridge factory was built in 1923.

The Naturalis from Lapua is a 99 percent copper hunting bullet. It includes "a novel, proprietary pressure-regulating valve that controls bullet expansion. This combination results in a bullet that expands symmetrically into the shape of a mushroom immediately upon impact. It works perfectly within terminal velocities of 500 m/s to 1000 m/s [1640 to 3280 fps] and retains 100 percent of its weight. This results in a more powerful shock effect, cleaner wounds and more latitude in terms of shot angle, distance to target and hit accuracy."

MagTech

Magtech Ammunition is a sister company to Sellier & Bellot in the Brazilian CBC corporation. Magtech opened for business with 20 employees in 1926 and now employs more than 1200 people producing small-caliber ammo.

First Defense and Hunting rounds are built with a 100 percent solid copper bullet, unlike traditional hollow points that contain a lead core covered by a copper jacket. Copper jackets can tear away, Magtech says, when fired, causing a loss of weight and a corresponding loss of power. Hunting rounds have a 6-petal design for terrific expansion with great weight retention.

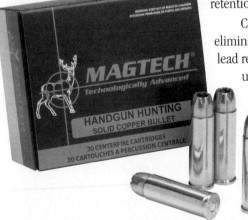

CleanRange loads are designed to eliminate airborne lead and the need for lead retrieval at indoor ranges. CleanRange uses lead-free primers, but its lead core is copper jacketed for a "fully encapsulated" bullet. This eliminates lead and heavy metal exposure at the firing point.

MagTech originally designed its solid copper, 6-petal hollow-point handgun bullets for law enforcement and self-defense. Known as "stoppers" they are also excellent for handgun hunting.

North Fork

In Wyoming, Mike Brady opened North Fork Bullets a dozen years ago because, he says, he was "obsessed with perfection." His first step was a line of premium bonded core soft point bullets. Next was a line of truncated cone flat point solids that would impact exactly the same down-range point, thus delivering a whopping amount of penetration, and he recently worked on a cup solid point as an "expanding solid." These cup point solids bridge the gap between softs and solids. Bullets are now manufactured in Oregon.

North Fork says its bullets begin as a bar of solid copper and are individually turned on a CNC lathe. "Pure copper is more difficult and time-consuming to machine, but it holds together better under impact than gilded copper jackets."

Nosler

Have you read Bob Nosler's comments about the lead-free issue? Just in case you haven't here they are:

"Regardless of your point of view, when the state of California banned the use of lead bullets in the condor range, sportsmen began the slow walk toward a lead-free mandate throughout the United States. ... There are several studies that focus on the effects of lead in the raptors that feed on prairie dogs. Whether well intended or not, environmentalists are using these studies to drive efforts to ban lead in the prairie dog range.... The California condor legislation came upon us quickly and Nosler responded...."

The E-Tip line is Nosler's response to the California condor; a solid copper bullet with an olive-drab plastic tip over a hollow "expansion cavity." Take that you big buzzard!

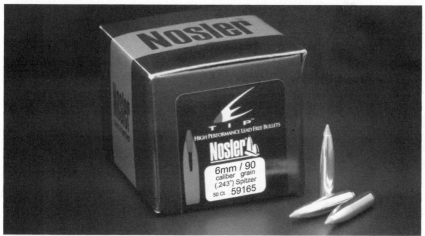

Nosler E-Tip lead free bullets with E² (Energy Expansion) Cavity give immediate and uniform expansion yet retain 95 percent of their weight for improved penetration.

Remington

Perhaps not everyone in the world knows the name Remington and associates the American company with shooting and hunting, but a whole lot of them do. Remington claims to be the only U.S. manufacturer of both firearms and ammunition and one of the largest domestic producers of shotguns and rifles, and in today's interlocking world economy that is some accomplishment.

In July 2009 Remington issued press release noting that it was "proud to announce" that its Premier Copper Solid Rifle, Premier Copper Solid Sabot Slugs and Premier Disintegrator Varmint lines of ammunition were "approved by the California Department of Fish and Game[4] for use in the hunting zones within the range of the California condor, pursuant to its July 2008 law prohibiting ammunition containing lead in those areas."

Premier Copper Solid rifle ammo is a polymer-tipped copper bullet that is designed to address – other than what every other bullet in every other manufacturer's line addresses, "extreme accuracy with devastating penetration" – the identified problem with condors eating gut piles, bullet fragmentation or the core's "weight retention."

In fact, the copper matrix construction, says the North Carolina company, ensures nearly 100 percent weight retention, while the polymer-tip and boat tail base provide high ballistic coefficient and flat trajectory. At impact, the polymer tip acts like a wedge, plowing back through a built-in expansion chamber and initiating a mushroom that's consistently 1.8x bullet diameter. At this time, the following calibers are available in a Copper Solid Tipped bullet: 243 Win (80 gr.), 270 Win (130 gr.), 7mm Rem. Mag (140 gr.), 30-06 Springfield (150 gr.), 300 Win Mag (150 gr.) and 308 (Win 150 gr.).

Premier Disintegrator Varmint ammo is loaded with a new frangible bullet, the Premier Disintegrator. This round looks like a typical JHP or jacketed hollow point; however, the specially-designed iron/tin bullet core is designed to disintegrate upon impact, fragmenting into countless tiny pieces. The new bullet offers a reduced risk of ricochet and is available in popular .22-250 and .223 Remington calibers.

Remington Disintegrator Varmint cartridges are approved for use in hunting zones within the range of the California condor.

Sellier & Bellot

The Czech ammunition manufacturer Sellier & Bellot says, "After firing the [non-toxic] cartridge is free from toxic exposure to barium, lead, mercury [and] antimony. [They mean the brass, not the bullet.] It does not pollute the environment, does not endanger the shooter's health with combustion products, and does not pollute the gun. It ensures safe shooting in closed premises and on target ranges. Unique patented primer design."

Sellier & Bellot loads a 110-gr. solid copper Barnes TSX for 6.8 mm Remington and a variety of handgun loads including 9 mm Luger, .38 Special, .357 Magnum, .40 S&W and .45 ACP. The company specifies Berdan 4.5 mm primers.

Read the fine print on the boxes though because what this European company considers a non-toxic load may simply be copper jacketed lead. For example, their .357 Magnum Nontox – SP cartridge is a "Semi-jacketed bullet - soft point. The bullet has a lead core. The lead core is bare in the front part. When hitting the target it gets deformed to make a mushroom-like shape, which ensures that kinetic energy is transferred fast. The bullet is characterized by the low ability to rebound. It is made in caliber's 9 mm Luger, 38 Special and 357 Magnum."

By "non-toxic," Sellier & Bellot implies that bullets in cartridges with Berdan 4.5 mm primers are also non-toxic, but not so. Primers, by the way, are small copper cylinders pressed into the base of the shell casing. Inside the cylinder is a pressure-sensitive explosive (not a gun powder that appears to explode but is actually said to burn rapidly) that is ignited when the firing pin strikes. A tiny hole in the brass base – two holes in the Berdan primer – allows fire from the exploding primer to ignite the powder. Invented by American Hiram Berdan in the 1860s, primers have remained essentially the same, at least functionally, to the present day.

Berdan primers have a reputation for being difficult to remove from a case after firing, which is certainly a conscious decision on the manufacturer's part to discourage reloading.

In the U.S. the Boxer primer, invented in Britain in the 1860s, is almost universal though it is only slightly different than the Berdan. Those small differences, however – having a single, larger ignition hole, for instance, rather than a double – make Boxer primers easier to reload.

Properly loaded, the two types of primers are almost impossible to distinguish and properly sized should work in any cartridge. Typically Berdan-primed ammunition, especially military surplus rounds, has often used corrosive priming compounds because they are cheaper to use. Boxer-primed ammo now is almost always non-corrosive and non-mercury-containing.

So yes, a primer matters in non-toxic shooting and if this is important to you, please read the fine print.

SCIENCE AND THE LAW

Just because a joke is old doesn't mean that it has lost its flavor. What's the problem with a bus loaded with attorneys driving over a cliff?

The answer, of course, is that it isn't two bus loads of attorneys.

No matter how often we tell that joke, we laugh. The very next day we stop the car at a traffic light and "WHAM" some guy headed to a salon to get his hair frosted and steering with one hand while texting his BFF with his other hand smashes us from behind. We land in the hospital. At that point, we would like to have one of those buses loaded with attorneys land beside us.

Lawyers of course perform services other than suing people. Big liability suits make the news, but if you have a brilliant idea, an "intellectual property," a lawyer can help you patent it and that patent will protect your idea from most of the R&C (research and copy) artists and engineers at work in every industry including the shooting sports. Maybe your invention cures world hunger, or your machine teleports people instantly from one place to another, or your design for a non-toxic bullet that performs just like lead will make millions of dollars. It could happen.

This brief chapter is about the patents behind the products ... and only indirectly you will be happy to learn about the attorneys. Still, thousands of patents are on file pertaining to bullets and this is only a sampler. If you have a free hour, researching them provides a fascinating look at the evolution of bullets and shooting.

A quick look at the patents helps us – even we non-scientists, non-engineers – see through the fog of the claims and counter claims. By taking the facts out of the hands of advertising and marketing, we reduce the fog of uncertainty. By laying bare the facts we are better able to judge what's best for our shooting situation.

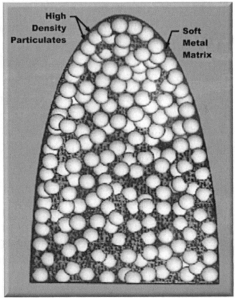

During the past generation, everyone from the U.S. Marine Corps to Canadian part-time gunsmiths have experimented – sometimes successfully – with alternatives to the basic copper-jacketed lead bullet. This bullet diagram is based on the work of scientists at Oak Ridge National Laboratory in Tennessee, otherwise known for research in nuclear energy.

A PATENT SAMPLER

U.S. Patent	Name and Date	Published Inventors	Owner/Assignee
5,012,743	High-performance projectile - May 1991	Jean-Paul Denis Marc Neuforge	FNH
5,131,123	Methods of manufacturing a bullet July 1992	Randy Brooks	Barnes Bullets
5,237,930	Frangible practice ammunition - August 1993	Germain Belanger Marc Potvin	SNC Industrial Technologies
5,259,320	Intermediate article used to form a bullet projectile or component and a finally formed bullet – November 1993	Randy Brooks	Barnes Bullets
5,399,187	Lead-free bullet March 1995	Brian Mravic, et al	Olin Corporation
5,616,642	Lead-free frangible ammunition – April 1997	Harley West John Mullins	Precision Ammo (RUAG AmmoTech)
5,679,920	Non-toxic frangible bullet October 1997	John Hallis Richard Proulx	Federal
5,811,723	Solid copper hollow-point bullet – September 1998	Jeffrey Stone	Remington
5,852,858	Non-toxic frangible bullet December 1998	John Hallis Richard Proulx	Federal Federal
5,877,437	High density projectile March 1999	Victor Oltrogge	Silvex
6,257,149	Lead-free bullet July 2001	Anthony Cesaroni	Cesaroni Technology
6,561,070	Bullet, bullet jacket and methods of making – May 2003	Dennis Weber	Alltrista Zinc
6,792,869	Expanding soft point bullet September 2004	Peter Pi	Zelda LLC

Primary Source www.freepatentsonline.com

FBI Ballistic/Ammunition Test Protocol[5]

As you study ammo and prepare to make a purchase, perhaps for concealed carry or for home defense, you will occasionally hear that a certain type or caliber has passed muster with the FBI. What does that mean and how does it square with your personal residence?

First, a handgun bullet has to penetrate a minimum of 12 inches of tissue to reliably damage vital organs in the human body regardless of the shot angle or intervening obstacles such as arms, clothing and glass. Obviously, penetration of 18 inches is considered better.

With minimum penetration, the only way to increase a wound's effectiveness is to make a bigger hole. A bigger hole increases:

a. the amount of vital tissue damaged,

b. the chance of damaging vital tissue with a marginal shot and

c. the potential for quicker blood loss.

These are important because, with the single exception of damaging the central nervous system, the only way to incapacitate a resisting adversary is to cause enough blood loss to starve the brain of oxygen and rapidly drop blood pressure. This takes time, so the faster hemorrhage can occur, the better.

The FBI Test Protocol results in an assessment of a bullet's ability to inflict effective wounds after defeating various intervening but common obstacles.

The test media used by the FBI to simulate living tissue is 10 percent ballistic gelatin (Kind & Knox 250-A) mixed by weight (i.e., one pound of gelatin to nine

The FBI Test Protocol results in an assessment of a bullet's ability to inflict effective wounds after defeating various intervening but common obstacles. (Photo Winchester)

pounds of water). The gelatin is stored at 39.2° Fahrenheit and shot within 20 minutes of being removed from the refrigerator. The temperature of the gelatin is critical, because penetration changes significantly with temperature. This specific gelatin mix was determined and calibrated by the U.S. Army Wound Ballistics Research Laboratory, Presidio of San Francisco, to produce the same penetration results as that obtained in actual living tissue. The 10 percent gelatin has been correlated against the actual results of hundreds of shooting incidents.

Gelatin blocks for handgun rounds are approximately six inches square and 16 inches long. Each shot's penetration is measured to the nearest ¼-inch. The projectile is recovered, weighed, and measured for expansion by averaging its greatest diameter with its smallest diameter.

The test using this gelatin has eight test events. In each, five shots are fired for a total of 40 rounds. A new gelatin block is used for each individual shot. All firing is performed with a "typical service weapon representative of those used by law enforcement," and the weapon used is described in each test report.

In addition to the tests described below, each cartridge is tested for velocity and accuracy:

• 20 rounds are fired through a test barrel followed by 20 rounds through the service weapon used in the penetration tests.

• Two ten-shot groups are fired at 25 yards from the test barrel, and two from the service weapon. Groups are measured center-to-center of the two most widely spaced holes, averaged and reported.

Test barrel results demonstrate a round's potential independent of any weapon factors which can affect performance. Test barrel results are the purest measure of inherent capability for accuracy and velocity. Repeating these tests with a service weapon shows how well the cartridge/weapon combination realizes that potential.

Test 1 – Bare Gelatin: The gelatin block is bare and shot at 10 feet. Greatest bullet expansion is customary in this test. (This test correlates FBI results with those obtained by other researchers, few of whom shoot into anything other than bare gelatin.)

Test 2 – Heavy Clothing: The gelatin block is covered with four clothing layers to simulate typical cold weather wear: one layer of cotton T-shirt (48 threads per inch); one layer of cotton shirt (80 threads per inch); a 10-ounce down comforter in a cambric shell cover (232 threads per inch); and one layer of 13-ounce cotton denim (50 threads per inch). The block is shot at 10 feet.

Test 3 – Steel: Two pieces of 20-gauge hot-rolled steel with a galvanized finish in six-inch squares are set three inches apart. The gelatin block is covered with light clothing (one layer of T-shirt and one layer of cotton shirt) and placed 18 inches behind the rear-most square of steel. The shot is 10 feet from the muzzle to the front of the first piece of steel. The steel used is the heaviest gauge commonly found in automobile doors and the test simulates the weakest part of a door. (In all car doors, there is an area, or areas, where the heaviest obstacle is nothing more that two pieces of 20 gauge steel.)

Test 4 – Wallboard: Two pieces of half-inch standard gypsum board six inches square are set 3½ inches apart. The gelatin block is covered with light clothing and placed 18 inches behind the rear most gypsum square. The shot is made at 10 feet from the muzzle to the front of the first piece of gypsum. This test simulates a typical interior building wall.

Test 5 – Plywood: One 6-inch square piece of ¾-inch AA fir plywood is used. The gelatin block is covered with light clothing and placed 18 inches behind the rear surface of the plywood. The shot is made 10 feet from the muzzle to the front surface of the plywood. This test simulates the resistance of typical wooden doors or construction timbers.

Test 6 – Automobile Glass: One piece of A.S.I. ¼-inch laminated automobile safety glass measuring 15x18 inches is set at an angle of 45 degrees to the horizontal. The line of bore of the weapon is offset 15 degrees to the side, resulting in a compound angle of impact. The gelatin block is covered with light clothing and placed 18 inches behind the glass. The shot is made 10 feet from the muzzle to the center of the glass pane. This test simulates a shot at the driver of a car from the left front quarter of the vehicle, not directly from the front.

Test 7 – Heavy Clothing (20 yards): This test repeats Test 2 but at 20 yards, measured from the muzzle to the front of the gelatin. It assesses the effects of increased range and consequently decreased velocity.

Test 8 – Automobile Glass (20 yards): This test repeats Test 6 but at 20 yards from the muzzle to the front of the glass, and without the 15-degree offset. The shot is made from straight in front of the glass, simulating a shot at the driver of a car bearing down on the shooter.

CHAPTER NOTES

1. Frangible bullets break into tiny fragments on impact with a hard surface, or at least a surface harder than they are, and you will read a lot about them in this chapter. According to the National Institute of Standards and Technology, "They are becoming increasingly popular in situations where ricochets or 'splash-back' from bullets is not tolerable: firearms training facilities and crowded places such as airports, courtrooms and office buildings."

The key to understanding frangible bullets – or penetration in general – is "hard surface." www.nist.gov/public_affairs/techbeat/tb2006_0608.htm

2. When studying ammunition and ballistics the term "SAAMI" which stands for Sporting Arms and Ammunition Manufacturer's Institute www.saami.org is frequently a part of the conversation. SAAMI is affiliated with the American National Standards Institute (ANSI) as "an accredited standards developer" and is, in the broadest sense, the technical governing body of the firearms and ammunition industry. SAAMI sets voluntary performance standards for pressures and velocities of rifle, shotgun and pistol arms and ammunition:

a. "Since 1926 SAAMI has been the principle organization in the U.S. actively engaged in the development and promulgation of product standards for firearms and ammunition. The U.S. military, the Department of Homeland Security, and many other state and local agencies frequently require that their suppliers manufacture to SAAMI specifications. SAAMI is the only trade association whose member companies manufacture and set standards for high-performance law enforcement ammunition."

b. Cor-Bon, for instance, is a SAAMI member. As such it follows established SAAMI specifications unless specifically noted. Thus Cor-Bon's 45 Colt +P and 45-70 +P ammunition are not within SAAMI specifications, and Cor-Bon requests that anyone having questions about these two cartridges should call their technical staff: (605) 347-4544.

c. According to Keith Porco at SinterFire, this SAAMI specification for frangible "has not been officially adopted yet however it has been in use for over 8 years:" To be considered "frangible" against AR500 steel targets for the purposes of law enforcement training, ammunition for centerfire pistol and revolver shall not produce any individual fragments weighing more than 5% of the nominal bullet weight when tested as follows: [10 rounds shot at 10 feet, recovering at least 85% of the bullet weight].

3. The IDPA (International Defensive Pistol Association www.idpa.com) is headquartered in Berryville, Arkansas. The statement of purpose says "IDPA is a shooting sport that uses practical equipment including full charge service ammunition to solve simulated 'real world' self-defense scenarios. IDPA shooting events require use of practical handguns and holsters that are truly suitable for self-defense. No 'competition only' equipment is permitted in IDPA matches since the main goal is to test the skill and ability of the individual, not equipment or gamesmanship."

4. These days manufacturers sometimes refer to a California list of certified non-lead ammunition for use in their condor areas. It is available through the California Dept. of Fish & Game web site at www.dfg.ca.gov/wildlife/hunting/condor/certifiedammo.html. Note that "non-toxic shot approved by the U.S. Fish and Wildlife Service for use in waterfowl hunting is certified to take appropriate non-game species within the non-lead zone. NOTE: The U.S. Fish and Wildlife Service reviews and may approve applications for other types of non-toxic shot throughout the year. A full list of approved shot types can be found at http://migratorybirds.fws.gov/issues/nontoxic_shot/nontoxic.htm.

5. The FBI report "Handgun Wounding Factors and Effectiveness" written by Special Agent Urey Patrick is a bit dated – July 14, 1989 – but is still idea-current and makes for fascinating reading. Access it on line at www.firearmstactical.com/pdf/fbi-hwfe.pdf.

Chapter 9

LEAD IN THE GREAT OUTDOORS

What levels of lead are normal in humans? The CDC has established a level of 10 µg/dl (micrograms per deciliter) as a point at which we should begin to be concerned or, if found in children, should investigate. It simply means they do not know, and the effects of lead are insidious.

Before we had industrial societies, lead was present in humans but only in trace amounts. Here are studies from opposite side of the earth, independently conducted a decade apart.[1]

• A study conducted and published in Japan in 1987 compared "Lead levels in ancient and contemporary Japanese bones." Researchers there found that "During the past few centuries, lead production, consumption and emissions, to our total environment have increased remarkably." Current lead levels were about eight times the levels measured from the bones of individuals who had been dead for 2,000 years.

• A study conducted in the Canary Islands, but published in the U.S. in 1997, discussed "Bone lead in the prehistoric population of Gran Canaria." Researchers in the islands found that "Higher bone lead values were observed in the modern sample than in the ancient sample.... Low bone lead observed in the prehistoric sample suggests a low lead exposure in pre-historic times in Gran Canaria." In this study, the current lead levels were about four times the levels measured from pre-historic individuals, dead and buried for hundreds of years.

NOW APPEARING IN COURT....

Death by a Thousand Cuts

In Connecticut Coastal Fishermen's Association v. Remington Arms Co., Inc., 989 F.2d 1305 (C.A.2d 1993) the Connecticut Coastal Fishermen's Association sued Remington[2]. The Connecticut Coastal case pitted two user groups against each other in environmental toxic tort litigation. It was based on the 1976 Resource Conservation and Recovery Act (RCRA) which requires the EPA to:

1. Establish standards for controlling hazardous waste generation, transport and disposal.

2. Enforce the standards with civil and criminal penalties.

3. Identify and list hazardous wastes.

RCRA requires permits and "cradle to grave" record keeping.

The Lordship Point Gun Club in Stratford, Connecticut had been in business since the '20s. Remington bought it in 1945. Open to the public, 40,000 people shot there each year. By 1990, it was estimated that 2,400 tons of lead and 11 million pounds of clay target fragments were deposited in the land and waters of Long Island Sound. The area was habitat for many species of waterfowl and shorebirds including the endangered Black Duck.

In May 1985 the Connecticut Dept. of Environmental Protection (DEP) began investigating possible contamination. DEP said shooting lead "reasonably can be expected to cause pollution" and required Remington to investigate, clean up the area and halt the "possible contamination" by August 31, 1986. Remington subsequently commissioned and DEP approved a study by Energy Resources Co.

Based on the results, DEP told Remington to cease all shooting and to submit a plan detailing remediation within four months.

Instead, Remington commissioned and DEP approved a study by Battelle Ocean Sciences to look into remediation alternatives for the lead only. Results were submitted January 1, 1988.

DEP then invited the Coastal Fishermen to comment and they expressed a concern that the millions of pounds of clay targets were not addressed. Remington and Battelle addressed this issue and DEP approved the report on June 8, 1990.

In 1991, DEP ordered Remington to supplement the remediation plan to include removal of visible clay target fragments from the beach surface above the mean low water mark of Long Island Sound and to study the possible removal of targets from the water. Remington submitted this report and is awaiting DEP approval.

Remington will have six months after DEP approval to submit final engineering plans and a construction schedule. Because the plan involves dredging navigable U.S. waters, Remington will have to obtain permits from the U.S. Army Corps of Engineers.

In its heyday, a shoot at the Lordship Gun Club regularly drew hundreds of competitors who shot at clay pigeons thrown over the fringe of Long Island Sound. Because the Sound is a navigable waterway, many governmental agencies and NGOs eventually became concerned that the volume of lead and broken clays was creating a toxic hazard. Legal wrangling took a decade and cost millions of dollars. Opened in the '20s and operated successfully for nearly 75 years, the Stratford, Connecticut, range is now closed, probably forever.

To date, no lead shot or clay target fragments have been removed from Lordship Point or the surrounding waters of Long Island Sound.

The fishermen argued that lead shot and clay targets are hazardous wastes. Therefore the Gun Club is a hazardous waste storage and disposal facility subject to RCRA requirements. Thus Remington needed a permit – which it had never obtained – and the fishermen wanted a court order to compel Remington to fix the situation.

The district court agreed and granted summary judgment to the fishermen. Specifically, the court found that "the lead shot was a hazardous waste, but believed there were genuine issues of material fact as to whether the clay targets were hazardous waste.

Remington appealed.

It said it did not need a permit because the debris did not constitute "an imminent and substantial endangerment to health and the environment under RCRA."

The court eventually ruled that the lead "which, due to its toxicity and the fact that it poses a substantial threat to the environment" was solid, hazardous waste and thereby subject to RCRA remediation and regulation. Remington must properly dispose of the lead shot.

Writing for the NSSF's National Association of Shooting Ranges, Richard Peddicord says, "Not only was this large and prestigious range closed, but site management actions continued for a period of more than 15 years and a cost of well over 10 million dollars."[3]

Clean Water, Clean Air – Youbetcha!

Who doesn't want clean water and clean air? As environmental stewards, we can have those things and pass them on to our children. Precious gifts, indeed.

Our shooting and hunting heritage is something else to pass along to our children. Bringing the two into a harmonious package is our challenge.

Not many years ago, gun clubs routinely fired at clay birds over lakes and wetlands. The practice was not identified as inappropriate or dumping or hazardous. We shot that way for generations. That has changed and, as we know, change usually brings conflict before equilibrium returns to a social system. Such is the case in America as we attempt to bring our need for a clean environment into balance with our traditional shooting pastimes.

It began with rivers catching fire in Ohio; neighbors developing cancer from toxins dumped in the ground in New York; and the use of dangerous chemicals in Viet Nam. In 1972, the U.S. Congress passed the Clean Water Act (CWA). Today, EPA calls the act "the cornerstone of surface water quality protection." The Act is a tool to reduce direct pollutant discharge into America's waters so that they can support "the protection and propagation of fish, shellfish and wildlife and recreation...."

Enforcement under the Act has gradually shifted, EPA notes, to a focus on "point sources" such as sewage plants and industry drains. Beginning in the late 1980s regulators began to look at runoff from streets, construction sites, farms, and other "wet-weather" sources. The approach continues to evolve from relatively simple source-pollutants to a "watershed-based strategy:" protecting healthy waters and restoring impaired ones.

And finally this critical notation: "Involvement of stakeholder groups [such as NRA and NSSF] in the development and implementation of strategies for achieving and maintaining state water quality and other environmental goals is another hallmark of this approach." It means that compromise and reason have a chance.

A Permit to Shoot

A permit to pollute is easily had by big business and it is called a "National Pollution Discharge Elimination System" permit. Lead shot and target debris (shattered clay pigeons and plastic wadding) are sometimes considered pollutants; sometimes traps at shooting ranges are "point sources" and sometimes they are not. It depends on the judge's politics and interpretation. Thus, what lawyers have argued is that any range from which patrons shoot over "Waters of the United States" must have a permit. And "Waters of the United States" is broadly defined to include virtually all rivers, streams, lakes, ponds, drainage-ways, wetlands and similar features, even those on private property.

In January 1994 the Long Island Soundkeeper Fund and New York Coastal Fishermen's Association – both non-profit environmental groups – filed suit in U.S. District Court, New York against the New York Athletic Club[4], a non-profit membership-based group. The Club had a private trap range at its Travers Island facility in Pelham Manor on Long Island Sound at which shooters stationed on

In January 1994 two non-profit environmental groups filed suit in U.S. District Court, New York against the New York Athletic Club[5], a non-profit membership-based group. The Club had a private trap range at its Travers Island facility in Pelham Manor on Long Island Sound at which shooters stationed on concrete platforms fired at clay targets tossed out over the sound. The Club had shot trap with traditional shells for 60 years prior to switching to steel shot in the November '94-April '95 shooting season.

concrete platforms fired at clay targets tossed out over the sound. The suit was titled Long Island Soundkeeper Fund, Inc. v. New York Athletic Club and plaintiffs sought "declaratory and injunctive relief, remediation, civil penalties and attorney's fees."

The Club had shot trap with traditional shells for 60 years prior to switching to steel shot in the November '94-April '95 shooting season.

In Affidavits filed against the Club, reasoning seemed intensely personal but was upheld in court as giving plaintiff's standing to bring suit:

- Wilma Turnbull visited the area four to five times a year for "personal recreational purposes" listed as hiking, bird watching and walking along the shoreline. Wilma said her enjoyment was diminished and that she was offended by seeing the target and shotshell debris.

- Jorge Santiago visited the area occasionally for hiking and bird watching. Jorge even said he cleaned up debris along the beach. "I am concerned that marine life and water fowl are seriously harmed by the pollution from the shooting debris and the poisonous effects of lead."

- Winthrop Parker was also disgusted by the shooting and the debris and gave this statement: "I do not fish any longer. My grandfather and father, who lived on Pelham Bay, used to fish from a rowboat, anchored in front of the NYAC, at a safe distance from the shooting. The discharged lead pellets would fall into the water near them, and often into their boat so that at the end of the day, the bottom of the boat would be covered in spent lead shot. I know that lead is very toxic. I would fish again if the water were clean, and not polluted by lead shot."

The New York Athletic Club countered that the above claims of "aesthetic injury" could not be taken seriously. Further, even the EPA which filed a brief on behalf of the Club, said pellets and broken targets were not discarded or abandoned materials; and even noted that a permit was not necessary because use of the materials were "proper and expected."

On the particular notes of standing to bring suit, the Club lost. On the particular notes of operating a non-permitted facility and "dumping," the Club's arguments were upheld.

Regarding the most pertinent points, however – whether the traps were a "point source" of pollution and whether shot itself was pollution – the Club lost. This in spite of an Affidavit from New York's Dept. of Environmental Conservation stating: "...the Department does not regulate shooting activities on ranges and that current environmental laws do not require permits for discharge of lead or steel shot on shooting ranges."

On March 20, 1996, the court ruled that the club must either apply for a permit [to pollute] or cease shooting immediately. The court ruled that even though the club had switched to steel shot, any shot was a pollutant for purposes of the CWA. The club elected to discontinue shooting rather than seek a permit.

A Litany of Lawsuits

Missouri: Daniel Brown moves to 12101 E. St. Charles Road in August 1984. In October 1996, Donna Brown also moves in. The Browns file a nuisance lawsuit in January 2004. Their target is the nearby 115-acre Cedar Creek Rod and Gun Club, a not-for-profit range that incorporated in March 1993 and is owned and operated by Ralph Gates of Columbia[5]. The Browns allege that the target shooting "caused vibrations and bothersome noise at their home night and day."

A Boone County jury awards the Browns $700,000. In a permanent injunction by Special Judge Jon Beetem of Cole County, the gun club is allowed to operate trap and skeet fields three days a week and host as many as six special events a year.

Filed in Boone County Circuit Court on April 4, the injunction says shooting at the club's trap and skeet fields is permitted on Tuesdays and Thursdays from noon to 6 p.m. and Saturdays from 10 a.m. to 6 p.m. The club may also allow shooting on the fields one Sunday or Friday each month from noon to 5 p.m. during months when a special event is not planned.

Full use of the facilities is permitted for as many as six special events per year during specific weekend hours, but a special event weekend must be preceded by and followed by a weekend of no shooting. No shooting is permitted on Easter Sunday, Thanksgiving or Christmas.

Shooting on all fields, ranges or other premises of the club south of the trap and skeet fields is permitted weekdays from noon to 6 p.m. on the condition that firearms are discharged in a direction away from the plaintiffs' home.

The Missouri General Assembly passes a bill (HB 2034 passed by a 139 – 6 vote in April.) to provide protection against civil and criminal liability to shooting ranges – including those operated by the Dept. of Conservation – and hunting reserves resulting from noise produced by shooting. Unfortunately it is too late for Cedar Creek.

WHERE'S THE BEEF IN THIS SANDWICH?

The four Federal Law Enforcement Training Centers (FLETCO; www.fletc. gov) – Glynco, Georgia; Cheltenham, Maryland; Artesia, New Mexico; and Charleston, South Carolina – serve more than 80 federal agencies as well as state, local and international agencies.

Glynco alone has "18 firearms ranges, including a state-of-the-art indoor range complex with 146 separate firing points; and eight highly versatile semi-enclosed ranges with 200 additional firing points."

Glynco alone trains 50,000 law enforcement officers annually, and students at the Firearms Division shoot approximately 20 million rounds of ammunition a year. For its training rounds, the center uses both lead and environmentally friendly or non-toxic ammunition. Reduced hazard ammo accounts for nearly three-quarters of expended rounds.

Is it really a problem?

We certainly accept that lead can be a problem in the bloodstream; that it is readily absorbed in fumes (hence the ban on leaded gasoline); and when children gnaw on toys made with lead-based paint, but is there truly a problem with lead leaching into our drinking water from shooting ranges, even ranges as heavily used as the one in Glynco? When you go to the range should you drink out of the water fountain or take your own bottled water?

SPRING CLEANING AT THE RANGE

Lianna Sanday, Marketing Manager for MT2 in Colorado, one of America's largest contractors for shooting range maintenance and lead recovery, says that outdoor ranges can avoid expensive, court-ordered clean-up of lead by developing an environmental plan that minimizes the possibility of contamination. Adding high berms to contain shot or bullets; recording and checking soil pH; planting to minimize runoff after a heavy rain; and having a time-table for regular lead removal will help prevent contamination … and lawsuits. In addition, finding bar-

Here is a random paper from Dr. Corinne Rooney of the Soil, Plant and Ecological Sciences Division, Lincoln University, Canterbury, New Zealand: "Lead is deposited at shooting ranges as spent lead shot (pellets) at clay target shooting ranges, and spent lead bullets in soil berms at rifle/pistol ranges. The lead is not insoluble in the soil environment, but is readily released in a soluble form.

"Soil lead concentrations greater than 10,000 mg/kg -1 (milligrams/decigram) of soil are commonly reported at shooting ranges around the world, in-

rels of an unmarked chemical in a storage shed on site is never a good thing.

• Selling reclaimed lead may offset range maintenance, and it can even be sold to club members for reloading.

• Removing lead from the soil is responsible environmental stewardship and complies with state and federal regulations.

• Reclamation demonstrates community responsibility and results in a clean and well-dressed shooting area. (Photos MT2 – Metal Treatment Technologies)

cluding in New Zealand, USA, England, Germany and Scandinavia. For lead, the ANZECC[6] guideline limit for further investigation is 300 mg/kg -1. It is the norm, rather than the exception, that shooting ranges are contaminated with lead."

According to Rooney, the deposition of lead on dry land shooting ranges has very different chemistry than in a wetland.

Wetlands: When lead falls into water, it is encased in a relatively anaerobic environment, an environment without oxygen that is free to combine with the impurities in the lead. Hence, there is little or no pellet corrosion and only minor sediment contamination.

Uplands: When lead shot falls on dry land shooting ranges, it falls in relatively aerobic environments – pellets are exposed to oxygen in the atmosphere and readily corrode. Soil contamination and therefore leaching from the topsoil downward into the water table is "high to extreme."

Curiously, although she shows photographs of corroded shot pellets in her paper, Dr. Rooney notes that it may take 10,000 years for a lead pellet to entirely corrode in a temperate climate – much of the U.S., for example – whereas in a tropical climate that time span might be cut to 1,000 years. She notes that 90 percent of the lead pellets that have been shot at any given range are still present in a relatively un-corroded state.

Rooney seems to go out on a limb when she argues that "Much of the range management information contained in U.S. Best Management Practices manuals is now incorrect. The following management methods are considered the most sound." Rooney says ranges should:

• Eliminate contact between ammunition and soil with a concrete pad or "geo-textile" covering the entire shot-fall area.

• Install a drainage collection system.

• Install bullet traps at static range berms.

On the negative side, Rooney adds that:

• Reducing the leaching of lead into the groundwater still does not control the leaching of arsenic and antimony.

• Lead shot must be sifted from the soil, and then the soil needs to be "chemically washed before return to the range."

• Current "non-toxic" alternatives to lead are also likely to cause contamination.

○ Steel shot: Iron corrodes about five times faster than lead and ammo contains "substantial heavy metal impurities including chromium and copper that have the potential to be released by corrosion."

○ Frangible ammunition: Newly introduced in the U.S., it appears to contain compressed, powdered metals which are likely to undergo the same corrosion and release process as lead shot.

When lead shot falls on dry land, pellets are exposed to oxygen and readily corrode.

Ultimately, it seems, there is no acceptable shooting solution for Dr. Rooney other than the closure of shooting ranges entirely…and this is precisely the attitude that the NRA and the NSSF have warned about when they talk about backdoor gun control.

Although Dr. Rooney apparently does not believe that any non-toxic bullet will prove to be "as advertised," SinterFire's MSDS[7] (Material Safety Data Sheet) dated January 30, 2006, for its copper (84-96 percent)/tin (16-4 percent) suggests otherwise.

The SinterFire Toxicological Information section reports:

"Copper is an essential element of mammalian metabolism. Copper metal has little or no serious toxicity. The most common adverse effect associated with copper is the acute inhalation of copper fume during refining or welding.

"Inhalation of copper fume may result in metal fume fever, which is characterized by upper respiratory irritation, chills, metallic or sweet taste, nausea and aching muscles. Attacks usually begin after 4-8 hours of exposure and last only 24-48 hours. Inhalation of fumes has been reported to sometimes cause discoloration of the skin and hair. Nausea and vomiting may result if large amounts of copper metal are ingested. This is probably due to the conversion of the swallowed metal copper to its irritating salts. It is unlikely that poisoning by ingestion in industry would progress to a serious point because small amounts induce vomiting, emptying the stomach of copper salts. High airborne concentrations of copper metal would be expected to cause mechanical irritation of the eyes and respiratory tract. Metallic copper may cause keratinization of the hands and soles of the feet, but it is not commonly associated with industrial dermatitis.

"Metallic tin is relatively non-toxic. Exposure to dust or fumes of inorganic tin salts is known to cause benign inflammation of the lung tissue (stanosis), a condition in which there is no distinctive fibrosis, no evidence of disability, and no special complicating factors. The U.S identifies no component of this product present at levels greater than 0.1% as a carcinogen by the National Toxicology Program, the U.S. Occupational Safety and Health Act, or the International Agency for Research on Cancer (IARC)."

Best Management Practices

The U.S. EPA says that lead at outdoor shooting ranges may pose a threat to the environment if best management practices – which it codifies in a manual – including reclamation and recycling, are not implemented[8].

The EPA's manual provides owners and operators of outdoor rifle, pistol, trap, skeet and sporting clay ranges with information on "lead management." It explains how environmental laws apply and presents a number of "successful practices" available. These practices, it says, have been proven to effectively reduce lead contamination.

Since every range is unique in both the type of shooting activity and its environmental setting, including soils type, EPA doesn't provide site-specific solutions. Rather, range operators can use the manual to select the best practices for their range.

Two things EPA says their manual is not intended to do:

1. address range safety or competition requirements, and

2. close ranges.

It specifically notes that for safety and competition questions, range operators should go to reference materials available from the NRA and NSSF.

EPA says four steps will usually result in a good program for controlling lead.

STEP 1: Control and contain lead bullets and bullet fragments. For bullets, this involves:

• Earthen backstops – 15-20 feet high, as steep as possible with a rock-free surface.

• Sand traps – Same as earthen backstops, EPA recommends a clay layer under the sand to prevent lead from contacting underlying soil.

• Steel traps – Deflect bullets into a "deceleration chamber" and perhaps into a collection tray, but may increase fragmentation and lead dust.

• Lamella or rubber granule traps – Lamella traps are tightly-hanging, vertical strips of rubber with steel backing; rubber granule traps are shredded rubber between a solid rubber front and steel backing – to recycle lead, bullets must be dug out of the rubber. Most effective traps are expensive, but many can be used indoors or outdoors.

• Shock-absorbing concrete – Used since the '80s, can be recycled.

• Reducing shotfall zones – For shot pellets, EPA encourages the compact layout of 5-Stand Sporting Clays. Although it is a highly condensed game, one of the attractions of sporting clays as opposed to trap and skeet is the ability to walk and shoot in different situations or to face different types of shooting problems. Hence, 5-Stand can become boring.

STEP 2: Prevent migration of lead to the subsurface and surrounding surface water bodies.

Adjusting soil pH – Ideal soil pH is between 6.5 and 8.5; check pH annually and if soil acidity increases (the lower the number the greater the acidity) consider spreading lime to raise soil pH. Lime is cheap, effective and easy to spread. Unfortunately, it is not a permanent solution.

Immobilizing lead – Spreading phosphate to bind lead particles (minimize their ability to leach into the water table). Spreading phosphate is also cheap, effective and easy, yet it is not a permanent fix.

Controlling runoff – Use vegetation, especially grasses, to control surface water run-off and to absorb water; use mulch or compost to cover the soil; use synthetic liners to immediately capture lead pellets. Plantings are relatively cheap and effective, but must be maintained; prior to reclamation, they must often be removed or trimmed and excessive vegetation interferes with reclamation efforts.

Using engineered solutions – Ground contouring or landscaping with filtration systems prevents hazardous runoff. May be initially expensive, but typically require little short-term maintenance.

STEP 3: Removing lead from the range and recycling it helps avoid reclamation and, the EPA notes, expensive lawsuits. Areas with acidic soils and/or high rainfall generally need to remove spent lead more frequently.

Hand raking and sifting or screening – Can be performed by club members with leaf rakes and progressively smaller screen from local hardware stores, but can be tedious and time-consuming.

Purchasing or renting mechanical separation machinery – Can be very expensive.

Working with a commercial recycler – Claim to recover 75 - 95 percent of lead in soil by vacuuming, screening (wet or dry), gravity separation, soil washing or pneumatic.

STEP 4: Documenting activities and keeping records. Record number of rounds fired and shot size, methods used, date and providers of services, keep records for the life of the range (including soil pH) plus 10 years and evaluate the effectiveness of steps taken.

"For shotgun ranges, tracking the number of targets thrown can help indicate when the lead shot should be reclaimed. For example, considering environmental issues, the market for scrap lead and common cleanup methods, one source indicated that when a range has thrown at least 250,000 to 1,000,000 targets, depending on the shooting area, reclamation of the lead shot is encouraged. Another reclaimer indicated that if at least two pounds of lead per square foot have accumulated on the range, reclamation is recommended."

Build Your Own

Ron Shema is a realtor in Gainesville, Florida. Home to a major research institution, the city has a very liberal political climate. When the only available shooting range was closed to the public, Shema decided to do something about it.

Shema researched area zoning ordinances expecting to build his range in some rural location, but the county had no provision for a target range. City codes, however, included a use-by-right provision for a range under its light industrial zoning category.

"Finding the zoning option was like winning the lotto," he says, "because there was no need for a special use permit, which would have opened the discussion to everyone in the state ... and in this state everyone would have gotten involved. Anyway, all I needed was a site plan."

Then he found a site with no possibility of residential encroachment. ("Lots of ranges get shut down because of that, but we're surrounded by industry and wetlands. With no homes for three miles there are no noise issues.") By following the NRA Range Source Book his plan "skated through" the plan board and city commission.

Shema has sunk almost a half-million dollars into his range. "I lost $10,000 a year for the first six years," he says, "but I have continued to make improvements."

The 50-acre Gainesville Target Range is celebrating its 11th year. Shema has 500 members, an on-site manager and actively promotes the range as a "community asset." Shooting, concealed carry and tactical instruction are available year-round.

"The range is a beautiful park where people can relax and shoot at their leisure," Shema says. "I have a 100-yard rifle range and two 25-yard handgun ranges, and each has covered shooting positions with room for 15 to 20 shooters. I also provide a covered pavilion with restrooms. The range is accessible to people with physical impairments."

The range entrepreneur has also found that people who target-shoot are more financially secure and become good real estate customers. "Everyone who buys or sells real estate through my company gets a one-year free membership. In addition, many of my real estate buyers send family members to obtain professional firearms instruction."

And the wetland? It is protected by 20-foot berms so that no bullets and no shotgun pellets – possible if someone were patterning a new shotgun because there are no clay games at the range – end up in the water.

The new shooting range in Gainesville, Florida distinctly shows the high berms that keep bullets from escaping into the surrounding wetlands. (Photo Ron Shema)

NRA Shooting Range Conferences

The NRA offers Range Development & Operations Conferences at various locations around the U.S. The conferences are five-day industry seminars focusing on fundamental aspects of building and maintaining a shooting facility.

Attendees receive a multidisciplinary perspective on major topics such as:

- Developing business and master plans
- Public hearings and zoning boards
- Environmental and sound
- Insurance
- Lead on outdoor ranges and OSHA lead standards
- Range maintenance
- Range safety

A new mini-industry has sprung up inside the shooting sports within the past 20 years. Companies such as Pennsylvania's SinterFire have been "aggressively developing and testing a wide range of ammunition components to address the growing needs for 'green' (lead free) and frangible (safer) projectiles."

The conference is designed to educate range owners and operators, of both existing and proposed range facilities, to identify potential problems associated with engineering, environmental issues and safety. This information is vital for government agencies, as well as commercial, public, private, school, club and casual ranges, of both indoor and outdoor types.

Presentations are given by range development experts, the ultimate goal being to give attendees a forum to share their knowledge, and ensure the public has a safe and convenient place to shoot in order to exercise their 2nd Amendment rights.

"A key element for advancement in any profession is continuing education," says NRA contact Kara Schlifke. "Today's shooting range operator needs the savvy of a businessman, the wisdom of a firearms enthusiast, and the knowledge of a health and safety professional. It's a lot to ask. The most successful professionals constantly strive to improve their knowledge and expertise by pursuing opportunities to learn from associates and experts."

Among many other questions, conferences discuss the fact that a trap field may distribute shot over four acres. While zones of shotfall from adjacent fields will overlap, each adjacent trap field adds about 1¾ acres to the total shotfall zone. The theoretical shotfall zone of a single skeet field covers about 14 acres, with an additional two acres for each adjacent field.

What the NRA does not mention, but a route which it often follows, is "going political." Backed by the NRA, members of the Florida Legislature passed legislation (SB 1156) by better than 2-1 to the governor to stop government lawsuits against shooting ranges.

"This bill protects shooting ranges, but it also protects the environment," said former NRA president and current board member Marion Hammer. "The law will stop damaging lawsuits by state agencies, protect the Second Amendment rights of law-abiding gun owners, and encourage environmental clean-up of shooting facilities."

SB 1156 prevents government lawsuits as long as ranges make a good faith effort to exercise sound environmental management practices. Government employees who proceed with such a lawsuit in violation of the act will now be charged with a first-degree misdemeanor.

"It was vital to protect these lawful establishments from malicious state agency lawsuits that could ultimately force them out of business," added Hammer. "SB 1156 helps ensure that Florida's firearm ranges will continue to serve law-abiding gun owners."

When your range is threatened, or even when you are in doubt, pull out your biggest gun, and in most cases that will be the NRA.

Insurance Anyone?

Lead leaching into groundwater is pollution and pollution is an "excluded peril" in writing insurance policies for shooting ranges. It isn't that insurance companies and their field agencies are unconcerned about lead, says Heidi Juttner of Sportsman's Insurance Agency[9], just that the expense of defending a lawsuit in court could be astronomical.

"We certainly want folks to be environmentally friendly," Juttner says, "but this is not something that is written into any policy I know of. Because we're endorsed by the Safari Club and by ATA, NSSA and NSCA, and because we have been around for 17 years, we help more than a thousand ranges in the U.S. get insurance.

"In theory, a range or club could buy a policy that includes a pollution clause, but it would be prohibitively expensive."

And the fact that one tenacious lawsuit – not to mention "doing the right thing" – can put most of us out of business fairly quickly even if we are ultimately vindicated and/or our range practices are upheld, is all the more reason to immediately begin or adhere to a program that addresses the possibility of lead contamination.

The author fires a new Mossberg at the shooting range with eye and ear protection in place. Whether or not it is true that anti-shooting, anti-gun activists are using the non-toxic issue to make the shooting sports more difficult and expensive, the author believes the shooting experience will be very different for the coming generation of outdoors people.

It's Not All Bad News

In 2003, six residents near the 45-year old Metacon Gun Club in Simsubury, Connecticut began to complain about noise from the 150-acre facility. Grumbling eventually migrated to discussions of possible zoning violations, noise, pollution and safety.[10]

In response, the 750-member Club vigorously defended itself by reviewing all ordinances with township officials. In addition, the state Dept. of Environmental Protection tested surface and ground water on the club's property finding that shooting at the club was not a source of pollution; neither had it had any problem in the 40 years of its existence.

In a letter to Connecticut Attorney General Richard Blumenthal, DEP Commissioner Arthur Rocque, Jr. stated that the Metacon Gun Club "operates at all times under strict safety rules that are specifically designed to prevent the occurrence of accidents, therefore I have no reason to believe that continued operation of the range represents any unreasonable threat to the safety of visitors of Talcott Mountain State Park."

The Club even hired safety consultants from the U.S. Army National Guard who reported that the Metacon Gun Club was one of the safest facilities in all of New England. In addition, the Club is adjacent to the State Police shooting range – which the homeowners did not complain about.

Homeowners next argued that the Gun Club was a safety threat. In an effort to mediate the dispute, the town of Simsbury hired NRA consultant and Florida-based engineer Clark Vargas to make an analysis, paying him a scant $2,780 to review the site and make a report. Vargas' September report recommended erecting several walls and buffers around the perimeter to allay fears that a stray bullet might hit someone on the nearby golf course or hiking trail even though nothing like that had ever happened before.

The Club proceeded immediately to implement Vargas' recommendations for the additional safety barriers. Nevertheless T.J. Morelli-Wolfe, attorney for the homeowners, stated publicly that design and safety experts simply liked guns. The complaining homeowners were not satisfied.

Vargas replied that groups which sue to close gun ranges typically begin with noise. If they are not heard, i.e. their objections are dismissed, they move on to safety and environmental threats. No matter what a club does to mitigate any situation, it is almost always insufficient for the complainers.

In May 2004, homeowners and former Club member Gregory Silpe filed a lawsuit which became Simsbury-Avon Preservation Society, LLC, et al. v. Metacon Gun Club, Inc. Five days later the homeowners incorporated as the Simsbury-Avon Protection Society LLC. Their argument was essentially that the Club was an unrepentant polluter. This time lawsuits leaned on the Clean Water Act and the Resource Conservation and Recovery Act.

Plaintiffs argued that there was a "tremendous amount of spent ammunition on the ground" – it was right there for everyone to see, they said – whereas gun club defendants countered that for 10 years members had raked the range to clean up spent casings, wads and other related materials.

The club dumped "thousands of pounds of lead" and other ammunition-related pollutants into the surrounding area by firing "large and small firearms, including shotguns, assault rifles and anti-tank guns at the site." Further, the six residents claimed, Metacon did not have a pollution permit. Homeowners wanted firing halted and penalties of $25,000 for every violation.

Supporting the homeowners' association – apparently without checking the facts or conducting any meaningful tests of their own – were such environmental luminaries as the National Wildlife Federation, Connecticut Fund for the Environment, Conservation Law Foundation, Environmental Advocates of New York, Farmington River Watershed Association, Natural Resources Defense Council, Rivers Alliance of Connecticut, Sierra Club and Vermont Natural Resources Council.

A Federal court upheld the EPA ruling that spent ammo is not waste product until a shooting range is abandoned.

Made from iron, tungsten and tin, Nice Shot is U.S. FWS approved. It is dense and pliable with a close physical resemblance to lead without the toxicity. Because it contains a trace of iron, it is also magnetic. It works like lead but performs much better, say the reloading experts at Precision Reloading in South Dakota. (Photo Alex Papp, RST)

"This is pure harassment," said Dennis Golden, the Club's chair of Safety and Education. The Club was going to fight and hired its own lawyers.

"The homeowners want to shut us down, period," Golden said. "We suspect that there are other agendas at work here that we might not be aware of."

In 2004, the Club was forced to hire an independent consultant to test a nearby stream and underground waters for lead pollution. The resulting April 2004 report found that "the ground water beneath the shooting range has not been impacted by lead from the shooting range," and that, with respect to wetland surface water, "the dissolved lead findings demonstrate that lead is not leaching out of the soil or surface water to contaminate the surface water." The homeowners hired their own expert and disputed the findings.

In July 2004, after the litigation commenced, Metacon adopted an Environmental Stewardship Plan. It provided for the annual raking of the range and screening of debris to recover bullets and fragments, as well as the use of "vacuuming machinery rather than hand-raking, and mechanical separation machinery in place of hand screening." The plan also provided for the mining of the berm to remove spent lead in the year 2024.

By September 2005, Metacon's attorney, Martha Dean, reported winning two small but promising victories. In July, a federal court upheld the EPA ruling that spent ammo is not waste product until a shooting range is abandoned. And in September, a state court ruled that the homeowners were not entitled to injunctive relief which would have otherwise halted range operations immediately.

In 2007, a state court ruled that Connecticut law provided Metacon immunity against noise complaints.

On March 13, 2008, the Connecticut Superior Court said that the homeowners' evidence against Metacon was "scant" and held that the environmental arguments were unfounded. Thus all of the lawsuits brought by the homeowners during a five-year period were decided in the gun club's favor. The homeowners continued to appeal each court ruling.

Upon satisfaction of the 2008 ruling, documents obtained from Connecticut's Dept. of Public Safety under the Freedom of Information Act revealed that several members of the homeowners' association probably expected a financial return from real estate opportunities if they could close the Club. The final disposition in the U.S. Court of Appeals for the Second Circuit was not decided until July 31, 2009.

CHAPTER NOTES

1. These scientific and peer reviewed articles and others can be found on www.spring-erlink.com and www3.interscience.wiley.com.

a. The Japanese study "Lead levels in ancient and contemporary Japanese bones" was published in *Biological Trace Element Research* (V. 16, #1, June 1988) written by members of the Dept. of Hygiene, Faculty of Medicine, Kyushu University (Akira Hisanaga, Miyuki Hirata and Noruru Ishinishi) and by Yukuo Eguchi of the Dept. of Public Health, Kokura-kita Health Center in Kitakyushu City. It incidentally found that lead levels in ancient women were higher than those of men and researchers assumed that the cause was facial cosmetics.

b. The study done in the Canary Islands "Bone lead in the prehistoric population of Gran Canaria" was published in the *American Journal of Human Biology* (V. 11, #3, April 16, 1999: on-line) written by Tenerife staff of the Departamento de Medicina Interna, Hospital Universitario de Canarias (E. Gonzalez-Reimers and F. Santolaria-Fernandez), Dpto. de Prehistoria, Antropología e Historia Antigua, Universidad de La Laguna (M. Arnay-De-la-Rosa and J. Velasco-Vazquez) and the Dpto. de Química Analítica, Universidad de La Laguna (L. Galindo-Martin and E. Delgado-Ureta). It incidentally found that lead levels were higher in older than in younger individuals, but only in the modern group.

2. The Connecticut case is summarized in the 1993 George Mason University Law Review, signed by James Kozlowski http://classweb.gmu.edu/jkozlows/lawarts/08AUG93.pdf.

3. "A Proactive Approach To Environmental Stewardship Could Save Your Range From Disaster" writes Richard Peddicord, Ph.D for the National Association of Shooting Ranges, a division of NSSF.

4. The case Long Island Soundkeeper Fund, Inc. v. New York Athletic Club can be read in full at the EPA web site: www.epa.gov/Region2/waste/leadshot/lisfnyac.htm. Aside from legal interpretations and findings of standing and pollution, this case also indicates that in America, any miserable pedant with sufficient resources can bring any project or activity – including your shooting range and the legal activities thereon – to a screeching halt if you are not aware and do not prepare.

5. Joe Meyer, Columbia Tribune, May 4, 2008 "Gun club suit triggers firing range measure" http://archive.columbiatribune.com/2008/may/20080504news004.asp

6. ANZECC stands for Australia and New Zealand Environment and Conservation Council. Dr. Rooney's study can be read in its entirety at www.lead.org.au/fs/shootingranges.pdf.

7. A Material Safety Data Sheet (MSDS) is a document that provides information about a given chemical product, in this case composition of a bullet. An MSDS includes the name, composition (chemicals in the product), hazards, first aid measures, fire fighting measures, information regarding the proper steps to take with spills, handling and storage, personal protection to be used, physical and chemical properties, and information about stability and reactivity, toxicology, disposal, transporting and regulatory requirements.

8. The EPA has a document called a BMP (Best Management Practice) specifically for outdoor shooting range owners. This manual is called *Best Management Practices for Lead at Outdoor Shooting Ranges* (rev. June 2005) and it can be downloaded from the Internet (alternatively, a paper copy can be ordered) at www.epa.gov/region2/waste/leadshot/download.htm.

A BMP is a recommended site management and/or maintenance activity, usually based on an approach that has been shown to work effectively. It is based on use of readily available equipment and/or technology. For outdoor shooting ranges BMPs are practices that range owners/operators can use to minimize the impact of lead on the environment.

9. Sportsman's Insurance Agency, Ormond Beach, Florida www.siai.net.

10. For a complete review of the Metacon story: www.ctsportsmen.com/issues/metacon_gun_club.htm.

Internet sites for companies mentioned in the text are: Gainesville Target Range www.gainesvilletargetrange.com, Metacon Gun Club www.metacongunclub.com, NRA Range Source Book www.nrahq.org/shootingrange, Remington www.remington.com and SinterFire www.sinterfire.com.

CHAPTER 10

INDOOR SHOOTING AND LEAD IN THE AIR

"**T**he firing of small arms ammunition for training, sport, law enforcement, and military purposes is a major source of environmental pollution. The lead from shot and bullets is a significant environmental and health problem at numerous public, private and government-operated shooting ranges. Many sites are contaminated with hundreds of tons of lead, the result of years of shooting and target practice. Lead is tainting grounds and water, and is being ingested by wildlife, and has thus become a serious threat to the health and safety of human and animal populations.

Shooting indoors has become more expensive because it is evident that lead dust and heavy metal fumes from the explosion of primers must be carefully controlled to keep range employees healthy.

"Indoor ranges pose other serious concerns such as increased lead exposure to the shooter due to the enclosed space and the subsequent need for high capacity ventilation and air filtration systems. Handling of ammunition and contaminated weapons can also produce elevated lead levels in the blood by absorption through the skin."[1]

The Indoor Equation

Thousands of independent indoor shooting ranges – 16,000 to 18,000 according to NIOSH, a division of CDC – offer gun owners an opportunity to enjoy shooting. Participants compete in leagues, train for live situations, practice for home or personal defense and just enjoy the thrill of shooting.[2]

Indoor shooting is of course a much different situation from shotgun clay games out-of-doors, or handgun and long-range rifle shooting outdoors. Whereas outdoors the problems with spent lead are wildlife poisoning and contamination of the aquifer, the indoor problems are related to breathing particles suspended in the air and maybe to handling and ingesting lead dust.

Still, clay shooters and manufacturers have become environmentally sensitive, perhaps because of the '70s emergence of the lead shot/waterfowl issue. Realizing the sensitivity of the issues facing gun clubs and shooting ranges, White Flyer for instance developed their biodegradable Bio line. These targets, the company says, are 95 percent degradable into elements found in nature within two years, depending on rainfall and moisture levels.

Nevertheless, over time, White Flyer notes, "the by-products of the degradation can affect soil Ph and vegetation growth. In high volume target areas, adverse soil impact can be avoided by raking up target residue on a monthly basis or by adding agricultural limestone to the soil if the Ph decreases abnormally. Soil PH in high volume target areas should be checked bi-annually." Other products are in the patent and production stage right now.

It may not be so easy indoors. Although the source of airborne lead inside a range seems obvious – a bullet hitting a target – this may not necessarily be the case. The primary source of airborne impurities is the explosion of a bullet's primer.

A cartridge primer is a small copper or brass cup containing a precise amount of stable but shock-sensitive explosive mixture, with ingredients such as:

• Mercury(II) fulminate – Used since the early 1800s in percussion caps for black powder shooting, this primary explosive is highly sensitive to friction and shock. Thus it is used to trigger secondary, but more powerful explosives. Although potassium chlorate is sometimes used in its place, the mercury(II) fulminate is less corrosive, but may weaken with time. Today it is usually replaced with materials that are non-corrosive, less toxic and more stable over time: lead azide, lead styphnate and tetrazene derivatives. It also causes brass to become brittle; a concern for reloaders.

- Tetracene – Winchester's MSDS says tetracene is an explosive, slightly more impact-sensitive than mercury fulminate.

- Lead azide – Also used as a primary detonator, lead azide is a highly sensitive inorganic compound that is usually handled and stored under water in insulated rubber containers. It will explode after a fall of around six inches or in the presence of a static charge. A related compound, copper azide, is even more explosive and considered too sensitive to be used commercially.

- Potassium perchlorate – A colorless, crystalline powder, potassium perchlorate is a common oxidizer in fireworks and sparklers. It has been even been used as a solid rocket fuel. Mixtures containing potassium chlorate or potassium perchlorate decompose leaving potassium chloride deposits as a by-product and necessitate frequent cleaning.

- Diazodinitrophenol – Abbreviated as DDNP, it is less sensitive to impact but more powerful than mercury fulminate and lead azide. It is used with other materials to form priming mixtures, particularly where a high sensitivity to flame or heat is desired. DDNP is used as an initiating explosive to substitute for lead styphnate in non-toxic primers.

- Lead styphnate – This chemical is sensitive to fire and static electricity, but less sensitive to shock and friction than mercury fulminate or lead azide. With other metals, it is non-reactive. The OSHA regulatory status of lead styphnate is: "Explosive, skin and eye irritant; lung, kidney, nervous system, blood and reproductive toxin; toxic, carcinogen."

A variety of traditional primers from CCI. The primer's explosion starts the chain reaction that puts dinner on the table, but all primers are not the same and specific primers are required for specific powder/bullet combinations. Traditional primers contain small amounts of heavy metals which, in a poorly ventilated range, can quickly become toxic and are always present in the air near a shooter's face.

When they explode to ignite the powder inside a cartridge, these chemicals produce traces of lead and other toxins such as a vapor or soot of mercury in the air of a shooting range. Although primers are sealed and are very small, typically .175 and .210 inches in diameter for handgun and rifle cartridges, the ingredients inside the primer are fragile and powerful for their volume, and highly toxic as well. Outside they readily dissipate, but inside the closed environment of an indoor shooting range, they are trapped unless precautions are taken.

A so-called "corrosive primer" uses stable, long-lived explosives that generate corrosive residues inside a gun barrel. These are usually metallic oxides that absorb water and form hydroxides even when exposed to moisture in the atmosphere; this causes quick rusting. Although it seems that "for obvious reasons" they would be on the way out, they are popular in military and some police applications because they work reliably under severe conditions.

The "non-corrosive primer" has a reputation for being somewhat less reliable especially when stored for a couple years, but they are far easier on guns because they leave behind less gunk. Today, most civilian ammunition uses non-corrosive primers. (Winchester's Super Clean NT (non-toxic) Tin in 5.56 has a 55-gr. jacketed soft point tin core. It of course "shoots and performs like lead, delivering superior accuracy and gun function. Ideal for situations where no down range lead is permitted.")

Without an up-to-date environmental plan, shooting range owners may find that negative air-flow and a lack of proper ventilation in and around the building circulates contaminated air into offices, restrooms and break areas. This can be not only a source of legal trouble, but a certain health hazard as well.

Sample Primers and Their Contents in Common Usage

Manufacturer	Primer	Ingredients	Physical Hazards
CCI-Speer	#525 Small Pistol Competition	Lead styphnate*, barium nitrate*, antimony sulfide, copper, zinc	Skin and eye hazard; reproductive, blood, nervous system and kidney toxin
CCI-Speer	#209M Shotshell Primer	Lead styphnate*, barium nitrate*, antimony sulfide, aluminum, tetracene, copper, nickel, zinc, zinc compounds	Skin and eye hazard; reproductive, blood, nervous system and kidney toxin
CCI-Speer	Rifle-Pistol – Clean Fire	Copper, zinc, DDNP, strontium nitrate, nitrocellulose, nickel	Skin and eye hazard
CCI-Speer	Rifle-Pistol – Lead-Free	Copper, zinc, DDNP, nitrocellulose, barium nitrate, nickel	Skin, eye and lung hazard
Olin-Winchester	Centerfire	Copper, zinc, lead styphnate*, barium nitrate*, antimony sulfide, lead thiocyanate	Eye and lung hazard; "It is unlikely that the amount of particles that someone would be exposed to from firing would be sufficient to cause any of these effects."
Olin-Winchester	Chlorate Base	Copper, zinc, potassium chlorate, lead thiocyanate*, paper, calcium silicide, barium nitrate*, glass powder	"It is unlikely that the amount of particles that someone would be exposed to from firing would be sufficient to cause any of these effects."
Olin-Winchester	Electric	Copper, zinc, lead styphnate* (normal and basic), barium nitrate*, polyvinyl chloride, antimony sulfide, calcium silicide	"It is unlikely that the amount of particles that someone would be exposed to from firing would be sufficient to cause any of these effects."
Olin-Winchester	Reduced Hazard Shotshell	Iron, copper, zinc, DDNP, bismuth sub-nitrate	"It is unlikely that the amount of particles that someone would be exposed to from firing would be sufficient to cause any of these effects."
Remington	Component – Electrically Initiated	Copper, zinc, barium, antimony, lead styphnate*, lead trinitroresorcinate*, aluminum	Skin, eye and lung hazard

* Indicates toxic chemical(s) subject to the reporting requirements of Section 313 of the Superfund Amendments and Reauthorization Act (SARA) of 1986 and 40 CFR 372.

Information from manufacturer Material Safety Data Sheets. Winchester explains the MSDS at www.winchester.com/SiteCollectionDocuments/pdf/msds/MSDSExplanationSheet.pdf.

Lead-free primers have been available for about a dozen years. They address concerns over the lead and other heavy-metal compounds found in older primers. Original lead-free primers were less sensitive, but had a greater susceptibility to moisture and correspondingly shorter shelf life than traditional non-corrosive primers.

When reloading, you must be careful to avoid inhaling fine dust from new or certainly from used primers. When reloading traditional primers, any yellow dust you might find in the priming station is a toxic lead compound. Clean the effected parts with a disposable towel dampened with a good cleaner. Don't use compressed gas to blow off the dust as it will become airborne where it can be inhaled, and will then settle back as a contaminant.

The primer chemicals are not alone in toxic compound deposition however. Microscopic lead and copper particles are also scraped off the bullet as it races through the gun barrel, and are propelled out the muzzle by the force of the burning powder. RSI (Recreational Software, Inc.) notes all barrels and all ammos foul and that copper residue especially, from copper jacketed rounds, is cumulative. Fouling accumulates and tears at the base of a bullet jacket, scarring it as it rushes down the barrel, and the more you shoot, the more dust and fouling is left inside the gun and blown into the air.

Plus, a bullet striking a steel target usually breaks or intentionally shatters. All of these things put lead dust in the air. Hence the frangible and non-toxic direction of bullet manufacture the last dozen years. Indoors the requirement for bullets is to mark a target clearly but to never bounce back or shatter in such a way that a shooter or spectator might be injured. Thus manufacturers of new RRLF (reduced recoil, lead free) bullets show photos or videos on their web sites of shooters standing just feet from steel targets and firing safely (with ballistic eye protection and hearing protection in place, of course). ICC has even posted a photograph of a law enforcement officer injured on the forearm by bounce-back from a bullet fragment from a non-frangible round.

Studies have shown...

But can a toxic incident happen here, and now, to you at your range?

Although the study "Result of Poor Ventilation in an Indoor Pistol Range" by Philip Landrigan, M.D. and others is dated 1975, it discussed three cases of mild lead poisoning among instructors at an indoor pistol range.[3a] "These cases were characterized by blood lead levels greater than 100µg/100 ml, free erythrocyte protoporphyrin levels greater than 450µg/100 ml of red blood cells, abdominal pain, and, in one instance, by slowing of motor and sensory nerve conduction velocity. Exposure to airborne lead produced during revolver-firing and bullet-molding accounted for the lead absorption. Ventilation in the range was inadequate."

NIOSH RECOMMENDS...

Proper ventilation, good housekeeping and basic personal hygiene will limit the risk of lead exposure. Examples of NIOSH recommendations for workers include the following:

• Wear respirators and full protective outer clothing when performing range maintenance.

• Wear gloves and eye protection when using chemicals to clean weapons or firing range surfaces.

• Wash your hands, forearms and face before eating, drinking, smoking or coming into contact (shaking hands, for instance) with others.

• Change clothes and shoes before leaving the firing range facilities.

• Wash clothes or uniforms from the firing range separately from your family's clothing.

A more recent study in 1989 by R.K. Tripathi and others for the Bureau of Toxic Substances, Virginia Dept. of Health[3b] wrote: "Significant overexposures to airborne lead were found in a covered, outdoor firing range among seven cadets during firing of conventional, non-jacketed, lead bullets." The investigators sampled air in "personal breathing zones" and air as far as 50 yards from the firing line. They found that air samples exceeded OSHA standards for occupational exposure to airborne lead (which was 50µg/m3) and that blood lead levels increased in all cadets after day two of shooting. None of the blood level values exceed the OSHA standard of 40 µg/dl however. "Based on environmental and medical data, it was concluded that a potential health hazard may exist due to inorganic lead exposure to cadets at this covered outdoor range during firing exercises."

The most recent study is from Germany. A 2008/2009 study in the International Archives of Occupational and Environmental Health[3c] said that "Recreational shooting in indoor firing ranges is very popular in Germany. Lead-containing ammunition is still in use. Therefore we checked the blood lead levels (BLL) from 129 subjects doing several types of shooting disciplines.

"Our results show clearly that many shooters have high blood levels; some of them are still exceeding threshold limit values for lead exposed workers. Especially for younger women there is a high potential risk if they become pregnant. So there is a clear need for improving the situation whether by use of lead-free ammunition or by better ventilation systems."

The study evaluated blood levels of 129 shooters (nine were women) from 11 different shooting ranges with a mean age of 49 years. Interestingly, median blood lead levels rose with caliber of gun: from airguns (33 µg/l) to .22 LR (87 µg/l) to large caliber handguns (100 µg/l). Eleven members of an IPSC shooting group had the highest median with 192 µg/l.

So, about reloading....

Other than breathing air with contaminants, there are other ways that one can develop a reaction to toxins in shooting ranges. If your range has its own reloading stations (perhaps including bullet casting, where molten lead is poured into molds), this will also be a potential source of lead or other toxic contamination. Melting lead produces a fume which can remain airborne for several hours, is easily inhaled and can contaminate surfaces.

The problem with handling lead bullets is that lead is dense, but soft. Any fisherman who has crushed a lead sinker with his or her teeth to tighten it around monofilament line knows that lead can be scratched and even scraped or flaked with a knife or pliers or sandpaper.

We suspect that lead may be a carcinogen and know that the cumulative toxic effects will make you sterile and brain dead – though not quickly. Just washing your hands right after reloading or handling lead, say the folks at Tacticool Products, and before eating or drinking, immensely reduces your exposure. With proper handling and good ventilation, casting your own bullets and reloading cartridges are absolutely safe.

The most common cause of lead poisoning is from swallowing lead. Lead oxidizes on its surface this soft toxin can transfer to your fingers. It can then be ingested when you eat, drink, smoke or place any item into your mouth such as chewing gum or chewing tobacco. It can be absorbed quickly if you rub your eyes or replace contact lenses. It can be transferred person-to-person when you shake hands or kiss; or from your clothing when you brush past in the hallway or give someone a hug.

The most common way to protect yourself is to wash your hands thoroughly with soap after handling lead or lead products. You can always wear latex or nitrile gloves when handling lead (many people have latex allergies, but options are readily available).

Because lead fumes are toxic it's a good idea to cast bullets outside and, if there is a breeze, even recognizing that moving air will swirl, to sit on the upwind side. Why contaminate the workshop with lead smoke and residue which, if undisturbed, can persist for years – maybe forever. Experienced reloaders suggest covering work surfaces with heavy duty aluminum foil before casting and once a session is over, carefully rolling up the aluminum foil with the lead contaminates inside – were you to run a slightly damp paper towel across the surface you might see a gray film, just what you want to avoid – and throw it away.

Keep the temperature on the lead pot as low as possible. Lead melts at 621 degrees F. When the temperature climbs toward 900, significant amounts begin to evaporate. Lead vapor quickly forms a fine lead oxide powder and can be inhaled.

It isn't a bad idea to wear a mask – something as insignificant as a dust mask helps – while casting and especially while clearing and disposing of the dross.

After casting lead, it's an excellent idea to shower thoroughly, especially washing your hair, and to wash your clothes separately from other clothes. Most people don't think about lead contamination when cleaning brass, but when using a tumbler remember that the inside of the case and particularly the inside of the spent primer contain lead compounds. Tumble cleaning removes these particles, but they remain in the cleaning media. They can become airborne and thus inhaled when sifting brass to separate it from the cleaning media. They can also settle on adjacent surfaces and concentrate there as contaminants.

Placing a used dryer sheet in the vibratory cleaning media helps collect the fine black dust that's generated during vibratory bowl cleaning. This not only helps prevent lead contamination, but cleaning media lasts longer, too. Still, when the cleaning media starts to become gray, replace it. Don't sift brass through an open colander to separate the cleaning media. Use a covered rotating basket style separator and always keep the lid closed while the basket is spinning. Keeping the lid closed for a minute after rotating allows the dust to settle. Clean the area around the tumbler and media separator after every use, by spraying a cleaner on the surface and wiping the damp surfaces with a paper towel. Be careful not to stir up the dust and allow it to circulate in the air.

Old timers, those who have been reloading for years, need to be careful for their children and grandchildren. Certainly, teach them the techniques of reloading, but the best strategy to avoid lead poisoning is consistent attention to maintaining a clean workplace and following some simple hygiene practices. Show them how to live a healthy life by doing the right thing.

Remember that lead poisoning is cumulative, so any reduction in lead intake helps prevent lead poisoning. The human body has a normal blood lead level

This NRA instructor is coaching a young shooter in the fundamentals of safety as well as the techniques of shooting. Unfortunately, an exploding primer – even in a .22 – can emit highly toxic fumes. Lead and other heavy metals are cumulative in the human body and, although poisoning can be reversed (blood lead levels decline when the source is removed) if caught in time, the effects can be terribly debilitating and in children can be permanent. (Photo NRA)

of about five ug/dl. The CDC recognizes that a level of 10 ug/dl is the early stage of lead poisoning and anything above 20 ug/dl requires immediate chemical cleaning of any contaminated environment or getting away from it. At 40 ug/dl, you need to see a doctor and consider chelation treatment.[4]

NIOSH and Your Right to Clean Air

Indoor shooting ranges can pose a health risk if they do not provide adequate ventilation. The ventilation system should positively draw air, fumes and ash from the shooter toward the target, where it can be vented outside, or filtered using a method that removes impurities. If you have a sore throat after shooting or you have a lot of congestion the next 48 hours with black or gray phlegm, consider that the ventilation is not adequate, and both talk to the owner of the shooting range and stop shooting there until the problem is corrected.

Obviously, the greatest risk is to those instructors and employees who are present in a range for long periods of time. Even a decade ago, the risk of cleaning filters and sweeping up lead and standing at the line for hours assisting shooters was poorly understood … and not well accepted. That has changed.

A 2009 report from NIOSH, the National Institute for Occupational Safety and Health, a part of the CDC, contains findings and recommendations to alleviate workplace problems with toxic air (and noise!) inside shooting ranges. The document says that employers should:

- provide sufficient information to shooters and employees to understand the problems,
- establish effective engineering and administrative controls,
- provide adequate personal protective equipment, and
- provide for health and medical monitoring.

How many shooters are there in the U.S.?

- 105,000 federal law enforcement of¬ficers (Dept. of Justice)
- more than 1 million state and lo¬cal police officers (Dept of Justice)
- 20 million active target shooters (NSSF) (13.8 million rifle, 10.7 million handgun)

Of course all of the law enforcement personnel are required to train regularly and remain proficient in the use of firearms.

NIOSH cites five lead and noise case studies.

Case 1[5a]: Members of the Colorado Department of Health conducted a study between February and April 1987 to determine lead exposure risk. In this study, 17 police trainees were studied for three months – prior to, during and after – firearms instruction at an indoor range. They found:

In one case study of law enforcement trainees described in a recent NIOSH Alert, blood lead levels at an indoor firing range rose from a pre-training mean of 6.5 µg/dl to 50.4 µg/dl post training. Mean airborne lead concentrations were more than 40 times the OSHA permissible exposure limit. After changes were made to the ventilation system, airborne lead concentrations dropped below detectable levels. In addition, using ammunition that had nylon-coated and copper-jacketed bullets substantially reduced (94 – 97 percent) airborne lead concentrations. (Photo CDC)

- Blood lead level rose from a pre-training mean of 6.5 to 50.4 µg/dL post training.

- Mean airborne lead concentrations were greater than 2,000 µg/m3, more than 40 times the OSHA PEL (permissible exposure limit) of 50 µg/m3.

During the study, two changes were made to the ventilation system.

- The first corrected a positive pres¬sure situation inside the range that had allowed lead-contaminated air to flow from the range into other parts of the building whenever the range door was opened.

- The second change consisted of placing fins on the air supply grille to cause smoother air flow across the firing line and to decrease air turbulence.

- Adjustments resulted in:

- A large decrease of airborne lead concentrations, depending on firing station.

- Airborne lead concentrations dropped to below detectable levels in the control room and classroom after the first adjustment.

- Airborne lead concentrations were reduced substantially (94 to 97 percent) by using ammunition that had nylon-coated and copper-jacketed bullets.

Controlling exposure is the best method of protecting range workers and shooters. Generally this means elimination of the hazard, substitution of a less hazardous material, engineering controls, administrative controls (to reduce time of exposure) and personal protective equipment. (Photo TSI Security)

Case 2[5b]: In 2002, Alaska's Division of Public Health, Epidemiology Section conducted an intensive study of blood lead levels in school-sponsored rifle teams after a team coach was found to have an elevated BLL of 44 µg/dl. They reviewed six rifle teams at three indoor firing ranges. Participating were 36 students and 35 adults (including family members and six coaches).

Two teams used a firing range with regularly scheduled cleaning procedures and had a written protocol for maintenance and lead concentration monitoring. Blood lead levels for those two teams were not elevated: 1.3 µg/dl and 3.9 µg/dl.

One team used a firing range/multi-use area that for 11 years had not been evaluated for lead. Student shooters showed small but measurable lead exposure with a mean of 8.1 µg/dl.

The other three teams used a firing range that had extensive lead contamination. These teams had blood lead levels of 27.9 µg/dl, 12.0 µg/dl and 12.2 µg/dl. Coaches of these teams had blood lead levels of 12.4 µg/dl. This firing range was voluntarily closed and arrangements were made for a thorough environmental evaluation.

"Following removal from a lead exposure source," Alaska's epidemiology specialists wrote, "blood lead levels should decrease by one-half within 25 to 30 days."

CASE 3[5c]: In 1997, NIOSH inspectors Joshua Harney and Michael Barsan conducted an inspection for the Forest Park (Ohio) Police Dept. They studied the department's five-booth indoor firing range to examine potential exposure to lead among the 30 police officers who used the firing range for training and firearms qualification. The firing range, which was located in a police department building, was used by other area police departments as well.

NIOSH inspectors found the following:

- The firing range ventilation system was independent of the rest of the building.

- Most of the range's exhaust air was re-circulated through 90- to 95-percent efficient filters before being directed back into the firing range.

- Users cleaned the firing range by dry sweeping and collecting shell casings from the floor by hand.

- The bullet trap was cleaned every 2-3 years.

- The firing range was under positive air-flow pressure; the smell of gun smoke increased noticeably when firing started.

- Air-flow rates were much lower than designed and yielded an average air velocity of 25 fpm at the firing line.

- Pressure gauges on the HVAC system were not working properly. Smoke tests revealed backflow patterns even when no one was at the firing line.

The operations led to the following conditions:

- Average airborne lead concentrations were an extraordinary 144 µg/m3 and 230 µg/m3 on two separate survey dates.

- Lead was found in the control room, in a hallway outside the firing range and at the rooftop air handling unit.

- Several filters were missing from the HVAC system, but were in place for the second survey.

An indoor shooting range used by the Indo-Tibetan Border Police illustrates some of the international difficulties faced by the green shooting movement: shooting into sandbags with no bullet trap, inadequate ventilation can be inferred from the broken gratings, no apparent vision or hearing protection and we can only hope that no one comes through the door at right while the line is hot. (Photo ITBP)

As a result, NIOSH recommended:

- changes in the ventilation system,

- a range standard operating procedure for maintenance,

- improved clean-up and personal hygiene practices,

- a written respiratory protection program,

- ammunition substitution, and

- blood lead level monitoring.

Detailed recommendations for employers and for workers are presented in the NIOSH report. Controlling exposure is the best method of protecting range workers and shooters. Generally this means elimination of the hazard, substitution of a less hazardous material, engineering controls, administrative controls (to reduce time of exposure) and personal protective equipment.

Proper ventilation, good housekeeping and basic personal hygiene will limit the risk of lead exposure. Examples of NIOSH recommendations for workers include the following:

- Wear respirators and full protective outer clothing when performing range maintenance.

- Wear gloves and eye protection when using chemicals to clean weapons or firing range surfaces.

- Wash your hands, forearms and face before eating, drinking, smoking or coming into contact (shaking hands, for instance) with others.

- Change clothes and shoes before leaving the firing range facilities.

- Wash clothes or uniforms from the firing range separately from your family's clothing.

Help is On The Way

The NRA manual titled The NRA Source Book: A Guide to Planning and Construction provides basic and advanced guidance to assist in planning, designing, constructing and maintaining shooting range facilities [NRA 1999].

Perhaps the first place to turn for range management of toxic substances is the National Association of Shooting Ranges (NASR), a division of NSSF. It has developed a manual titled Lead Management and OSHA Compliance for Indoor Shooting Ranges [NASR 2004]. Developed in partnership with OSHA and NIOSH, this manual addresses the potential of lead exposure at firing ranges and presents methods for managing exposures as well as compliance with the OSHA lead standard [29 CFR 1910.1025].

Cold Welding and Bullets at Oak Ridge National Laboratory

Scientists and engineers at the U.S. Dept. of Energy's Oak Ridge National Laboratory in Tennessee have worked on the issue of non-toxic, all-metal replacements for lead in bullets using a process called "cold welding." In this process, metals are ground into powders and then mixed together at room temperature. Finally, once the composition is right for the intended purpose, the powder is pressed into a mold and jacketed.

Cold welding allows bullets to be built in custom sizes, weights and densities; it lets bullets in theory be developed for exact situations and performance (though in practice when a gun is drawn there will almost never be enough time to think about which bullet would work best in the situation).

Heavy tungsten, for instance, can be mixed with different amounts of tin to make bullets that are either highly frangible or very dense and almost unbreakable. And thus, the search for true frangible bullets – fast, hard-hitting, but that will not penetrate several layers of sheetrock or

bounce off sidewalks and brick walls to kill or injure innocent bystanders, thus giving work to attorneys and fodder for the anti-gun, anti-hunting press – coincides almost perfectly with the search for effective green or eco-friendly bullets.

The work done at Oak Ridge developed over more than a decade and results with powdered-metal replacements for lead have gradually filtered into the commercial world. Today there is plenty of ammo based on non-lead bullets and even some with fully non-toxic primers. One of the tricks is to adjust the powder weight and style so that velocity and chamber pressures are safe and yet sufficient. The Oak Ridge scientists felt that their new bullet performance was consistent with performance of lead-based ammo.

Oak Ridge was a member of the Interagency Working Group for Non-Toxic Small Arms Ammunition, the Dept. of Defense "Green Bullet" team. They found a non-lead bullet material composed of tin and tungsten to be "the leading candidate for use in military ammunition." Eventually, tens of thousands of rounds were tested by independent contractors and the military with good ballistic results and a million rounds were acquired in the second step of the testing process in 1999-2000.

At the time, the Green Bullet team anticipated that the procurement system would generate significant orders, but subsequent findings indicated that the tungsten could leach into an area's drinking water and soon enough emerge into the public water supply. Procurement was halted until scientific studies could determine the effects and consequences of leached tungsten.

The Oak Ridge National Laboratory is managed by the University of Tennessee-Battelle for the U.S. Dept. of Energy.

CHAPTER NOTES

1. www.ms.ornl.gov/researchgroups/SPM/methods/powder/NTammo/Ntammo.htm

2. NIOSH (National Institute for Occupational Safety and Health) Science Blog "Take Aim At Protecting Yourself" www.cdc.gov/niosh/blog/nsb051809_firingrange.html.

3. Studies have shown:

a. Journal of the American Medical Assn. (Vol. 234, No. 4: October 27, 1975) by CDC members (Philip J. Landrigan, MD; Wallace W. Rhodes, Jr, PE; Dennis H. Cox, PhD), Emory University (Alexander S. McKinney, MD; Linton C. Hopkins, MD); and DeKalb County (William A. Price) http://jama.ama-assn.org/cgi/content/abstract/234/4/394

b. International Journal of Toxicology (Vol. 6, No. 6: 1989) by employees of the Bureau of Toxic Substances, Virginia Dept. of Health (R. K. Tripathi, P. C. Sherertz, G. C. Llewellyn, C. W. Armstrong and L. Ramsey) http://ijt.sagepub.com/cgi/content/abstract/8/6/1189

c. International Archives of Occupational and Environmental Health (Vol. 82, No. 4: March 2009) Investigators Matthias Demmeler, Dennis Nowak and Rudolf Schierl for the Institute for the Occupational, Social and Environmental Medicine, University Munich, Munich, Germany.

4. A controversial medical practice, chelation therapy is designed to remove heavy metals like lead and mercury from the human body. Typically, a chemical called dimercaptosuccinic acid (DMSA) is used. DMSA or another chosen agent is be administered intravenously, intramuscularly or orally, depending on the agent and the type of poisoning. DMSA binds to heavy metals in the body and prevents them from binding to other agents. They are then excreted from the body. Some physicians have tried to extend chelation therapy far beyond its obvious ability to do good, claiming that it has benefits for autistic children and in the treatment of heart disease so beware of frauds using proven techniques in unacceptable situations.

5. The NIOSH report is Publication Number 2009-136 and dated April 2009. It can be viewed on line at www.cdc.gov/niosh/docs/2009-136/pdfs/2009-136.pdf.

a. Case 1: *American Journal of Public Health* 79(8): 1029–1032 August 1989 (Valway, Martyny, Miller, Cook and Mangione).

b. Case 2: Alaska Dept. of Health and Social Services, Epidemiology Bulletin 1 John Middaugh, MD, Editor January 9, 2003: www.epi.alaska.gov/bulletins/docs/b2003_01.pdf.

c. Case 3: U.S. Dept. of Health and Human Services, Public Health Service, CDC, NIOSH: NIOSH HETA Report No. 97–0255–2735 (Joshua Harney and Michael Barsan): www.cdc.gov/niosh/hhe/reports/pdfs/1997-0255-2735.pdf.

6. Internet sites for companies mentioned in the text are: International Cartridge www.iccammo.com, Tacticool Products www.tacticoolproducts.com, White Flyer www.whiteflyer.com.

Gun Digest Store.com
Providing you with firearms details you need.
Get the best deals around on:
• Books
• Subscriptions
• Videos, CDs, and DVDs
• Online Courses
• Magazine Issues
New products being added daily!
Check our weekly newsletter for updates.
SAVE 25-30% on many products!
PLUS!...save an extra 10% on all purchases when you join the Gun Digest VIP.
GUN Digest Store

Free Download:
AMMO TODAY feature
from Gun Digest Annual

Ballistic Products' new "ITX" shot sports a sharp cutting band around the circumference.

AMMUNITION TODAY: Ammunition, ballistics and components BY HOLT BODINSON

Get a free download of the Ammo Today feature from the World's Greatest Gun Book, *Gun Digest 2010*. The feature contains an in-depth analysis with photos of today's hottest ammunition options from 27 leading manufacturers. Everything from shotshells, to rimfires, to handgun and rifle centerfire cartridges and bullets is included.

To Get Your Free Download visit
www.gundigest.com/AmmoToday